Sense Think Act

A collection of exercises to experience our elemental human abilities

Stefan Szczelkun

Routine Art Co

Copyright & Acknowledgements

Copyright © by Stefan Szczelkun 2016

All commercial rights reserved. This book or any portion thereof
may not be reproduced or used in any manner whatsoever
without the express written permission of the author
except for the use of quotations in a book review.

Printed in England

Second Deluxe Edition, January 2018

ISBN 978-1-870736-12-1

Routine Art Co
An imprint of Working Press/ WP

http://www.stefan-szczelkun.org.uk

DISCLAIMER

This book and the content provided herein are simply for educational and entertainment purposes. Every effort has been made to ensure that the content provided on this website is accurate and safe for readers at the time of publication. The author cannot accept liability for any injury that follows doing any of the exercise suggestions in this book. If in any doubt please refer to your local gym trainer or doctor. No liability is assumed for losses or damages due to the information provided. You are responsible for your own choices, actions, and results.

ACKNOWLEDGEMENTS

To the original geezers at Wildwood House who encouraged the whole project in the late Seventies as a follow-up to my Survival Scrapbooks and paid me a forward. Then before the book, then called 'Total Ability', could be published Wildwood House went bust. A special thanks to the young editor who worked on my primitive English so diligently; also to Oliver Caldicott, Snowy and others.

To Clifford Harper who designed and marked up the Senses section in the Eighties (without pay) for a journal version of it that never happened.

This design work inspired the current layout design.

To my wife Chloe who put up with me scanning and OCRing old pages of typescript all summer of 2004 but still married me in the autumn.

To Gordon Joly MediaWiki master who made the wiki version possible and is an enthusiast for all the lifeworld.

To James Stevens at SPR.ORG in Greenwich.

To 'MedO' who did useful copy editing for free on the wiki version.

The illustrations are largely from my original research notebooks. It's been a long process...

CONTENTS

Introduction

Sensing introduction   11
Thinking Introduction   34
Acting Introduction   55

SENSING exercises

Seeing exercises   68
Hearing exercises   71
Touching exercises   75
Smelling & Tasting exercises   79
Thermal sensing exercises   82
Moving exercises   84

THINKING exercises

Memory exercises   87
Association exercises   99
Meditation exercises   103
Intuition exercises   105
Imagination exercises   112
Dreaming exercises   119
Reasoning exercises   128
Emotion exercises   145

ACTING exercises

Posture exercises   149
Breathing exercises   152
Sleeping exercises   158
Relaxing exercises   164
Sitting exercises   167
Standing exercises   171
Walking exercises   176
Running exercises   180
Jumping exercises   184
Handling exercises   186
Vocalising exercises   189

Bibliography   195

Sense Think Act - Introduction

History has given us arbitrary cultures, religious practices and educational curricula. Most contain much of value but also much that seems to be redundant. In this book, I suggest that such practices should relate to our elemental human faculties.

Who are we as humans? Thinking elementally, we are made from our basic faculties and the subsequent articulation of higher-level skills. By experiencing our basic abilities in a systematic way, we may be able to get a new idea of what we are capable of.

To take full control of our abilities it is helpful to be able to get to know them in an embodied and organised way. This text provides a clearly structured presentation of our basic abilities and ways to experience them. These elements of our power underlie more complex abilities and tasks; like rearing children or making art.

We are motivated to seek out sensations by the pleasure that every sense flux gives us.

> *"All pleasure is creative if it avoids exchange. Loving what pleases me, I have to build a space in life as little exposed as possible to pollution by business, or I will not find the strength to bring the old world down, and the fungus among us will rot my dreams."* Raoul Vaneigem, 'Book of Pleasures' 1984

A new global approach to human ability could signal the end of our development as victims of the largely irrational, mechanistic and barbarous process of history and the emergence of a mature period of conscious evolution in which we decide what we want to become rather than passively accepting our fate.

Mythology has provided us with many stories of witches and wizards who could change their shape at will, often taking on the shape of animals with supra-human qualities. This vision of metamorphosis was an imaginative insight into our true being. Existing religions and systems of self-improvement address and improve some abilities to a degree. However, all deny the power of each person to take charge of their own development both alone and with their peers. The function of traditional practices is often not made clear. We are not invited to make an assessment of the usefulness of any ritual or practice. We are certainly not invited to discard old rituals and practices if they seem to no longer serve a purpose. Religion is all to often a mish-mash of hocus-pocus which we are asked to take on as an act of faith. Modern culture insists that each sense has its own scene of expression and critical apparatus controlled by experts. We are expected to be relatively passive consumers.

I am suggesting a system which is divided into elemental abilities only as a temporary expedient to get the idea across. Any exercise that was not working for a group or individual could always be replaced or improved on. The whole system and its categories is open to criticism and change. It could grow in response to what is learnt in practice and as conditions change.

Although such exercises may be amalgamated and built into cultural rituals or educational practices they should always refer to the experience of our concrete human faculties. They need not become vacuous rituals whose origin and purpose is lost in the mists of time. As they in turn become redundant they can be replaced. Culture, education and religion could always be under review and reinvented in response to changing needs. However, it should always relate to the universal of the faculties we humans have in common.

Literary book based knowledge repressed the common oral-visual knowledges in the early Enlightenment period in Europe. This led to a demotion of oral skills and knowledge from the realm of 'serious' learning which had to be written and published by a dominant literary class.

> *"The mind-shaping powers of the ocular, tactile, kinaesthetic, and auditory skills remain scarcely articulated in the tale of Western civilisations turn to the cultivation of the interior."* Barbara M. Stafford, 'Artful Science: enlightenment entertainment and the eclipse of visual education' MIT 1994 pXXII

Imagine an education system based on basic principles of sensory pleasure. My guess is that it would result in a much less culturally predetermined and more joyous person. The goal of education would be quality of life rather fitting people into a system of waged work. Culture would become more clearly a matter of heritage, choice and play rather than an obligation to the past.

> *"The important thing is that the question of the relationship between aesthetics and politics be raised at this level, the level of the sensible delimitation of what is common to the community, the forms of its visibility and its organisation."* Jacques Rancière, The Politics of Aesthetics 2004 p.18

A world culture made from such a conscious view of ourselves would be one in which people would be aware of local needs and have widespread access to channels of expression in all of our sense media. My definition of culture is the ongoing assessment of our totality in all sense media. A culture that derived from basic human abilities would tend towards a globally and rationally defined human being rather than culture as a set product of particular traditions. Although traditional cultures could be a rich source of inspiration and choice, the drive would be to make going into the future a conscious and playful process. We would take charge of who we are to become.

> *"The idea of culture is a general reaction to a general and major change in the conditions of our common life. Its basic element is its effort at total qualitative assessment... What it indicates is a process not a conclusion."* Raymond Williams, Culture and Society: 1780-1950, 1958 p. 285

I became aware of the idea of remaking cultural totality from scratch from the many experiences I had in the late Sixties with people who were approaching the creative process in this way. Apart from the Scratch Orchestra, which I was a part of, there were people I was inspired by meeting; people like John Steven's Spontaneous Music Ensemble and The Exploding Galaxy performance commune.

The idea of collecting exercises to explore our basic abilities arose from previous research into basic human life supports published by Unicorn Bookshop in Brighton as the Survival Scrapbooks: Shelter, Food and Energy. Whilst researching the book on energy I came across a detailed description of an ideal way of standing in Iyengar's classic book 'Light on Yoga.' I then thought of Francis Bacon's Idols of the Mind as similarly basic thinking about human mental ability. I wondered if a collection could be made which covered all the elemental human abilities. At the time, I was doing bodywork with the X6 Dance Collective in London who were rethinking the relation of dance to the human being. This fed me with many ideas, especially in the area of muscle action. After a couple of years, a structure emerged that seemed a good compromise between simplicity and catholicity. This was the dynamic triad;

SENSE

THINK   **ACT**

The senses pick up information in various media from outside and inside the body. They monitor what is happening. This sensory information travels along nerve pathways to the brain where it is compared with our experience before it is analysed and evaluated. The result of this processing is a decision to do or not do. Doing something inevitably requires movement and muscle action; whether it is writing a poem, taking evasive action in the face of attack or chewing the top of your pencil.

This sequence provides a model for the organisation of the information in this book. In reality, it should be remembered that senses, mind and muscle are a interdependent and closely integrated unity. In particular we can only experience the senses through their mental effects; our perception. However, it is arguably useful to distinguish between direct sense perception and mental processes that have a secondary relation to the senses.

The knowledge we gain through experience is in some ways the most potent type of knowledge. It is the experience of doing that impresses us most deeply. You can read a book about driving, but until you get behind the wheel and switch on the ignition you don't really begin to know about driving. This information is about the faculties through which all our knowledge flows: The key knowledge that precedes all other knowing; To look to learn how to see; To think about how to think better; To flick through an archives index cards to find an exercise on dexterity. I wanted at the end of the day, to catalyse insight into our fundamental functioning rather than prescribe what other people should be doing.

Stefan Szczelkun 2015

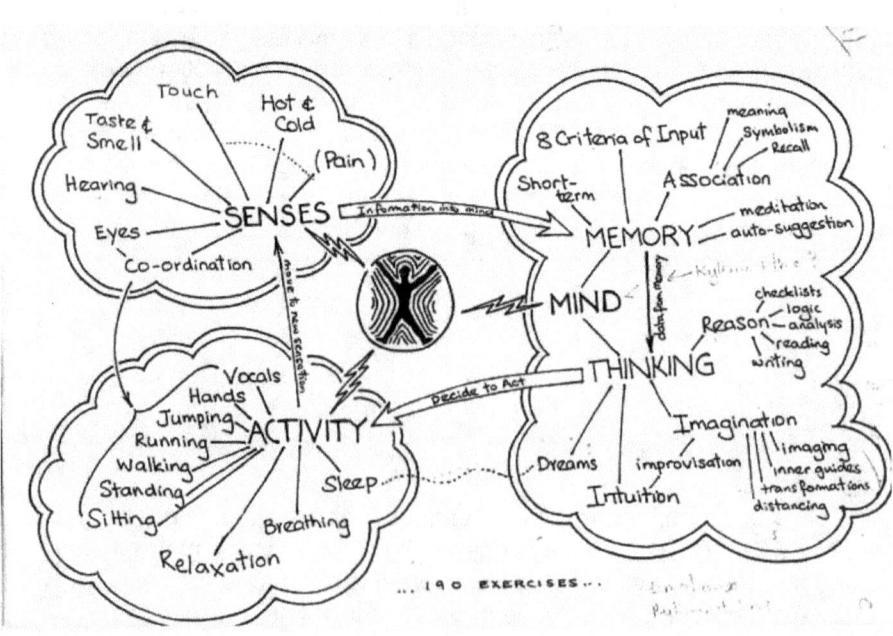

STA is a simplistic model and in reality the three categories operate simultaneously and in close correspondence. Certain areas of our basic abilities do not fit into the tripartite model.

Time & Rhythm Our perception of time and rhythm seem to be a synthetic function of all three S-T-A areas. Our perception of time passing is a function of sense data looping through some mental awareness of pulse and sequence. It works with information from all the other senses to establish relative speeds of time. A pulse is a regular variation in the intensity of sensory perception. A fundamental example of which is our awareness of our own heartbeat. Add to this a conceptual ability to be aware of things happening sequentially, one after the other, with a certain degree of regularity or a rhythm.

Pulse patterns, or beats with accents, may reappear and be recognisable often with other sensory associations that give them meaning. The patterns can also relate to mathematical regularities of proportion that we appreciate through our senses. Clearly rhythm can be perceived in every sense although it is largely associated with the sense of hearing.

A sense of time that can recognise a precise regular beat may be a learnt faculty. The omnipresence of clocks and other precise beat keepers in modern life makes it difficult to say what the perception of regular time intervals would be capable of without this reference point. Although the heart muscle is fundamental to the idea of beat it is of course not regular. Other muscle groups can be important like those that make hand-claps or thigh slaps and foot stomps. Blues rhythm often referred to walking as the reference point. Shoes and pavements certainly gave urban life a newly clipped sense of rhythm and motion.

Rhythm is somewhere between sense, mind and muscle. It is a function of the wholeness of our being and a reminder that the structure of S-T-A is a temporary expedient.

Emotion STA posits that there is a flow of data in through our senses to our mind and on to muscle action. The data flow may also result in the production or circulation of hormones and other bio-chemicals such as endorphins or adrenaline. These may lead to feeling states and emotions as well as other body changes.

Emotions are included under the heading 'Thinking' but may be quite physical and even muscular in their expression.

Pain The alarm system of the body that defends the integrity of the organism and ensures its continued survival is felt as pain. We feel pain from free nerve endings rather than sense receptors.

Organisms have a common reaction to the noxious or harmful in their tendency to constrict or contract away from such stimulus. The reaction to a pleasant and need-fulfilling stimulus is to open up, expand, relax and generally dilate.

In this way pleasure and pain mediate survival on the most basic level. The major activity of the brain is concerned with awareness of pleasure and pain upon which the survival of individuals and the species may depend. The perception and handling of pain is not yet fully understood, nor have specific pain receptors been identified. There are two qualities of pain that are carried along fibres of different diameter. Larger fibres carry the knowledge of pain, whilst smaller fibres transmit a suffering quality. Painful experience seems to be the interaction between these fibres in the central nervous system.

Is pain a sense or is it the antithesis of the pleasure producing senses?

The destruction or mechanical dislocation of body tissue that is sufficient to constitute damage to our organism may stimulate pain. Other knowledge of threats to our survival or integrity will trigger a psychic anxiety commonly expressed in the emotions of fear and grief but when insistent may also be felt as mental suffering. Such threats may also result in the release of hormonal chemicals by the body, but pain is often felt when there is no actual threat to our integrity. There are various ideas as to why this is. Such experiences of pain are probably intense memory recordings of past pain. The pain recordings may be thought of as somehow locked into the body-mind from which they can at times erupt uninvited.

Draft definition: Pain is the alarm system of the body that defends the integrity of the organism and its continued survival. Pain can also become embedded in the body-mind long after the event of threat.

If the threat is great enough to put the survival of the organism on the line then anxiety or distress results and can accumulate. This accumulated distress is ideally released through emotional discharges; such as laughing, shaking, raging, screaming, crying and yawning that seem to accompany healing processes. If this kind of healing is inhibited the distress will be impressed on the body and may lead to psychosomatic illnesses and postural dysfunctions. Distress may also interfere in the brain and nervous system causing later neurotic behaviour or confusion when it is triggered by current events.

SENSING introduction

"For there is no conception in mans' mind, which hath not first been begotten upon the organs of sense."
Thomas Hobbes.

It is common knowledge that we have FIVE senses. This view is rooted in a past where mystical symbolism of number was more important than a basis in fact. The inclusion here of the vital temperature sense expands the famous five to six. This number senses can be increased when we consider that our sense of movement and balance in the inner ear is picking up information of three types - gravity, body movement and muscle action (position). So we could then say we have eight or nine senses.

This number increases again if we categorise senses by their different nerve endings rather than by environmental conditions sensed. We would then include taste and other common chemical receptors as separate from the more sophisticated organ of smell. Rods and cones in the eyeball separately perceive shade and hue. There are three types of touch receptor in our skin. By now we are up to about thirteen. An article in New Scientist suggested a 'radical' breakdown of sensory functionality leads to a total of 33 senses. This is without complicating things with our 'sense' of time, rhythm and pain.

Sensory pleasure is fundamental to our functioning. In our society pleasure has been made secondary to, and sometimes completely segregated from, work. Our senses evolved so we might survive, enjoy the goods of our earth and be productive. Yet too many of us find ourselves persuaded to live a life of sensory paucity.

Reevaluating the essentially pro-life function of our thirteen or more senses by engaging directly with them, we may whet our appetite to evolve a new culture. One of whose main criteria would be to gain the maximum pleasure from our sacred time on earth.

There is also a challenge here to the culture of the screen. Cybernetic culture hardly acknowledges the diversity of our sensory manifold. We must break away from the screens flattening of our experience.

At the end of the day the senses seemed to settle into six chapters: seeing, hearing, touching, smelling and tasting, thermal sensing and finally the sensing of gravity and movement.

_____

SEEING

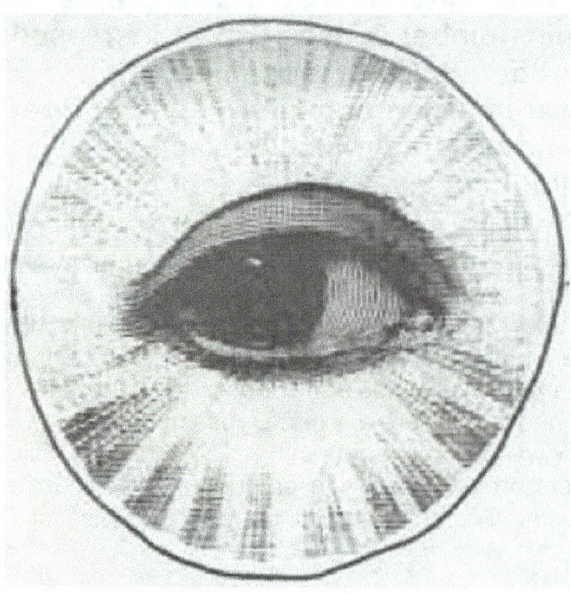

The eyes are capable of taking a much greater amount of precise information in a shorter time than any other sense. This is largely due to the nature of light.

The very high speed of light means that we can see things very quickly after they have happened. The time lag is so minute that it is of consequence only when we are looking deep into space. On earth the event and our visual perception of it are, in human timescales, simultaneous. Light normally travels in straight lines. This enables us to place things with great precision. This means that we can locate detail very accurately. It is also capable of traveling long distances in clear conditions. From a suitable viewpoint, we can have tremendous breadth of vision. From the cathedral spire we may compare the whorls of our fingerprints, landforms 15 to 30 miles away and the crescent of a new moon.

Colours depend on the wavelength of the light. Shorter wavelengths are seen as blue. Then as the wavelength gets longer we see green, yellow, orange, and red. These pure colours are known as hues. Normal sunlight is a mixture of all the wavelengths and appears colourless. The human eye can discern a remarkable 10,000 different hues. The colour of objects is caused by the surfaces of objects reflecting some wavelengths and absorbing others. Tonal variations are caused by the amount of light of each wavelength that their surfaces absorb. Between the extremes of pure hue and blackness we can see about 20 shades of grey.

Therefore, the combinations of shade and hue enable us to distinguish as many as 200,000 colours. Light's huge capacity for carrying information means that vision has become the boss sense of the information oriented age of modernity. The cultural dominance of sight is shown by phrases such as 'world view' and 'how you see the world'.

We value the wooly look of our cardigan rather than the acrylic reality. The visual emphasis of our culture will also devalue or ignore that which cannot be conveyed visually. The look of an apple becomes much more important as a sale criteria than its taste or texture. An otherwise bland product may sell if it looks right. Advertising will even go so far as to discard any real characteristics of the product in favour of a more exotic visual fantasy. Desirable images are artificially associated to a bland product by an advertising campaign. Mundane motorcars convey to the user an imagined air of sexual potency or social power.

All this encourages a retreat from the direct use of our other senses into a misleadingly fanciful visual domain. The result is not only a loss of sensation from the other senses but a confusing overload of visual perception. We are provided with such an onslaught of petty visual information that the untrained eye sees a lot but takes in very little. We can't see the wood for the trees. We are often left registering familiar

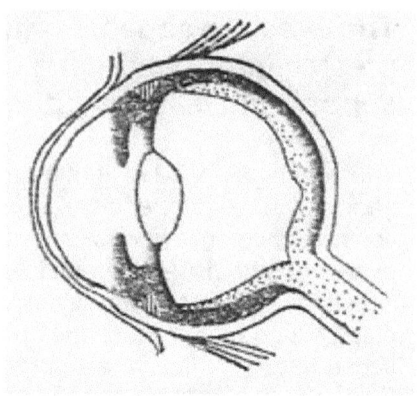

shapes without ever seeing the new; the detail; the variation; or the growth. Rather than seeing the world as a habituated blur, our eyes could be used as a tool to obtain much more satisfying information.

Optical illusions

There are exceptions to the simple rule of physics that light travels in straight lines that may sometimes mislead us. Light travels in straight lines only in media of uniform density. When light enters water it will change direction. This accounts for the coins in the fountain not being exactly where they are seen to be.

The human eyes are evolved to make the most of light's complex characteristics but they do have their limitations. If we are looking at a bright red picture and then turn to look at a pale faced friend we may be excused for thinking they have a greenish pallor. This is because the eye has tired of seeing the red component of white light. The remaining wavelengths give the greenish tint.

Our mechanisms of memory and recognition will effect how we interpret the patterns of light that we see. We may know that a sheet that appears grey in dim conditions is 'white' when seen in good daylight. On the other hand in some conditions we may perceive a sheet that is grey as 'white.'

Factors in these three areas can mislead us. It is important to check for sources of error when making crucial observations or when what we see is unlikely or controversial.

Recent studies have shown that the impact of colour sensation relates to the intensity of hue rather than to particular colours. Objects of brighter colour seem to be closer, larger and more prominent. Bright colours reflect coloured light onto adjacent surfaces and are more stimulating. The superstitions associated with colours are largely unfounded. Green is calming and red exciting only if a person has internalised this association. The association of red with heat and so danger, clearly has a basis in reality.

When understanding sight, it is also useful to remember that light is a form of energy the eye captures and the brain then uses to create a picture. The important point being the picture is generated by the brain and is not external to you. Although it is congruent with reality to a useful degree!

HEARING

Sound is a simpler and less precise medium than light but it has one overwhelming advantage, it is always with us. The sun sets and leaves us in darkness; then sound dominates. Listening has a central place in the evolution of humanity and social coordination happens through the use of language.

The source of sound is not only the external world; our own bodies produce sounds. Even in a sound free room we can hear the rushing of our own blood. Even in the womb, when we had never seen a thing, we registered the pulsing rush of our mother's blood. We are constantly and forever immersed in the sounds that surround us.

Perhaps this is why we first communicated and developed our language in sounds. We needed a medium that was always available to us. Language and hearing abilities are intimately linked. Oral language is the basis of reading and writing skills and so central to the modern culture.

Sound is a vibration; a pulse of pressure that emanates from its source out through a continuous material. The motion uses up the energy of the vibration so that it gradually fades as it moves outwards. Sound vibrations travel at a constant 765 mph in air at 18°C. Compared with the speed of light this low speed suggests a more local and intimate medium. Sounds can vary in pitch from a high whine to a low rumble. This quality of pitch depends on the 'wavelength' of the vibration. Although it is the same word it is a very different thing to a light 'wave'.

Regular variations are heard as a pulse, beat or rhythm. So the three variables that are discriminated by our hearing are volume, pitch and waveform. Our conceptual sense of time passing gives a fourth set of variables, around such things as pulse, rhythm and duration, which become an essential part of the hearing experience.

As we have little or no control of our ears, as we do with our eyes;

which we can swivel and focus, much of our hearing faculty is perceptual. There is a mental capacity to sort out sounds into their component parts. We can listen to one instrument in a band when many others are playing or listen to one person in a room buzzing with conversation. This is similar to our ability to distinguish detail from mass with our visual perception.

The fidelity of our hearing perception breaks down in certain conditions. When a sound phrase is repeated repeatedly a perceptual breakdown occurs and we begin to make imaginative changes. This may lead us to trancelike or dream states and is an effect that also might be obtained through the chanting of mantras.

Although the solar forces of light have taken over much of our information handling, our ears still retain a primal importance. If we 'are not heard' we feel profoundly powerless, misunderstood and alienated. Through language loaded with oral nuances of emotion we resolve and share our feelings with others. Given adequate non-reactive listening we can precisely pinpoint causes of emotional block or turbulence. Skilled listening to each other's histories seems to be the only reliable path to understanding between people who appear to hold irreconcilable positions. In this sense hearing may even hold the key to global peace.

Musical Pitch

Production of Notes. Traditional Western melody is usually produced on a pipe or string instrument. This is probably because these resonators produce a smooth and mellifluous waveform.

Pipes. When the air in a pipe is resonated wavelengths that are whole fractions of the length of the pipe are produced (One half, a third, a quarter, a fifth, a sixth, etc). The wavelength, sound or note that is equal to the length of the pipe is called The Fundamental. The fractions are called Partials or Harmonics. The fundamental and all the harmonics will always be present but usually one note will be considerably louder than the others. In a simple pipe instrument like the bugle it is possible, by the way we initiate the resonance with our tongue and lips, to cause any of the simple fractions to dominate. In this way a series of notes can be produced.

The notes that comprise whole fractions of the length of a pipe or string are called the Harmonic Series.

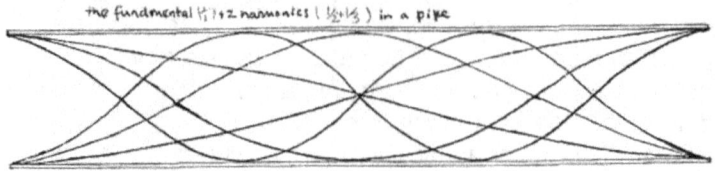
the fundamental f_1 + 2 harmonics ($\frac{1}{2}$, $\frac{1}{3}$) in a pipe

Strings. When a taught string is plucked it will also produce notes that are whole fractions of the length of the string. The dominant wavelength will depend on three factors: length, tension and mass. The relative loudness of each partial will depend on the resonator to which the string is attached and the manner in which the string is plucked. The specific distribution of loudness and softness amongst the partials constitutes the 'timbre' of the instrument.

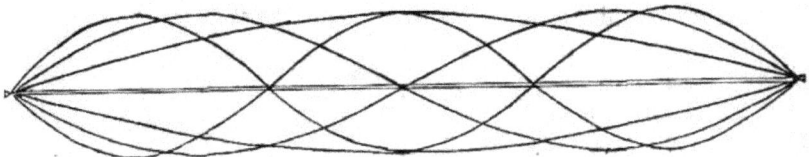

This diagram shows the fundamental (1/1) + 2 harmonics (1/2 + 1/3) of a string

The fundamental and other partials can be cancelled by lightly touching the string, whilst it is vibrating, at one of the nodes. If it is touched at the node midway along the length of the string, the fundamental and all fractions of the string that are odd numbers will be cancelled. If it is touched one-third of the way along the string, the fundamental and any fractions that do not divide by three, will be cancelled.

The above diagrams show the curved shapes of pure notes, but waveforms may take other shapes depending on what produces them. On top of the variations in waveform there may be variations in amplitude or loudness.

Consonance: A Western Preference?

When wavelengths are in simple numerical ratios the result is smooth and pleasing. This effect was originally observed by the Greek philosopher Pythagoras, and later researched more thoroughly by the C19th scientist Hermann von Helmholtz.

> *"When two musical tones are sounded at the same time, their united sound is generally disturbed by the beats of the upper partials, so that the greater or lesser part of the whole mass of sound is broken into pulses of tone, the joint effect is rough. This relation is called dissonance.*
>
> *There are certain determinant ratios between pitch numbers for which this rule suffers an exception, and either no beats at all are formed, or at least only such as have so little intensity that they produce no unpleasant disturbance of the united sound. These exceptional cases are called consonance."*

The Fundamental, Half and Third are almost perfectly consonant. The Quarter and Fifth are consonant with the Half and with each other. The upper partials become more dissonant. The Half and Ninth are dissonant to an extent commonly found to be agreeable, but most partials above this are dissonant in a manner many people consider unpleasant.

The first nine notes of the harmonic series are approximately consonant and it is amongst these notes that the bugler must find a melody. These consonant notes were the basis of western harmonic music.

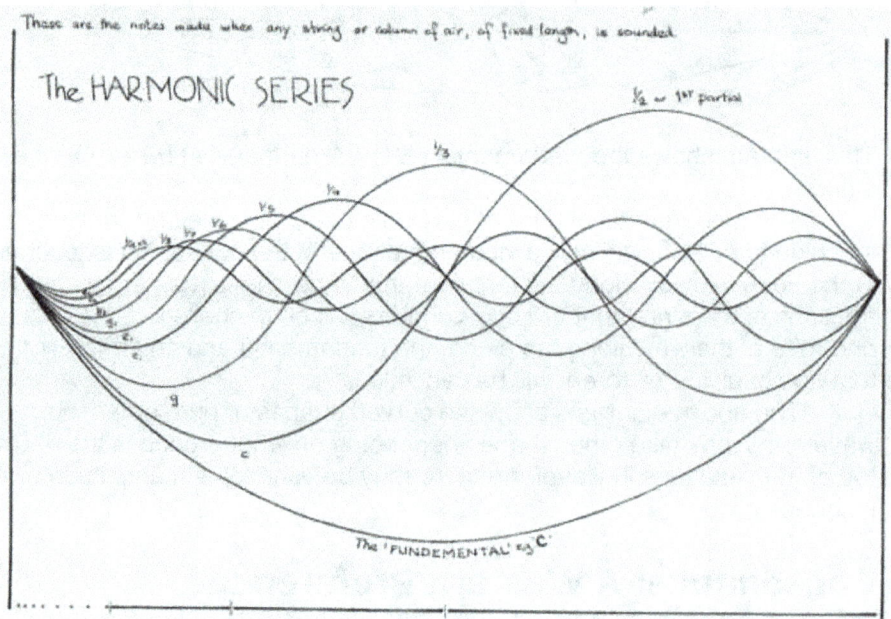

Beats. When two different notes are sounded together, the combined note is found to fluctuate between maximum and minimum intensity at a regular frequency. eg. notes of frequencies 500cps and 499cps sounded together will produce one loud period or beat per second. The number of beats per second is the difference between the two frequencies in cps (cycles per second).

SMELLING

The sense of chemistry: the sense that can tell us of molecular differences that are invisible to any other

sense. The sense that reaches into the atomic nature of matter; the sense that can detect minute traces and differences of great subtlety.

The fact that our sense of smell can respond to such minute quantities has led to difficulties in the scientific investigation of the field. Effects of smells on our psychology have been claimed, although there is some doubt how much suggestion effects the results obtained rather than the chemical nature of the smells. For instance: Lavender, Orange Blossom, Rose, and Sage are said to be calming, whilst Sandalwood, Patchouli and Jasmine may alleviate mild depression. Treatments using smell are called aromatherapy.

Personally, I have my doubts about such things although there is probably something useful amongst some pseudo-science and quackery. The relationship of smell to the process of breathing and to anxiety is, perhaps, more interesting. Attention to smell is attention to breathing. Attention to the rise and fall of breathing is thought to be calming. The other point here is that pleasant smells are a powerful sensory pleasure, and pleasure dilates and relaxes the body.

Its original survival function in the selection of nonpoisonous foods has become obsolete for most of us. Most of our ten million or so olfactory cells lie dormant. Occasionally, specialists in a variety of industries or connoisseurs of wine or cheese have reawakened this ability; the subtlety and precision of their skill is then a cause of wonder in ordinary mortals. There are also chefs, herbalists, florists, perfumers, and real ale buffs who have achieved a super-nose level of performance. Their training methods are, however, rarely shared in public. One imagines that perhaps there is no conscious method and it is just a conjunction of a 'gifted' individual and a long acquaintance with a subject of interest.

Our senses of smell and taste, however undeveloped and vestigial compared with many animals, are still capable of guiding our food choice fairly well; but only amongst natural products. There is no naturally occurring toxic vapour that is odourless. However, synthetics will often give false, sometimes dangerously false, impressions to our senses and then our natural preferences can no longer be relied upon.

The sense impressions given by natural foods also guide us to eat a balanced diet. Processed or purified foods make these sense judgements less reliable. Refined sugar is a case in point. Our mouth recognises sweetness as a source of fast energy. Natural sources of sweetness are usually combined with various other minerals and useful nutrients that are necessary for the utilisation of this sugar. Refined sugar has none of these minerals and vitamins. In this way, it tricks our sense of taste. For children, who are naturally drawn to sweetness, sugar may lead to an unhealthy diet.

If the use of our noses was to be included in our educational curricula perhaps we would begin to eat more healthily. Unfortunately, the commodity food market has structured its business on our lack of olfactory discernment.

The vested interests behind the sugar industry can be traced back through a history of repression and exploitation to the days when African slaves were used to produce sugar in the West Indies under inhuman conditions. The sugar was then imported as a cheap energy food for the working class in England with the resulting tradition of malnourishment and dental caries.

Foodstuffs are often processed to reduce their smell to an acceptably banal level. Other products have smell added to them, often on a subliminal level. A product will sell better if it is slightly scented. Domestic products are often given strong floral odours to conceal their chemical nature; like disinfectant that smells of Lavender.

On a local level this kind of deodorant culture may seem harmless enough, but it is all part of an alienating whole in which things are not what they appear to be. Commercial research on 'vapours as hidden persuaders' has obvious implications as a means of manipulating consumer desire.

Part of the problem of the scientific understanding of smell is the difficulty that has been encountered in creating a universal classification of smells. It is interesting to quickly look at some of the attempts that have been made, if only to give us a range of adjectives to describe certain smells and group them as a memory and learning aid.

One of the neatest systems was proposed by Hans Henning in 1916. He tested more than 400 different scents on people, and then decided on a smell prism of only six main odour qualities:

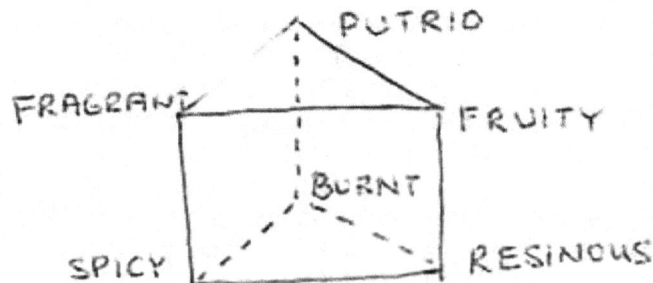

Each of Hennings six categories can be further subdivided.

A more recent classification of ten categories was proposed by Castro,

Ramanathan, and Chennubhotla (2013) based on Andrew Dravniek's Olfactory 'Atlas' of 1985.

Fragrant

Fruity

Citrus

Woody and resinous

Chemical

Sweet

Minty or camphorous

Toasted and nutty

Pungent (like blue cheese)

Decayed or sour

However, it may be noted that none of these classifications has gained popular currency. Smell tends to resist a standardised classification.
Trace airborne chemicals may effect our sexual attraction for each other. This may, however, only be a part of a broader chemical interaction that happens between people during social intercourse. In recent years, we may have been obscuring these signals through our obsession with hygiene. It would seem to be quite possible that we all give out smelly signals that are picked up by other people, often unconsciously, in a similar way to many animals. This may even be the way that actors gain rapport with their audience.

Note: There are two types of sweat gland, the Eccrine and the Apocrine. The products of neither emit a smell. The Eccrine are distributed over the whole body. Their sole function is to increase heat loss when necessary by excreting odourless saltwater on to the surface of the skin. The Apocrine glands are concentrated in specific areas of the underarm, groin and buttocks. These excrete perspiration in times of stress, anxiety, and other emotional activity and excrete a small amount of fatty substances. It is these substances which, if left on the skin to decompose, will cause body odour or BO. This smell will not be so bad if the bacteriological community on the skin is intact. Some conditions such as anxiety seem to upset this.

Daily washing with soap destroys these symbiotic bacteria and the body odour becomes acrid, requiring more soap or deodourising chemicals. Which in turn seem to perpetuate the conditions under which body odour thrives. Rinsing the skin with plain water is sufficient to remove the products of excretion and will leave the bacteriological ecosystem intact. Soap should only be used if the skin is so dirty that rinsing is insufficient. On the other hand, the use of soap may be an excuse for self-massage which may have positive effects.

TASTING

Taste is a separate chemical sense and one that is simpler than smell. The taste buds are on the tongue and I learnt they were arranged in four quite distinctive areas of sweet, salt, sour and bitter. Some other cultures recognise a fifth - umami; the taste of glutamates or meaty flavours.

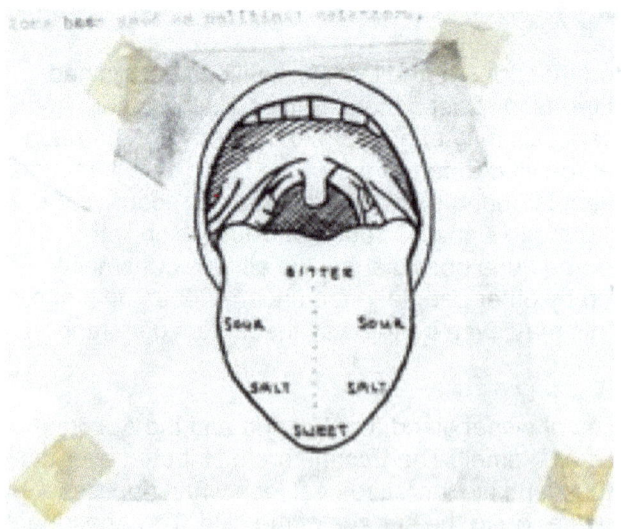

NB This diagram c1901. Separate areas is a myth!

Regarding food, the experience of smell and taste is often simultaneous and indistinguishable. Taste is often used to mean flavour which is the trans-sensory experience of touch, heat, smell and taste.
　　The word taste has acquired a strong historical meaning of

conformity to a set of upper-class aesthetic preferences and social manners. It would seem that the rigid and simple classification of taste and the anarchic complexity of smell have long been used as class defining metaphors. As I have noted earlier one of the key confusions of our inborn taste instincts, the desire for sweetness, also has a violent class history.

THERMAL SENSING

Perhaps more than any other, this is the sense that connects the inner world of body organs to the outer world of climate and cosmos. Our sense of temperature tells us all about the flow of heat in and out of our bodies. Heat flow happens all the time, whenever there is a difference between our body temperature and that of our environment.

This sense has in the past been included as part of the touching experience, the receptors being distributed in the skin and functioning simultaneously. We feel heat at the same time that we feel textures. In some ways, this is a useful confluence of senses. Some important characteristics are shared. Temperature shares with touch a primal importance; the steady warmth of the mother's womb can be shattered at birth and our adaptation to the varying temperatures of life after birth can be happy and smooth, or a matter of bare survival. It also seems likely, by the way our skin encloses us, that it is important to our sense of being and of our self-image.

In other ways, the sense of temperature is very different from touch and the twinning of these two senses has led to confusion. Sense of temperature has a constant and absolutely crucial function in keeping us alive. As mammals, our body metabolism must maintain a constant and steady temperature of 98.4°F or 36.67°C. This varies only within one degree F during a normal day. Changes greater than this have drastic results on our body functions.

Continual warmth is essential to life. So, the thermal senses must report continual changes of temperature and make body changes that retain or give off heat. This is done through a series of automatic reflexes which dilate or constrict blood vessels below the skin, initiate sweating or raise goose pimples. The central control that coordinates this complex process of temperature balance is the Hypothalamus, a substantial brain structure above the back of the roof of the mouth.

Another important difference between the sense of touch and that of temperature is that the temperature sense does not have to be in contact to give us sensation. It can, like the eye, monitor electromagnetic radiation, this time in the infrared or heat spectrum. We can feel the heat of a fire without touching it!

As well as the automatic function, we are also conscious of temperature sensations that give us an experience of comfort. This information directs our choice of shelter and clothing. It is often unacknowledged that this sense is central to the creation of those pillars of our culture - Architecture and Fashion. When we realise its use in the formation of these art forms we begin to realise its importance as a sense in its own right. Previously it has been seen as an alarm to avoid discomfort rather than a source of sensual delight with enough complexity for cultural expression. This mistake has come about because architecture's visual qualities, together with its visual methods of production and dissemination, have obscured its true basis, which lies with the sense of thermal delight.

The sense of shelter. From womb to room our experience of warmth signifies the living against the cold dead. We hope for a warm welcome rather than the cold shoulder. Hearth is closely associated with home.

The reason this sense has so much power, apart from its significance to life, is that through temperature difference it informs us of four quite different and important variables of the environment that effect our comfort. These are:

1. The temperature of the air and of adjacent substances.
2. The radiant heat emitted from surrounding objects and especially from the sun.
3. The movement of air across our skin.
4. The amount of water vapour in the air (ie humidity)
5. Besides these external factors it monitors conditions within the body.

Air Temperature

Different materials have different capacities to hold and conduct heat. When we touch or have our skin near to objects, we are given clues to what they are made of; by the heat flow to or from them. A steel rod will hold a large amount of heat and it will quickly pass it to or absorb it from your hand. Wood holds less heat and will feel warmer and 'softer' in this respect.

Air holds little heat and is therefore a good insulator. However, whether we feel air as cold or not will also depend on air movement and humidity. Generally we are comfortable in air in the temperature range 60° to 70°F (or c16° to 21°C).

Radiant Heat

Radiant heat has some of the same properties as light. We can locate a heat source by feeling the radiant heat emitted from it on our skin and moving towards it. The sun feels hot because of invisible radiant heat. Visible light has almost no heating effect. In this way we can locate hot bodies without having to touch them.

Our bodies also radiate heat themselves. If we radiate more than we absorb, we can feel this heat leaving our bodies. Nearby surfaces that are at a lower temperature than us feel cold and may abosrb our heat. Wall materials that feel most comfortable in fluctuating conditions are those that provide a constant source of radiant background warmth. This provides the kind of thermal stability that is required for the body to relax. If a wall material is cold we may insulate against the effects of negative radiation by covering the wall with heavy curtains, wood panelling or similar material. As water has a high heat capacity, a damp wall will feel cooler than a dry wall. Surface evaporation will give an additional cooling effect.

We are remarkably sensitive to radiant temperature. We will notice a change in wall temperature of 5°C although we may well attribute this sensation to a 'cold draft'. This common mistake implies a general lack of recognition in British culture of the importance of low-level background radiation as a major component of thermal comfort. The reason living in caves is healthy is that the radiant temperature does not fluctuate.

Air Movement

We can feel air movements that are not strong enough to effect our sense of touch by the loss of body heat. In hot conditions, we sweat to produce a moist skin surface that can be so effective in cooling us.

A barely perceptible movement of air is the requirement for comfort in equitable conditions. Still air dulls the sense whilst too much air movement cools us unnecessarily. Air movement is more stimulating if rising rather than sinking. This may be because warm air rises and cool air sinks.

Humidity

Humidity is the amount of water in the air and is relative to air temperature. Hot air will hold a lot more water vapour than cold air. The amount of water vapour in air is therefore expressed as relative humidity or RH. This is the amount of water vapour in a sample of air compared with the maximum amount of water vapour that air of the same temperature could hold. This is expressed as a percentage. 40% R.H. is considered a minimum for both health and comfort. The implications of humidity being relative to air temperature are:

Cold 'damp' air will become dry if it is heated up. This is why it can be fruitless to try to improve the humidity in a dry centrally heated flat by opening the windows.

The ease with which perspiration evaporates depends on the RH. Sweating is not so effective in humid conditions.

Very dry air, especially moving hot dry air, will absorb body moisture too quickly, drying eyes, bronchial tubes and sinuses. This may lead to soreness or the production of excess mucous and lower our defense to respiratory disease. 'Dry air' is air with an RH. of 35% or less. 30% RH is often found in houses with central heating.

Although our sense of heat flow does not measure humidity as such, we get a good indication of humidity by the sensed air temperature compared with the skin cooling we feel around the nose and mouth as we breathe in.

Internal Body Conditions

The body produces heat as a necessary byproduct of the body's internal and muscular activity. The rate at which we produce heat will depend on how active we are. Doing physical work, we are producing around 150 kilo-calories whilst asleep we're still producing 50 kilo-calories of heat. Calories are a measure of energy. Nearly three quarters of the calories that we consume as food are lost from the body as heat. This heat is lost by convection to air, radiation and evaporation of moisture from skin and lungs. We are acutely aware of this temperature balance between the heat we produce and the heat we lose. As I said earlier our internal body temperature can only be allowed to vary within 1°F. Outside this small range emergency measures are brought into play. Too cold and we get goose pimples, go paler and finally start shivering and looking for shelter. Too hot and we flush, begin to sweat and look for a cooler environment. If it is cool the muscles will tense, and body systems alert; if it is warm they will relax. Even the mental association of warmth helps us relax.

In normal conditions, we sweat between three quarters to a half pint per day. Strenuous exercise or very hot conditions cause this to increase to as much as ten pints per day.

This sense keeps us very much in touch with the weather. Anyone who comes from a rural district in the United Kingdom will know how important this has been to our survival. The weather is still the first essential topic of daily greeting and conversation. *"Good a morning, Bert. It looks like we're in for a bit of rain."*

The sense of weather, the sense of architecture, the sense of fashion, the sense of security, the sense of living being. Perhaps more than any other sense the need for thermal stimulation is unrecognised in a world of controlled but static thermal environments.

> "Whilst we may provide for all our nutritional needs with a few pills and injections, no-one would overlook the fact that it also plays a profound role in the cultural life of a people. The thermal environment also has the potential for such sensuality, cultural roles and symbolism that need not, indeed should not, be designed out of existence in the name of a thermally neutral world." Lisa Heschong, Thermal Delight in Architecture 1979

TOUCHING

For the first nine months of our existence we are firmly enclosed in the womb of our mothers. The tactile sense of enclosure is one of our most important prenatal experiences.

After birth, it is essential that holding and touching provide us with continuity and allow us to form an idea of our independent physical existence. Touch continues to reaffirm this existential security throughout our life. Touch is a sense of the skin which contains us, separating inside from outside, defining our form. Completely deprived of touch after our birth we would almost certainly perish. A great deal of touching continues to be a primary need at least until we are through the dependent stage of our development. It will retain associations of security throughout our life.

As adults, we have needs for affection that are well satisfied through this sense. Direct contact with another person has the capacity to communicate caring with an intensity that no other sense can. However, sexuality and frozen needs from infancy often confuse any simple implementation of such meetings. Infant needs that went unmet at the time cannot be satisfied in adulthood. However hard we try, the anguished feeling of need remains because it is a memory, a recording fixed by hurt, rather than a current need that is capable of satisfaction. Resolution is not through touch but by an emotional expression of the original experience.

Touch is the sense without flux, without medium, making direct contact with the outside world. A dependable sense. When we touch an object, we know for sure something is there. We are certain it exists. The lucky prizewinner may be heard to say: *'I won't believe it until I get my hands on it.'*

Touch, more than any other sense, reassures us that the external world exists and is not just a dream. You pinch yourself to check you are not dreaming. This certainty and intimacy that touching gives us has imbued it with strong symbolic power.

The master lays his hand patronisingly on the head of his servant. Should the servant ever do likewise it is taken as an insolent and threatening reversal of etiquette. Relations between men and women are a good illustration of the power of this class custom. A man is expected to touch a woman first. For a woman to initiate an uninvited touch upon a man is usually interpreted as a sexual provocation through which the woman must appear as a 'whore'. Only when a woman clearly has higher social status than a man can she initiate touch without breaking this taboo.

Sexuality is mediated through touch and is a powerful instinctual drive. For many people, the enjoyment of touching another person is almost entirely tabooed by a myth-laden sexuality. It is possible, however, to learn to enjoy touch without it being weighted down with sexual innuendo. In addition, sex might become easier, lighter, if freed from the burden of our touching needs. Fortunately hugging is becoming more acceptable in recent years.

It did not seem feasible to make any comprehensive attempt to deal with the touching aspects of sexuality, or provide exercises here about experiencing sexual pleasure without attracting a distraction from my overall aims.

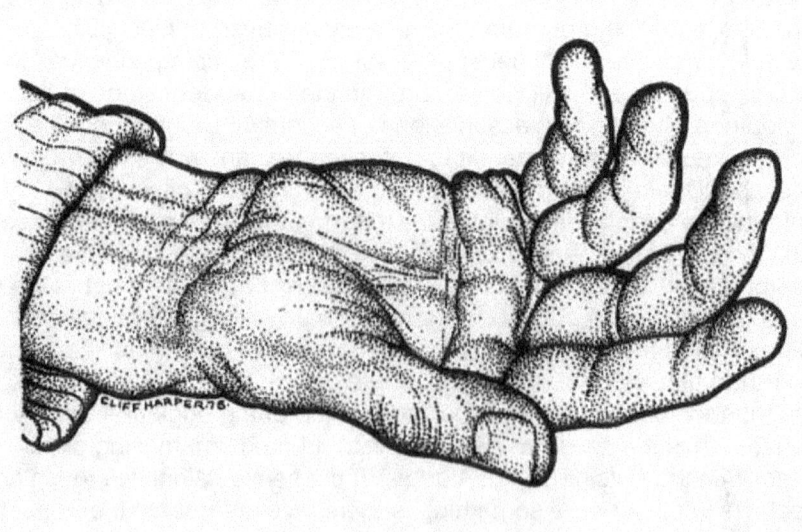

MOVING IN GRAVITY

This integrated complex of four or five receptors will give us information about the physical realities of our bodies. Mass, acceleration, balance, orientation to gravity, relative position and movement of parts of the body, muscle tension and stretch, and the coordination of all these things. These 'mechanoceptors' will give us information about our postural and gestural expression and give us a picture of how we feel about ourselves.

How we feel about ourselves is usually derived from how we were treated in the past rather than the reality of how we are physically in present time. As we move and enjoy and explore this sense we regain a strong sense of our true physicality: a self-image that is not distorted by cultural expectations, misinformation and stereotypes or the past; a self-image that has a much more real basis in mechanical efficiency, biological health, and most important, sensory delight. In this way we can short-circuit conditionings which demean our innate joy of being. This can be a great source of self-confidence. It can allow us to feel grounded and at home in our bodies.

As with all senses, this compound sense provides a source of pleasure that is ours for the taking. Moving for its own sake is normally considered crazy behaviour so our pleasure has to be framed in all kinds of game structures or other acceptable physical activities. Only small children may freely explore this sensual area of pleasure, spontaneously playing with movement expression without rules and boundaries.

There are four main receptors that contribute to this compound sense. They are different from the preceding senses in that most of their messages do not enter the conscious mind. The information that they gather is subconsciously coordinated in a brain structure called the Cerebellum or is part of fast reflex loops that pass through the spinal column.

The four main sense organs

1. The Pacinian Corpuscles. A type of touch receptor that is found in the skin of hands and feet but also in the tendons, inter-muscular septa, and around the joints. They are responsive to pressure.

2. The Labyrinthine receptors. These are located in the inner ear. Three semicircular tubes are arranged in the planes of the three space coordinates. They are filled with a fluid called endolymph and lined with sensitive hairs. These hairs pick up the movement of the endolymph as the head is moved. A neighbouring tubular structure called the Utriculus is also filled with endolymph and lined with sensitive hairs. Crystals of calcium carbonate, known as the Ontoliths, indicate the direction of gravity, which is always down towards the centre of the earth.

3 & 4. The Golgi Tendon organs and Muscle Spindles work together. The Golgi Tendon organs are tension recorders initiating inhibitory safety reflexes. The muscle spindles, which are complex organs, respond to the amount and velocity of stretch in muscles.

Posture

Posture is the integrated pattern of muscle use that keeps our skeleton upright against the pull of gravity. Ideally it is a clever balancing act in which vertebral bones poise one on top of the other with the need for the least amount of muscle action to keep us upright. This is rarely achieved. Whether through accident, hostility or ignorance of our developmental needs our survival has usually required the building of various protective expressions into our posture. Cowering or thrusting the chin forward are common examples. These reduce the efficiency of the balancing act and of the coordinated use of the body as a whole.

In addition, it is possible we simply mislearnt some physical actions by copying wrong models. The poor alignment of bones is compensated by muscle action. This can result in these muscles being tense most of the time. These hypertonic muscles further interfere with healthy body functioning.

A postural expression of pride, lack of fear, self-esteem and joy corresponds to an efficient alignment of the skeleton.

However, it seems likely that negative feelings that are denied a physical expression will not disappear but find another expression in cellular distortions, allergies or other disease. To resolve postural idiosyncrasies without going to the original root of the expression is like treating a symptom and ignoring the cause.

As we rearrange our posture to obtain better functioning we should ideally allow any feelings expressed in the old body patterns to surface and be discharged. However, this is not so easy as the appropriate memories and associated emotions may not be available at the time the posture is changed. If feelings can be 'let out' the muscle tension eases and posture will tend to return to its natural state of efficiency. Perhaps the process of emotional release can be speeded up if accompanied by realignment work.

Taking a posture of pride and self-esteem is useful to contradict certain early negative conditionings.

The dynamic relationships between emotional expression and correct alignment have not yet been clearly worked out. It does seem unlikely that alignment work on its own is sufficient for holistic change. What alignment work or massage can do is give us a useful temporary relief from body misuse, backaches, headaches, tension, and possibly prevent harmful effects from accumulating.

What is 'realignment work'? Efficiency of movement is an ideal that comes from a consideration of the skeleton as a weight supporting articulated structure. It is the ideal alignment of the 200 or so bony levers of the skeleton that is our aim. This is the arrangement that will use the least energy for posture or physical actions. Our bones are pulled into action by muscles. This effort of the muscles is achieved not by volitional control of muscles, but by having the correct 'image' of the intended movement in mind. So, if we aim to improve skeletal alignment towards a mechanical ideal we must condition our mind with ideal and accurately imagined movement. At the same time preparing to deal with possible emotional fallout.

To ensure that this idea of movement is correct or mechanically efficient it must be based on an understanding of the anatomical, neurological and mechanical facts involved. So, the first requirement, if we want to improve our own body use, is to gain at least some knowledge of the skeleton and musculature as a dynamic mechanical unit. Second, images depicting the forces involved and their ideation and direction of acting must be adopted. These images must relate to your own knowledge and experience if they are to be vivid. They are best expressed in the vocabulary of your personal imagination. The anatomical knowledge, which is a basis for the widespread use of alignment imagery may be learnt in the following ways:

1. From the study of a full-sized skeleton considered as a dynamic mechanical frame.
2. By drawing muscles and skeleton.
3. Study of muscle charts alongside the palpation of a person.

If this factual knowledge is not absorbed the ambiguous nature of imagery can lead to mistaken and fanciful ideation that may do more harm than good.

Every bone will have at least two lines of force that express the direction in which the contracting muscles act upon it. So the detailed picture is a complex one. The forces involved, and the images we use, may fortunately be much simplified and yet still be effective. The most essential of these compound lines of force is the function of the spine as a central axis.

> *"Imagine the central axis of the trunk as a sliding curtain rod, and watch it being elongated upward to raise the head to a higher position. This should be alternated with watching the spine lengthening downwards in the back like a kangaroo tail."* Lulu Sweigaard, Human Movement Potential 1974

The spine is imagined as a central line or axis around which the body action maybe balanced. If we feed this idea to our imagination it will pass it on to the cerebellum coordinating centre and gradually, if we stick with it for many weeks, we will find ourselves being able to move more freely.

> *"You need a long axis, I need a long axis. Everyone needs a long axis."* Barbara Clark, Let's Enjoy Sitting, Standing, Walking 1963

There are other less DIY methods of improving the efficiency of our muscular coordination:

The Alexander Method: In this technique, a student is shown better ways of using his body through gentle guiding in the hands of an experienced teacher. The old habitual relationships of the body are inhibited whilst the feeling of the correct use, as judged by the teacher, is experienced and gradually brought into daily practice. The wrong patterns of use are often quite subtle, and even when more obvious, they are often not felt as wrong. What we feel as 'right' is simply what we have adjusted to feel as normal. The correct posture may at first feel odd and awkward.

Feldenkrais Method: Moshé Feldenkrais taught that efficient posture could improve human functioning. Feelings of self-esteem are fed to the cerebellum to create a 'awareness through movement'. Needs to be taught by professional teachers.

Many of the ancient methods of self-knowledge include postural directives as part of their training in an explicit or implicit way, for example:

Hara: Hara is a Japanese term that literally translated as 'belly' means the centred, balanced and imperturbable person. The essential three instructions on the way to Hara are:
    1. Drop the shoulders; let the arms hang heavy.
    2. Release the belly; but allow some tension.
    3. Breathe with belly on exhalation only. Inhale at ease.

Zen: The famous Zen Buddhist 'empty head' is often misunderstood to be some kind of metaphysical joke. However, it may be understood as a straightforward physical instruction that relates to the feeling of an efficient relaxed posture. The head balanced on the spine will feel heavy if posture is in any way wrong. When accurate bone through bone alignment is achieved the head will feel light and 'empty.'

Revitalising this sense with serious realignment work or playful exercise will enable us to move through the earth's gravitational field with an increased sensitivity to our bodies and what they are capable of. Further training of this sense would facilitate the learning of all other physical skills and form a strong basis of self-knowledge for all activity. More than any other sense time spent in this area can lead to a profound sense of well-being and openness to change.

A note on 'Interoceptors'. The 'New Scientist' magazine of January 2005 introduced a whole new category of internal senses to me, that are not included in the Sense Think Act collection. These are the 'interoceptors', which measure things like three types of blood pressure, blood oxygen content, cerebrospinal pH, plasma osmotic pressure (or thirst), artery and vein blood glucose difference (or hunger), bladder stretch, lung inflation, stomach fullness, etc.

THINKING introduction

Some popular ideas of the mind and intelligence are based on ignorant superstitions. These limit us from realising anything but a fraction of our potential capability. Not until the Renaissance period was it accepted that our thinking centre was located in our head and it is only in the C20th that our knowledge of the brain has had much of a basis in scientific knowledge.

The division of students into Arts or Sciences was considered soundly based educational philosophy that was particularly convenient for the development of an efficient technocratic society. It has recently emerged that a 'scientific' or 'artistic' bias is simply an unbalanced brain; for it seems that the right-hand side of the brain is concerned with mainly creative work whilst the left half does mainly calculation work. There is no good reason why the two 'halves' of the brain should not be encouraged to develop in a complimentary way.

Another common misconception is that the brains ability decreases with age. The reduction in number of cells by those cells that die as part of the aging process is a very small proportion of the whole and not enough to effect intelligence. The accumulation of knowledge and experience we get with age more than compensates for any loss.

Irretrievable forgetting is another idea that seems to be wrong. When we can't remember, the information is only temporarily inaccessible, and may be remembered if we know the reason it is obscured. It now seems likely that we permanently store most of our experience from the period of our fetal development in the womb when our sensory faculties first formed.

Another fallacy is that we inherit a level of intelligence (IQ) from our class background. Although we may acquire characteristics of the culture that we are brought up in they are transmitted through the behaviour around us rather than on a genetic level.

These examples of misconceptions about our thinking abilities serve to illustrate the confusion that surrounds our common power to think. Thinking is everyone's prerogative. It is only negative conditioning that leaves most of us feeling dependent on the thinking of experts and authorities. This is a core myth of class society.

We are the product of our senses and the sum of our conditioning. The accumulation of experience creates the characteristics of human behaviour and intelligence. There is no reason why we should lose our soulfulness or poesy as a result of this prosaic explanation. As we become adult this process may become more consciously directed and if we have the knowledge we can choose to become whoever we want to be at any time.

The Physical Construction of the Brain

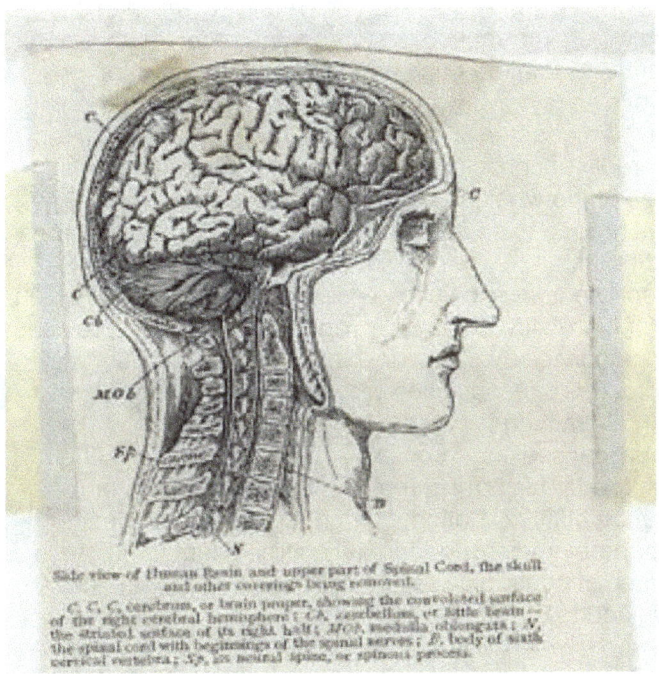

The brain is physically composed of several hundred million nerve cells. Their surface is extended into a mass of filamentous dendrites. These bring information to the cell. A single thicker nerve, called the axon, carries information away to other cells. The millions of brain cells are thus interconnected by a complex network of fibres. Areas of the brain with specialised functions may be identified, but they do not seem to be structured differently or to have centres.

Information travels between brain cells as an electromagnetic pulse which travels along at about 300ft per second. Each cell will need to receive information from several sources before it is triggered to send an impulse *out* along its axon. A 'decision' will not be made until verification is received from various sources. This allows us to sort out priorities, and acts as a safety check against overhasty responses. It also allows for subtle judgments of timing.

Repeated responses develop preferred pathways through the network. These pathways become habitual routes, which may be used in a semiautomatic, unconscious or intuitive way. Both muscular movements and patterns of thinking develop preferred pathways. These busy neural routes will change only when we deliberately change our habitual thoughts or actions.

I have structured the mental section by popular conceptions of mental functioning. Memory and Association are relatively mechanistic mental processes by which information is stored in an orderly way and retrieved. Memory and Association each has a separate section of exercises. Meditation is a way of slowing the mind and being aware of its processes and its given a chapter.

Intuition is a largely unconscious and multidimensional process utilising the resources of the whole mind to reach a decision, often at lightening speed. It is hard to experience but the ground can be prepared for it to give the best results.

Imagination represents a sophisticated level of functioning in which playful use is made of our ability to mentally replay and combine previous experiences. It may be conscious or unconscious and may be seen as a combination of the process of association with the mysterious thought processes of intuition. Dreaming is given a separate chapter.

Thinking that is goal seeking, problem solving and logical is the last category to be considered. This may in reality also be conscious or unconscious, rational or intuitive. Rational thought is the more linear and conscious process of problem solving, primarily utilising language. As languages are a means of communication that define culture; rational thought is forever welded to the social and cultural.

All five processes happen all the time in different proportions. The reality is not of separate abilities, but a unity of body-mind directed to a purpose. However, for the time being the mind exercises are roughly organised into these five categories.

A section on Emotion is appended here as it effects the clarity of our thinking or at least colours it with value.

MEMORISING

The memory mechanism of the brain may be crudely likened to a computer. Its operation depends on definite real conditions. It reacts to information from sense

impressions and thoughts and, if conditions are right, stores the information in relation to our existing experience. Current perceptions and conceptions are recognised by their similarities with past events in the memory store. This operation is largely automatic and can happen without the overriding control or direction of the conscious mind.

The infant comes to recognise certain repeated experiences as significant to her ongoing comfort and development. These become key impressions in the development of memory and of mind. Other repeated or powerful impressions are also coded, remembered and their use or meaning sought. This evolution of key groupings may later become conscious, but for at least the first 6 to12 years it is dependent on prompts from the environment.
     The mind remembers by connecting key impressions, signs and words. To some extent you can become aware of this process going on in your own head. For instance, you are telling a friend about an experience. Key images, words and feelings seem to be simultaneously present. Linear sentences of speech are spontaneously constructed around the more diffusely structured basic memory information. This mundanely wonderful improvisation is what defines us as human.
     Memories are automatically referenced, to give meaning and value to current experience.

Short term memory

Most of the information continually pouring in through our sensory windows is of momentary value only. It serves to give experience continuity and allows more important events to happen in a particular context. Most of this input vanishes within a few seconds. You might not remember the pattern of linoleum in a much-frequented bathroom not because your memory was bad but because you had never created the conditions for it to enter your long-term memory; it was not significant. Another example of short term memory is with telephone numbers. You can look up a number in the book, cross the room and dial it correctly, but five minutes later you may have no idea what it was.

Short term memory is limited to about ten digits repeated consecutively, or equivalent in other media.

Long term memory

The more powerfully an experience is remembered, the greater effect it will have on present day activity. Memories are not just passive lumps of data. 'Memories' make up who we are and how we react to the world. Our experience becomes us.

The strength of the memory trace is dependent on the following criteria of retention:

1) Primacy and recency

2) Categories

3) Difference

4) Sensual power

5) Repetition and review

6) Personal interest or use value

7) Attention

8) Preparedness.

These factors will decide the prominence of any perception in the mind.

Diversified review for flexible recall

A memory is not usually an isolated piece of data, but a part of the total experience within which it occurs. Memories of facts are therefore linked to a particular context, to other similar facts or whatever. One of the keys to creativity is to relate facts not normally found in the same context to each other. This is difficult if the context within which a fact is remembered is always rigidly similar. A person always seen in a particular setting may be difficult to place when she or he turns up somewhere different.

A fact linked to various contexts, in the process of reviewing it, will be able to be recalled in a greater variety of circumstances.

'Bad' Memory and Forgetting

Sigmund Freud was the first to point out that forgetting was often due to the repression of a painful experience associated with that memory. This theory has been borne out and expanded in recent times by researchers.

If the right conditions are present any experience will be remembered and will easily be recalled when the prepared signals are given. If the memory doesn't work it is because the necessary techniques were not used. If the memory still doesn't work then it may be that accumulating hurt associated with that experience, has isolated that memory recording. Recourse to techniques of obtaining emotional release or discharge of the hurt may release the memory.

On the other hand, old memories can be awakened by simple associations in our lives and will be replayed like a stuck record, often playing havoc with how we feel, and obliterating our capacity to think well. Such old recordings can become played throughout our lives without invitation; giving out a constant barrage of negative messages that we aren't good enough or whatever.

The simplest strategy to avoid forgetting is to over-learn. This means not stopping learning when you can 'repeat it without looking', but continue to impress the material upon the mind. Fear of the consequences of forgetting is not a useful method of producing results.

ASSOCIATING

First, a memory is stored with the total environmental experience in which it is perceived; then it is categorised within the brain by being linked to other items with similar characteristics. This mental linking is known as the faculty of association. To remember a new thing, we need to think of something associated to it. We need to make a connection with something we already know. In this way, our thinking continues by a complex and subtle chain of association or interconnections. Another way of type of association is pattern matching. This ordering of similar patterns is perhaps one of the most fundamental aspects of thinking.

Some items are stored in a sequence or in a particular set that can only be recalled by the name of the group as a whole. Other things will be linked to an enormous range of different facts, feelings, objects and sensations.

Repeated associations may become habitual, and provide a line of least resistance; a particular perception always invokes a particular response. If this response becomes unsatisfactory or obsolete then we may consciously decide to associate along weaker non-habitual links to find a more appropriate chain of connections or ideas. This breaking out from the normal pathways of thought is sometimes known as lateral thinking.

The particular pattern of habitual association that anybody accumulates is seen as their outlook, personality, preference, priorities and values. Two people may be crudely compared by the different associations they make with a basic object, word or shape. A habitual association with an early experience of trauma can produce quite irrational or bizarre behaviour in later adult life. To some extent this can be countered by taking on a positive direction. However, long lasting relief may only come after an emotional catharsis or even a mental breakdown.

I spoke in the 'Thinking' introduction about the formation of habitual patterns of thought or preferred pathways. They have the advantage of facilitating quick response. There is a strong analogy that can be drawn here with routines in daily life. Routine allows one to develop efficient methods of doing mundane tasks; leaving more time for what you want to do, above and beyond the mundane. Preferred pathways also have this sort of function in allowing much repeated behaviour to be done without rethinking it afresh each time.

The same disadvantages follow to some extent on both levels. Rigidly developed and repeated routines lack flexibility and may not be able to adapt to changing conditions. The same is true for fixed modes of thought. However, flexibility seems to be a natural quality of the brain's preferred pathways which only become rigid or entrenched through association with hurtful experiences.

Core associations

Contrast or opposites eg. sharp and blunt

Resemblance eg. icing and snow

Cause and effect eg. money and wages

Whole and parts eg. engine and piston

Contiguity eg. factory and worker

Genus and species eg. mammal and whale

Sign and thing signified eg. cross and Jesus

Meaning and symbolism

Association is an important mechanism for it gives the objects and processes of our world meaning. A thing and its associations are one. The total meaning of anything is the sum of its associations. A thing may have associations from:

1. Its use. eg. plough - furrow - earth.
2. Mental connections.
3. By ritual or repeated connection and subsequent use as a symbol - the communion wafer that is 'transubstantiated' by the ritual of mass into the body of Christ.

In this way, a simple thing may not be so simple in the mind. Mentally it may be associated with powers or qualities that it does not, of itself, possess. It represents values possessed by the something else it is associated with.

Clearly strong symbols can focus the emotional power of our needs and fears with incredible vigor. In primitive times the objects were chosen to represent the supernatural powers and forces beyond everyday experience and comprehension. This served to reduce fear of the unknown by ritually calming the power of frightening phenomena. In modern times many of these symbols still exist as objects that retain some of their psychic and emotive powers.

Everything shares the values of the things associated with it to some extent but symbols do this most powerfully. They can represent in one object, a belief which is otherwise an abstraction or a complex ideology. eg. a tree represents 'life.' If you choose to wear a gold key around your neck to represent your ambition to overcome the difficulties of life and get what you want, then you might do well to invent a ritual to 'give life' to the key. The main invocation of which might be: *"With this little gold key, I'm going to get all I want."* Note the difference between the above phrase and the weaker: *"This little golden key is going to give me all I want"*.

Environmental influences

Memory recordings include all environmental perceptions. If you experience a certain state of mind in a room with orange walls or when a particular melody is playing, the two things become linked. In this way, we develop a range of personal values or tastes by the subtle associations that new things evoke. Our cultural group will also inform us of values that have been produced by our social history. Gold signifies wealth and power because of its rarity and by association with the sun.

Your surroundings will imbue your life with meaning by association both from your personal history and from social consensus. As well as that your surroundings will become associated with the life you have in them. We normally choose our present experiences in sympathy or in reaction to our early experiences. Poor associations, like a drab environment, can exert a continuously enervating effect. Our surroundings are commonly chosen for:

    Irrelevant economic and political reasons.
    Purely functional' reasons.
    Social reasons - to be in fashion or socially acceptable.

A revolution is needed to upgrade the quality of the surroundings that most of us live in!

MEDITATING

It is possible to isolate the basic memory and perceptive functions from the higher-level processes, which occupy so much of our time, simply by not thinking. This allows us to look in a relatively objective way at this whole process, and seems to have a number of positive features.

Our thinking mind is rested from racing around in circles, chasing its own tail. When the dust has settled our consciousness is allowed a refreshing draught of present time reality. This can be a profoundly reassuring awareness. We are more clearly aware of a perception starting, being considered by the mind and the associations which it brings. This is closely allied with physical relaxation.

    Meditation can allow you to separate what is happening now from the associations that often cloud present reality. Things take on their actual unique identity in the present and are not confused with associated feelings from the past.

    Intermediate meditative practice also allows the awareness of thought itself. The principle being that if a thought or impression may be observed in its arising, its continuance and its dying away, we have come to know it objectively. Once it is known in this way it will not have any mysterious power over us.

INTUITING

The word intuition is used here to include all types of problem solving or goal orientated thought, from simple value judgements to theoretical hypotheses which entail a complex and simultaneous use of all mental resources. Special qualities of intuitive thought that result from its nonlinear use of the whole mind are high speed of operation and the decisive evaluation of many possibilities. If we are attuned to its use this 'faculty' will allow us to respond quickly and yet flexibly to new and complex situations.

Intuition manifests itself on both mundane and magical levels. Many results of intuition are assumed to be instincts. We seem to just 'know' the answer to a request for advice without thinking. An appropriate response is made without a pause for thought. It all seems quite 'natural' and therefore instinctive. Most of our judgements on which we make daily choices are based on unconscious thought processes that are a form of 'intuition'. It is difficult to draw a clear line between 'instinct' and 'intuition' and I have a hunch there is a close rapport between the two. I'm defining instinct as preexisting whilst intuition relies on experience accumulated since conception.

It is when intuition gives answers to original questions as if from nowhere that its incredible potential is noticed. It may often provide such penetrating insight that we assume it must come from an outside source. eg. an answer to prayers or a symbol seen in the random patterning of tea leaves. We find it hard to credit our own minds with this mysterious capacity to seemingly leap through the unknown.

Preparing the Ground

Without doubt the greatest obstacle to the free flow of intuition is physical tension and mental anxiety. Tension and anxiety tend to happen together. However, we may change our situation so we are more physically relaxed and not plagued by worries. We may also neutralise much of our anxiety by consciously striving to have a positive frame of mind. Never forget that negativities interfere with mental functioning. The other preparation we can make is to saturate the mind with relevant information.

> *"It is always necessary first of all, that I should have turned my problem over on all sides to such an extent that I had all its angles*

> *and complexities in my head and could run through them freely without writing. To bring the matter to that point is usually impossible without long preliminary labour."* Herman von Helmholtz 1891

This priming of information is better absorbed as multimedia presentations, live events or contextual environments, as a total experience will provide more mental connections than reported verbal information. The more diverse and rich the relevant mental landscapes that can be prepared, the more likely intuition will turn up a choice of fresh and appropriate answers.

Most of the judgements we live by are intuitive, in that they are not based on rigorous rational analysis, objective evaluation or proof. For instance, I would say that a large part of our personality is formed by conditioning rather than hereditary factors. The evidence indicates this but doesn't prove it conclusively. The weight or value attached to each piece of evidence is decided intuitively. Many such questions with important implications for social organisation are, finally, intuitive judgements on factual evidences and should be held in some degree of doubt.

When people hold an intuitive judgement in common it gains considerable weight. The judgement is sometimes spoken of as 'normative'; and yet this is not itself any proof of its correctness, eg. only a few hundred years ago practically everybody firmly believed the world was flat.

Estimation of the value or usefulness of information received is the main day-to-day business of intuition. It is the facet of intuition that continually and invisibly supplements rational thought. These judgements are very reliable when they are based on recent direct experience. They become less reliable as they are based on less intimate and recent acquaintance. Intuitive judgements as to the intrinsic values of normative moral, ethical and aesthetic precepts are the most doubtful.

> *"Where there is conflict the more self-evident proposition is to be retained and the less self-evident rejected."* Bertrand Russell, Problems of Philosophy 1912

As intuition is unconscious, how do we train it? Well, it seems that we cannot improve it directly. It is more a matter of preparing the ground and removing obstructions; being receptive to results in any form and checking them with rational procedures wherever possible.

Being Receptive

People often assume an intuition will appear in the form in which their thoughts tend habitually to operate, but an 'intuition' may appear as a picture even to an intellect that has tuned itself exclusively to words. An intuitive answer may be symbolised or 'hidden' in a found object.

You will have to 'follow your nose'. You turn left earlier than usual because a curious house facade has caught your eye. Further on you take an alley to get back onto your route. Down the alley is a dustbin with an intriguing box of old papers beside it. You rummage furtively and out slips a copy of 'National Geographic' October 1935 which has 'Demon Possessed Tibetans and Their Incredible Feats' with 12 natural colour photographs. Which turns out to be a great source of inspiration for that street theatre piece you are currently working on.

Too much conscious focus on getting results may interfere with this process. If you 'look' for an intuition you may not find it. Results will be presented as an integral part of your life.

There are ways of coaxing the intuition to supply verbal answers to questions. The simplest of these is the Ouija Board. The disadvantage of this sort of crude manipulation of intuition is that mental filters are by-passed and the questions used may dredge unwelcome material from the subconscious. Emotional needs create fantasies, which are incorrectly interpreted as fact. However, the Ouija Board does seem to demonstrate a 'group mind' facet of intuition.

Checks and balances

Intuition is fast and comprehensive but it is also subject to our weaknesses. The vested interests of our present situation and background may bias the intuitive process in many subtle as well as crude ways. Superstition and our inherited culture will condition us with much outdated information. Intuition can only work within the totality of who we are. The more aware we are of our personal and cultural background and our emotions within this framework, the more we can see when the clear light of intuition has been clouded by emotional pollution or consensual irrationalities.

On a more specific level we can check intuitions of particular importance with rational procedures. It is noteworthy that the speed of intuition can provide crucial information before emotion occludes clear thinking. We may see a man's evil intent for a fleeting moment before his charm or beauty enamours us. We can make use of this in a situation where we feel stuck. The rational mind is not getting anywhere, so we may decide to spontaneously strike out at a tangent and do what seems to be a random action (hopefully it is guided by intuition). Repeated, this will sometimes lead us out of the deadlock.

By being open to the unknown power of our body-mind intuition may be capable of feats at present considered metaphysical or magical. As with imagination, we are unsure of the limits of its power. It seems feasible that our understanding of physics will soon get to the point were the connection of thought and matter may not seem so outlandish. The electrical energies of thought do seem to exist and interact on a molecular level.

Another idea is that intuition can tap the cultural wisdom of a people. By being open to transpersonal values, symbols and gestures we may engage our minds in a kind of collective consciousness. Such intuitive thinking, animated by the imagination, is an integral part of our socialisation.

For the present, we should be open to the possibility that each of our minds is probably capable, at its best, of making a synthesis out of our accumulated experience and knowledge which goes well beyond any mundane ideas we may have acquired of our capabilities. At the least, intuition gives the mind limitless creative potential.

Improvisation could claim to be the activity in which our potential is most fully extended. Intuition allows us to improvise thought and action at great speed. This enables us to deal with complex, dynamic situations faster than we could ever think them through consciously. Improvising freely, we can achieve a unity between our sensory experience, our intuitive power, and rational ideology. I have included a range of improvisation exercises covering all sense media plus language, as the most apt field of 'practice' for intuition.

IMAGINING

To imagine is to form experiences in the mind. These can be recreations of previous experiences as they happened such as vivid memories with imagined changes, or they can be completely invented and possibly fantastic scenes. We can also imagine sensations abstracted from their matrix of experience.

An imagined experience is such a rich and complex mental process that it may appear to gain a life of its own. In other words, an imagined experience may take off and progress through time, with 'unexpected' twists and turns like a real experience. Because it is a fabrication of our own mind we can also control or guide this experience, manipulating it in a way that we can never manipulate reality. In our imagination, we can take risks and be more playful than is possible in real life.

So, imaginative experiences, however fantastic, are constructed from the bricks of sensory experience. The ability to fully take in sensations and draw on them to create vivid imaginative reconstructions has, to some extent, been lost to most of us in the West through the emphasis on words and labels. The natural ability, to draw on memories of sensation rather than their labels is easily regained through training.

Imagination will naturally tend to include images from all the sensory areas in the same way that real life is a mingling of all sensations in varying proportion. We can, however, decide to imagine one particular sensation predominantly or exclusively. The exercises suggest we practice the memorising and recollection of sensations in each of the senses. The extent to which our imagination provides a total experience is demonstrated by our physiological responses which will often react as if the imagined scenario was real. Imagine a monster and your heartbeat will rise and adrenaline increase, even though there is no need to 'fight or flight'.

Even body functions that are normally regulated automatically may be changed and even controlled by suitable imaging. More general images may be used to aid healing processes and improve postural functioning. In these ways, the profound relationship that imagination has with our body functioning may be glimpsed. Some insight into the extent of body-mind unity may be gained. It is of course in this area that the imagery of spells and other sorcery have their 'magical' effects.

Because of the mental complexity of the imaginative flow a myriad of associative connections are possible at any moment. This explains the unexpected directions in which the imagination can go. It means that imagination is a very creative mode of thinking. A major component of creativity is that endless possibilities are presented to the mind. An abstract idea given a form that has life in our imagination is useful because new associations are more easily made to an imagined form than to an complex idea.

Although imagination is usually playful it can also have a survival function in providing 'sensory pleasure' that is lacking in the environment. People can survive the most adverse realities by retiring into their imaginations. Children survive parental neglect by inventing parental surrogates from their comfort blankets and having fantasy playmates.

Another function of imagination is to give one a change of viewpoint. We can imagine ourselves seeing the world, and ourselves in it, from places we do not in reality occupy. Plato was said to view everything as if from a lofty rock. We can also imaginatively enter the viewpoint of another person and may learn something of what their experience is like. We can imagine change to ourselves and to the environment to motivate ourselves and imagine how things might develop in various ways. We may then make decisions about present actions by considering their imagined consequences.

The danger of a weak imagination is that it will not accurately predict reality. We may then either reject an imagined possibility when the reality would have had unimagined but advantageous qualities; or we may be drawn by lurid fantasy to live in a reality that is, actually banal.

The weakness of our imaginations is continually exploited by the image merchants of the advertising industry. The confusion between reality and image can be most disastrous in the images of ourselves that we try to live up to. Our real selves might feel inadequate so we assume a glamorous media personality. As a boy, I thought walking with cowboy bowed legs would make me more macho. All it did was wear down the outsides of my soles and give me backache. People will often fabricate a complete personality or body image for themselves made of commodified images. In this way consumer ideology alienates us not only from the world but from ourselves through the colonisation of our imaginations.

Imagination, because it is not in itself a focusing method of thought, will often require an entry vehicle, context or direction from the real world to set it in motion. Sometimes a cardboard box is all we need to imagine ourselves in a moon buggy. Other times more complex rituals have enabled people to have spiritual experiences or appreciate a larger reality. Spring rituals allow people to have a deeper appreciation of seasonal change.

The danger of imagination may be that we can get lost in it. Fearful imaginings and worries can separate us from a connection with the safety of our present time reality. A meditation exercise is included as an antidote to imaginative follies.

DREAMING

Our conscious mind, of which we are aware during normal waking hours, is only a fraction of our total thinking mind. A great deal of sorting / evaluating / symbolising / choice making goes on in our unconscious mind without us knowing about it. Dreams give us a direct access to this veiled area of the mind.

Our sleep alternates between two types of sleep. Each night deep sleep is broken up by four or five periods of dream sleep. Everyone has dreams, although the extent to which they are remembered is another matter. The function of dreams is not known for certain. This is not so surprising when we consider how little is known about why we need sleep.

It is also possible to reach dream states whilst we are awake. Some people will naturally 'daydream' more easily than others but there are techniques available that allow everyone to generate waking dreams.

Dreams can vary from those that seem to have a life of their own to imaginative fantasies whose every twist and turn is willed; from a series of inconsequential images to the most profound insights; from a sensual erotic aquatic delight to a nightmare so disturbing one is jolted awake as ones only escape.

To some extent dreams may be directed and controlled, and practice increases our ability to do this. Consciously directed waking dreams may be seen as exercises in the use of imagination. There is some doubt whether we should regularly interfere with our sleep dreams as their biological function is so little understood.

If dreams are semiautomatic and of unknown function then what use can we make of them? It has been suggested that deliberately 'dreaming' of clear sunshine, bright stars, huge rivers, can help to keep our bodies healthy. This is possible if one considers the fantastic claims made for the psychosomatic powers of visualisation.

Dreams may be used to solve problems or throw up ideas whilst our minds are released from inhibitions during sleep. Dreams may be used to obtain original images and ideas for stories, poems and pictures. However, perhaps the most important use of dreams is to give us insight into the subconscious pool of our past conditioning: to throw up clues that help us better understand the construction of our personalities; the unique living result of our personal histories.

The images in dreams are often masks for feelings not normally available in our present time. These repressed feelings may derive from early memories, which do not have their own clear memories. Such feelings without form will be 'dressed' by the mind in images plausible to or palatable to the intellect.

As there are no universal interpretations for the meaning of dream symbols, trying to analyse dreams in this way is often a hit or miss affair unless you gain a clear understanding of your own symbols.

REASONING

Reason is the ordered use of language to ascertain the truth or validity of statements. It has gained tremendous prestige in the last few centuries through the immense achievements of science. This prestige has led to an unhealthy domination of thinking. We try to apply reason

to areas of intuition or emotion in which it is inappropriate and at best crude and heavy handed. The appearance of reason can confer authority to any common rhetoric; the politician who will dress up his emotional appeal in the appearance of rational analysis.

Rationality can be thought of as very straightforward. It uses simple principles that we all find intuitively self-evident. Accepting these we may then derive valid implications from combinations of simple statements. For example: If apples, grapes and bananas cost the same price per pound, then three pounds of apples and one pound of grapes will be the same price as two pounds of bananas and two pounds of grapes. If it is true that all women are mortal, and if Maggie Thatcher is a woman, then we may deduce it is true that Maggie Thatcher is mortal. This has proved to be the case since I first started this research.

Put in this simple form, logic seems ridiculously obvious but that just shows how natural an ability is rationality. The trouble is that in the real world the examples we come across are much more complex than the simple forms I have just given, and this leads to all kinds of error. The more we can be aware of these areas of error, the more we can allow our inate reasoning ability to take its course unimpeded.

The errors that creep in to complex chains of reasoning are easier to spot if the reasoning is written down and examined in written form by a range of people to whom the reasoning is relevant. Below is a list of fifteen sources of thinking error. In the exercise section each of these heading is discussed in more detail and can be used as a checklist to examine an example of reasoning.

Key checklist of thinking errors

1. Definition of key words or terms used

2. Equivocation

3. Incorrect basic ideas

4. Cause (or antecedent)

5. Attribute (or association)

6. Generalisation

7. Classification

8. Emotion

9. Personal experience

10. Context

11. Viewpoint

12. Logical arrogance

13. False validity

14. Analogy

Some of these points will overlap and merge into each other.

Some Fundamental Assumptions of Rationality

1. Frequent repetitions of similar sets of events give us good reason to expect a similar result in the future. We continually act with faith in this Principle of Induction. We buy a chair in a shop without testing it because various visual clues convince us from past experience that it is in fact a sound chair. However, we must remember exceptions are possible. Some degree of doubt should be retained.

2. What follows from a true premise is true. If it is true that stars are in the sky, then as we look up at the blue sky we deduce the existence of stars we cannot see, or, if it is known that Y is true if X is true and if X is indeed found to be true, it follows that Y is true. This is known as the self-evident principle of deduction.

3. The universe is consistent. No elemental event in one place will contradict the same event in another place. Technically this is now challenged when applied to distant parts of the universe, but for our more everyday purposes the principle is useful.

New knowledge can only be understood with our previous experience. The less things are capable of attachment to things we already know the less they are capable of being understood.

Rationality is given a social definition by Jürgen Habermas. Rationality is communication that is "*oriented to achieving, sustaining and reviewing consensus - and indeed a consensus that rests on the intersubjective recognition of criticisable validity claims.*" Theory of Communicative Action Vol. 1 p.17 1981

EMOTION - feeling is not thinking

Emotions seem to be chemical excretions, which effect how we feel and are triggered by sensory or mental events. There is also a physiological expression associated with many emotional states - crying, shaking, laughing and so on. So, in a way emotions are not entirely situated in the mind and could be seen as a fourth arm of the sense, think, act triad.

Our fundamental requirement is to survive and thrive; firstly, as individuals, and secondly as a species. What is the psychic channel of this organic drive? The most credible theory is that it is our desire for pleasure. Our sensations and thinking seem to stimulate an area of the brain that gives us a positive feeling of pleasure. This drive is modified first by our thinking which budgets our resources to ensure longer term security; we think ahead, and second by our perception of pain.

Pain is our warning of survival threat. In psychic terms pain is incurred whenever there is a threat to the integrity or power of our organism. As well as damage to our body this can take psychic forms such as loss, fright, frustration, boredom or ridicule. The perception of pain causes the body and mind to protect itself in various ways and then later when the threat is no longer present and we are feeling safe, it will heal the hurt. A process accompanied by emotional expressions especially when the hurt was psychic.

These releases of emotion or discharge processes include animated talking, laughing, yawning, trembling, and possibly things such as sighing, scratching, retching and stretching. It seems that a range of these are needed for a thorough healing process to occur. Certain conditions of safety need to be present for these processes to occur. The main requirement is usually the uncritical caring attention of another human.

If these resolving processes cannot occur after a painful experience there is a shut down, repression or rigidity in the memory areas associated with the hurt. Accumulating or catastrophic pain, that is unresolved, causes serious general interference with the functions of the body/mind. The symptoms of this disturbance vary from severe depression or feelings of inferiority to irrational dislikes or erratic memory recall, from 'nerves' and 'tension' to disease or psychosis. Fortunately, these blocks may be cleared by simple techniques. It does take time. It seems that a large part of human potential is probably occluded in this way.

"What is repressed exercises a continuous straining in the direction

of consciousness, so that the balance has to be kept by steady counter pressure." Sigmund Freud, Collected Papers Vol 4 1959

The resolving processes are commonly confused with the hurt itself. A sympathetic parent will often distract a child from her tears, thinking that all is well if tears can be stopped by distraction or other means. Teardrops are not the hurt. Quite the opposite, tears are a visible sign of the resolution of the hurt. The value of quiet listening and appreciative attention is often not realised and instead the healing process is interrupted.

A high premium is put on our children displaying self-control. Emotional outbursts are not encouraged, as their cathartic healing function is widely misunderstood. A pain is stored as part of the whole sensory experience in which it occurred. When something happens to us that is similar to the experience in which the pain occurred it will bring up those feelings by association and we will experience a change of mood. This can be quite dramatic!

We frequently experience irrational feeling, the cause of which, we look for in the events around us. Often as not, the cause of the feeling is an upset that happened years ago in our childhood that has simply been triggered by an association in our present time experience. By this, process a patently innocent event can resurrect a strong feeling, which is quite irrational when applied to the current situation.

To make things more confusing several feelings can arise at the same time to produce a gamut of bad feeling. The thing to remember is that there is always a concrete origin in past events for an unhappy feeling in the present.

This process of hailing events from that past happens subconsciously as part of the continually association of our experience with present sensations. When people see a sad movie, they cry because it brings up sympathetic feelings in themselves. Many people will 'pull themselves together' and inhibit crying because they think it is immature to cry in a situation that in reality is 'just a film'. What they do not realise is that they are crying about a past incident that really was once sad and upsetting in their own lives.

It is easy to see how people equate crying with weakness - 'You cry baby!'; trembling and raging with lack of control - 'Pull yourself together!'; yawning with insufficient sleep and so on. These conditioned responses to emotional expression, particularly while we are young, have seriously interfered with our capacity to heal from past trauma.

What do I mean by a survival threat that causes psychic pain? Any denial of our potential is a threat to our integrity. Helplessness on any level is the most common and hurtful experience. It conditions us to be dependent and feel powerless. Any of our infant needs, which were repeatedly denied, will be felt when evoked by later events as an emotional upset that reduces aspects of our ability live well now. These unmet infant needs that have later repercussions on our mental well-being include: the need to be touched; to be allowed to sleep in peace; to nurse on demand; to be dry and fed properly; be appreciated; never to be left unattended; to be freshly stimulated but have a tranquil environment; to be consulted and informed; to be treated with respect and love; to be weaned from dependency with consideration and so on.

Another key need is to receive uncritical attention when hurt and be allowed an emotional response. This is key because it leads to the later difficulties we have dealing with our feelings.

Denial of our power is of course more widespread than the infant realm. It extends through the class structure, in which most people are conditioned to internalise a feeling of being inferior to a superior ruling minority. All the pervasive and often subtle put-downs that are the building blocks of oppression are profoundly hurtful and leave most of us struggling in the mould of second-class humans.

I'm not saying that anger at our current situation should be ascribed to infant causes. If, however, our anger does not lead to powerful action to rectify the cause of the problem then there may be early occlusion of our power in the mix.

Summary

Emotional release is an automatic physiological reflex that is triggered when the right conditions exist. You can create these conditions and allow it to occur with evident benefit to emotional health. Some attention must be given to the hurt but some must also be put onto present time safety. The present time 'safety' is usually provided by the presence of caring human who will not interrupt the process for an agreed amount of time.

With sufficient time and space emotional processes will take place, hurts will heal, and mental limitations will vanish or wither away. Body/mind functioning in areas associated with the hurt will improve, tensions reduce and thinking becomes sharper.

As little children we have all internalised an immense amount of hurts and as oppressed adults we get more. These hurts interfere with our body and mind functioning leading to disease, irrational and antisocial behaviours and a shut down of flexible thinking.

The resolution of this coagulation of hurt we are all caught up in is to be found in a revolutionary uprising that will include widespread release of pent-up emotions! We need to learn how to handle it well.

ACTING introduction

Having obtained experience through our senses and analysed it with our mind there is nothing left for us to do but act on the information received. Action is produced by a complex system of contracting muscles pulling on a flexibly jointed frame of 208 living bones. The action produced can vary from breathing and blinking to singing and eating.

Eating and breathing; are the key muscular activities that supply the food-fuel and oxygen necessary for muscle contraction. These raw materials are transported to muscles by the disc shaped cells of the blood. This red fluid is circulated by a centrally located pump, which has acquired a mythic status. Just six weeks after conception the fetal heart starts to beat, before there is even blood or a circulatory system.

The gut, lung and heart are themselves, operated by muscles. The gut and heart will benefit from exercises but are otherwise automatic functions that cannot be improved or further experienced by practice, except by raising the quality of the raw materials we ingest. Lungs are similarly automatically regulated but can also be under more conscious control and awareness. The movements involved being larger and more external. The eternal cyclic and rhythmic action of the lungs, make them central to our focus on muscle borne activity.

This section opens with a variety of breathing exercises and follows these with a sequence of elemental movements from resting and lying down through sitting, standing, walking to running and jumping. This sequence covers the main mobility functions of the human animal. There are two more areas of muscle action that give us our power over other animals and make us potentially godlike. These are the dexterity of our hands and the expressive range of our voice.

General Principles of Practice

Before going on to the myriad of muscular actions and skills here is a short guide to general principles of practice.

1. The character of the movement must either be demonstrated for imitation as slowly, and as often as required, or the limbs must be physically guided to the pattern of the act. In this way, the general shape of the movement is acquired.

2. Verbal instruction is of little use at fundamentals levels. Where the

elements of an act are known and labelled then verbal use of this 'skill vocabulary' may act as sufficient cue.

3. If a complex act needs to be broken down into parts to be learnt, the meaning and place of each part in the whole should be well understood.

4. Once the movement has been roughed out by the learner the only way to achieve improvement is practice, practice, practice.

5. At the roughing out stage care should be taken that the principles of good posture are attended to.

6. Corrections at all stages should consist of relaxed caring physical guidance and demonstration rather that verbal fault finding.

7. As the action is practiced a few core features should be kept in mind at any one time moving on to other features only when these have been successfully assimilated.

Constant feedback of some kind is essential. It may be by the reflections in a mirror or through verbal encouragement and correction of errors by a coach.

The categories that the muscle action exercises are in have arisen from the process of collecting rather than having any overall schema that relates to the body. No doubt this reflects my cultural viewpoint and research experience. The workbook presented here is not meant to be definitive in its structure or selections.

POSTURE - Expressing Being

Although action can have an ideal of the efficient and safe use of the skeletal frame and its muscular pistons, it also carries social meanings. An efficient balance of the spine with the use of minimal muscular tension is also a posture of pride and self-assurance. It is a posture that has the association of being regal and 'belonging' to the upper classes.

> *"The shoulder, in rising, is not called upon to teach us whether the source of the heat or vehemence which mark it, arise from love or hate. This specification does not lie within its province; it belongs entirely to the face, which is to the shoulder, what the barometer is to the thermometer. And it is thus that the shoulder and face enter into*

harmonious relations to complete the passional sense which they have to determine mutually and by distinct paths... The shoulder of every man who is moved, rises sensibly, his will playing no part in the ascension; the successive developments of this involuntary act are in absolute proportion to the passional intensity whose numeric measure they form; the shoulder, therefore, may be fitly called the Thermometer of Passion and Sensibility." Francoise Delsarte quoted by Ted Shawn, Every Little Movement 1975

"The physical expression of a gestural mood is, however, not always the most appropriate for the situation... Anyone not thrusting up his shoulders when startled but gathering his strength in his lower belly must certainly have practised in some way." Sato Tsuji quoted by KG von Durkheim, 1960.

People in cities often suffer with tense shoulders and neck because their gestural reaction to urban stress has become stuck in the 'stressed out' mode. To make matters worse this somewhat rigid postural expression is socially contagious.

Each part of the body is capable of some expression of internal feelings. The body as a whole is communicating meaning all the time. Activities are dealt with here as functional processes but it should be remembered they are also expressive states and sometimes we choose to trade efficiency for expression.

BREATHING

Breathing is the cyclical and continuous pumping action by which air is brought into the body. Air is sucked into the lungs so that oxygen in the air may be absorbed into the blood and carbon dioxide and water exhausted. The oxygen is necessary for the combustion of the foods that produce our energy. The energy fuels all our body processes. As a whole, this biochemical activity is known as our metabolism.

The lungs are composed of an elastic sponge-like structure of tiny and delicate compartments called alveoli. It is in the thin walls of these minute chambers that oxygen is absorbed and the waste products carbon dioxide and water vapour are released from the blood. This process is called respiration. The lungs themselves are not muscular and play a passive role in the process of breathing.

The rib cage protects and supports the lungs. It is the intercostal muscles between the ribs and a sheet of muscle that forms an upward curving floor to the rib cage, known as the diaphragm, that motor the breathing process. To suck air into the lungs the diaphragm contracts, moving down in the trunk like a piston. Simultaneously the ribs expand out and up to increase the girth of the ribcage.

In the first stage of exhalation the diaphragm and intercostal muscles relax; the elasticity of the inter-rib cartilage and lung tissue return the lungs to their original volume and the air is gently expelled. Further expulsion of air may be achieved by use of the abdominal muscles.

The capacity of the human lungs is about six to seven litres. Only about one-fifth of this is exchanged in relaxed exhalation. This is called the tidal air, which comes and goes steadily. With forced exhalation, up to four-fifths of the lung capacity may be used. This is known as the complemental air and the remaining litre or so is known as residual air.

At rest an average adult will take 10 to 14 breaths per minute. With light activity, this goes up to 17 to 20. People practiced in sitting meditation claim to be able to manage as little as three. In each breath about half a litre of air reaches the alveoli and takes part in respiration. The rate of breathing is automatically regulated and related to the pulse rate.

Breathing practice does not serve to increase skill as much as remove obstacles to efficient breathing. Breathing practices also seem to be used for their effect in calming the psyche and as a meditative metaphor.

The initial instruction in breathing exercises is often to let it happen. Don't *take* a breath. Deep breathing is a natural function; all we have to do is to relax enough to let it happen.

> *"The first thing that has to be learned is to let breathing happen. This is possible only to the extent that the person is able to cease directing the breath from his I. Just how difficult this is, becomes clear when he first observes his breathing, for then the effect of the fixing I, interrupting the natural rhythm, becomes immediately apparent. Breathing falters and the beginner frequently has the impression that he is no longer capable of breathing properly, and that he is short of breath. It takes a long time before such a person, even one who breathes more or less rightly, is able to breath consciously in the right way. To learn this is a basic exercise - exercitum - which is needed by both the sound and the unsound... Again and again, he resists exhalation half-way and half intentionally he assists the inflowing breath."* K.G. von Durkheim, Hara, 1960

Another school of thought would say that poor breathing is an effect of generally faulty skeletal alignment. The way to improve breathing is only through a general improvement of coordination. Defects which are often attributed to people who have learnt 'deep breathing' include: undue depression of the larynx; stiffening muscles in the throat, vocal organs and neck; undue lifting and depression of the front part of the chest and insufficient use of the back.

Yoga breathing exercises are somewhat different in that they do not apply to normal breathing. As in other yoga practice they put a controlled strain or stretch onto the breathing faculties, which stimulates them and their allied functions. Abdominal breathing will massage the gut. This will aid peristalsis and invigorate the digestion. This serves to flush out poisons, make the organs tougher and more flexible and have beneficial psychic effects.

Perhaps the best breathing exercises are those done as a part of movement sequences. The conscious mind focuses on the movement: breathing is just allowed to happen in response.

The diaphragm, the main breathing muscle, is closely connected to parts of the nervous system in the solar plexus. The old prescription to 'take three deep breaths' in times of stress has a basis in our physiology. Achieving smooth deep breathing does seem to have some calming effect on the 'nerves'. Massage of the solar plexus seems to happen especially during forced exhalation.

Along with the calming effect energy seems to be released. This energising effect is imaginatively described in many oriental practices. The breathing is seen to be a pump of our 'intrinsic energy' which moves in channels through the body. Probably the same channels as those identified in acupuncture practice.

The intrinsic energy or 'Chi' rises from the base of the spine up the spinal column. It is pumped up these channels by deliberate abdominal breathing in a relaxed mood of concentration with the exclusion of everyday thoughts. The 'chi' is said to be stored in seven centres as it rises through the body (the perineum, sex organs, navel, heart, throat, pineal gland & brain). When this energy is accumulated it is claimed to power some of the more extraordinary practices of the Eastern martial arts. It is difficult to assess whether this is due to the physical process of breathing or a mental image that is evoked.

The exercises provided fall into roughly three types:
1. Improvement of everyday breathing by identifying and avoiding bad habits of body coordination.
2. Strengthening of the breathing apparatus by synthetic methods of breathing.
3. Breathing as a cosmic metaphor and rhythm that helps us get in touch with present time realities.

"Nature has provided two familiar muscle responses to help maintain a long spine in breathing. They are automatic, which makes us feel they are unimportant. But anyone who starts trying them out begins to find their true value. One response is called the yawn, the other is called the sigh... The yawn acts as a muscle barometer for the breath. Without being aware of it you can shorten your breathing over a period. This can happen in either a rapid or prolonged buildup of tension. It can be occasioned by physical or emotional impulses or both. This tension creates a desire within the muscular system to stop holding the structure rigid. Result... you yawn or sigh." Barbara Clark, Lets Enjoy Sitting, Standing, Walking 1963.

SLEEPING

Sleep, rest and relaxation are all kinds of non-action. Non-action is as important as action. Sleep is another area that does not fit easily into the tripartite classification of STA. The mental side of sleep, dreaming, is covered in the thinking section. A good perspective to take on the importance of sleep is the thought that if we have lived for 75 years, then 25 of those are likely to be spent in bed.

There are two types of sleep that alternate four or five times during the night. The basic dreamless sleep, during which the body tissue is restored, is divided by shorter periods of Paradoxical or dream sleep. During paradoxical sleep nerve connections are strengthened and nerve tissue restored. There are four conditions which go to make good quality sleep:

1. Pre-sleep period - mental and physical repose.

2. Environmental conditions - warmth and ventilation.

3. Correct support - bed, pillow and posture.

4. Waking up.

Pre-sleep prescriptions: Because we know so little about sleep and because it is, on the whole, a non-experience, we tend to wish that it would look after itself. Like any conscious activity it can be done well or not. The most effective general prescription for sound sleep is to allow at least half-an-hour to prepare oneself

---

RELAXING

Informal relaxation does not mean that any permanent improvement of posture is necessarily achieved. However formal relaxation does allow the tension patterns that interfere with our body's proper functioning to subside for a while. This gives our body essential relief from the restrictions imposed by stress.

Tension arises when gestural expression becomes rigidly or chronically held. For instance: a person who once had a good reason to be afraid of the world may habitually have tight muscles around the upper torso and neck with a tendency to have raised shoulders. This tension becomes habitual even though the original cause of the fear is no longer present. As youngsters, all of us have had experiences which have left a pattern of tensions in our musculature. Such muscle tensions can interfere with breathing and other basic functions, including the constriction of blood vessels and nerve routes. Apart from the shoulders other common areas of tension are in the neck, stomach and back.

Neck tension often causes headaches by restricting flows to the brain. Stomach tension results in stomach upsets or intestinal malfunctions. Back tension gives us crippling pain and can lead to slipped discs and Sciatica. Temporary relief is afforded by relaxation techniques. Permanent relief may require complementary therapeutic work.

Relaxation is also the first step in achieving waking sleep in which the consciousness may get in touch with the creative powers of the unconscious.

Fruitful relaxation is not slumping into an armchair. It is creative inaction similar to meditation. Systematic relaxation allows us to be more in tune with our intuition. It allows us to see the less obvious possibilities by finding a neutral space outside of our routine program. The highest forms of relaxation and meditation practice achieve an inner poise that allows us to observe some of the emotions and fantasies in which we are usually immersed.

Apart from the exercises described here, baths are very good for relaxation. Turkish, Russian, Sauna and Aerotone, are a worthwhile weekly treat if they are available in your vicinity.

SITTING

Sitting is a postural compromise between standing up and lying down. Sitting is often a perfect position for creative (in)activity.

The requirements of keeping the trunk erect whilst taking weight off the legs and feet help keep us alert for long periods without getting tired. You can sit behind a table to work or you can just sit. You can sit up on a chair or sit down on the floor.
    If you sit most of the day it is worth spending some time getting it right. If you don't often sit then is good to enjoy doing it well when you have the opportunity.

STANDING

Standing is a complex task of subtle muscular coordination. The central structural member is the spine that is made up of 33 individual vertebrae. Ideally it is the deep muscles lying close to the spine that lend us the most efficient support to keep us upright.

However, bad posture stemming the expression of emotionally distressing experience, tends to bring other muscles into play as the skeletal structure becomes more eccentric. Apart from inefficiency, this can lead to all sorts of health problems.
    It was Iyengar's long description of standing yoga or Tadasana that inspired me to start collecting the exercises in Sense Think Act.

> *"Erdem Gunduz is a legend. And all he had to do to earn this status was to stand completely still."* Richard Seymour, Guardian 18-6-2013

WALKING

Walking includes much of the postural principles mentioned in the last section on standing and in the previous section on coordination. In walking the spinal balance becomes complicated by a dynamic weight exchange from one leg to the other.

The weight of the body is supported first through one leg and then the other. The rhythmic use of our muscular symmetry often makes walking for long periods easier than standing for a similar time. However, as with all posture, walking is not just a matter of mechanical efficiency but a whole mode of communication and source of rhythm. When we walk we express our deepest feelings about ourselves, and we perform walking in a way that we would like others to see us.
    When out walking we are ensured a continual change of stimulation. We're aware of the interrelated detail of the world and are able to interact with our surroundings.
    Walking is our most ancient and basic means of travel.

RUNNING

The difference between running and walking is that, in running, both feet leave the ground. It is really a series of small leaps. The leaps can be made so efficient, the exchange of weight so smooth and rhythmic that a healthy fit and physically average person can run for miles without undue strain.

Jogging or long distance running allows us to experience the limits of our metabolism. We can run as fast as our circulation can bring sufficient oxygen and glucose to the muscles and carry away waste materials. This intensification of our circulation flushes out our system in a way few other physical activities can.
    It is exhilarating to realise how fast we cover distances when we have learnt to run properly. The sensation itself, if we are not struggling through the pain barriers of competition or personal best times, can be like floating along whilst our feet beat time. It can be encouraging to run with

other people and some people may find it useful or exciting to compete. However, especially when beginning, it is important to find your own pace and progress gradually.

Some claim that a daily running schedule burns off negative 'energies', cleansing the psyche as well as invigorating the body.

JUMPING

We jump for joy. The exhilaration of leaving the ground under our own power and flying through the air, however short an experience it is, cannot be equaled by any other unaided muscular action. Jumping is an expression of tremendous vigour and energy.

> *"I was never a class clown or anything like that, but I do remember being in the first grade and my teacher, Mr. Chad, told the class one day that we were going to do some exercises. He meant math exercises, but I stood up and started doing jumping jacks. To this day, I don't know what possessed me to do that, but all my friends cracked up."* Will Ferrell

---

HANDLING

The dexterity of the hands produces tools, which make machines, which produce the wealth of all the things made by humans. Things that now provide every imaginable extension of our basic functions.

The abstracted development of dexterity does not seem to be a common element in physical education programmes. However, it is the hand that provides the most important synthesis of our sensing and thinking in the production of things. Improvement of dexterity is usually an integral part of some specific craft only a few of which seem to have separate hand exercises. For most makers, it is repeated practice with their preferred tools that brings the higher levels of achievement.

As with other muscle uses hands produce communication as well as things. Here is a selection of British hand gestures.

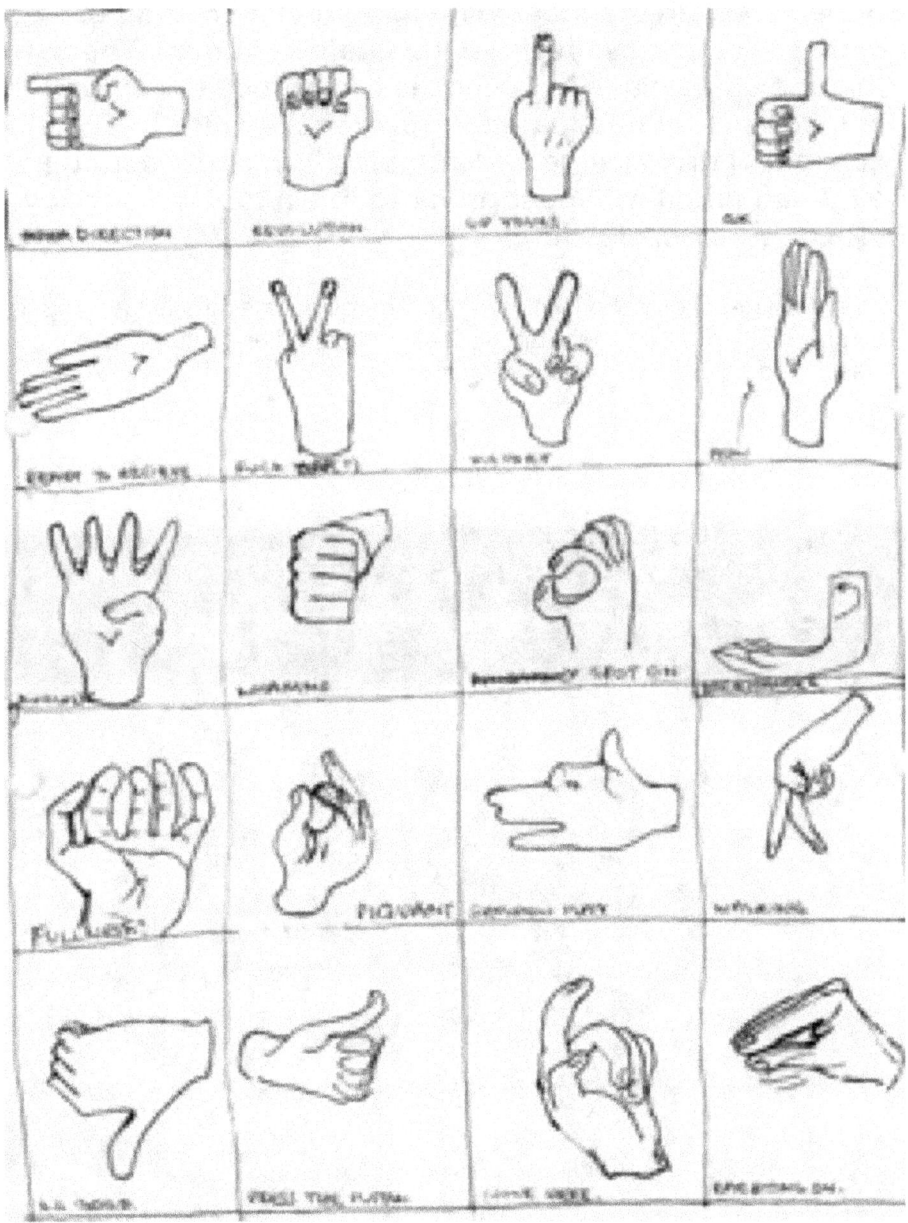

VOCALISING

Speech is both the most vivid and precise method of communication available to the unaided human. The part that the voice plays in speech is to produce the myriad component sounds that make up vocal quality. It is capable of great range and complexity. It is the sound that a human infant will most prefer to listen too. It is the key tool of our socialisation.

The result depends not only on the vocal cords but also the lungs, tongue, mouth cavity, skull, lips, etc. Each area must be under control and yet elastic and not rigid with muscle tension.

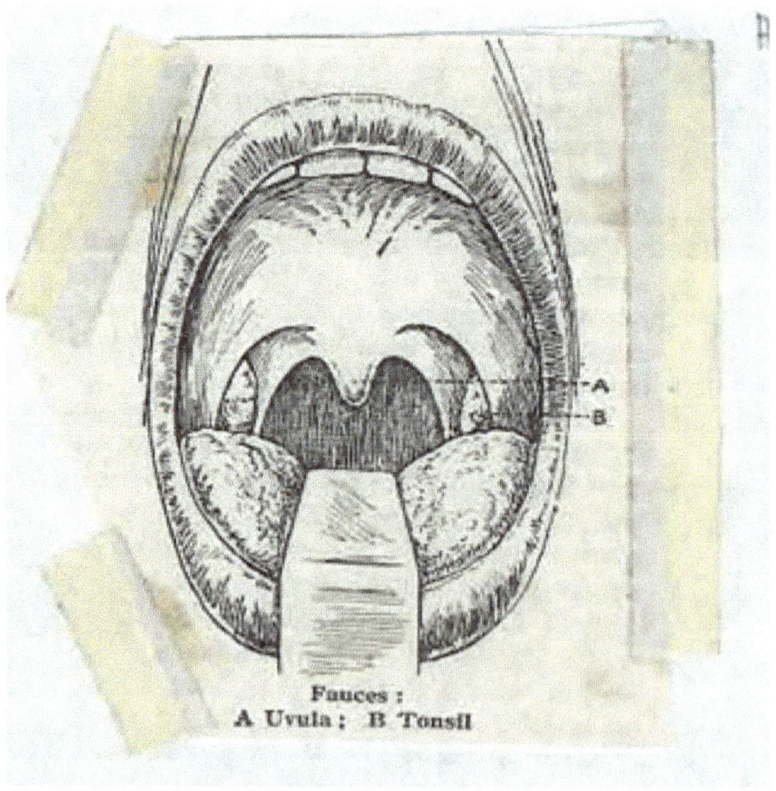

Fauces:
A Uvula; B Tonsil

"If I cannot fly, let me sing." Stephen Sondheim

EATING

There is an old controversy about how we should physically eat our food. There are old customs that it is good to chew each mouth seventeen times or so. These advices seem to have a basis in the fact that digestion is aided if the food is fully mixed with saliva before swallowing. Saliva contains a digestive enzyme called Ptyalin. Chewing also means we eat at a steady pace and are so, perhaps, able to avoid the indigestion which occurs when food is gulped down in lumps.

A good case against the careful chewing approach is made by a Persian Dervish related by G. Gurdjieff in his classic: 'Meeting with Remarkable Men'.

> *"By chewing your food so carefully you reduce the work of your stomach... At your age, it is better not to chew at all... We eat chiefly to gratify our taste and obtain the accustomed sensation of pressure, which the stomach experiences when it contains this particular quantity of food. In the walls of the stomach there branch out what are called wandering nerves which, beginning to function when there is not a certain pressure, give rise to the sensation we call hunger. Thus, we have different hungers: a so-called bodily or physical hunger and, if it may be so expressed, a nervous hunger, and a psychic hunger."*

There are no exercises on eating at present.

SEEING EXERCISES

exercise: **Eyeball Muscles** It is claimed that holding the eye positions shown for a few seconds each day will restore a true rotundity to the eyeball. The exercise will also massage the eyeball. The order indicated in the diagram may be followed or you may choose your own. However, be methodical, be precise and increase time gradually to avoid strain. Movements between the positions should be slow and steady, the eye focusing naturally. Do not neglect to blink regularly.

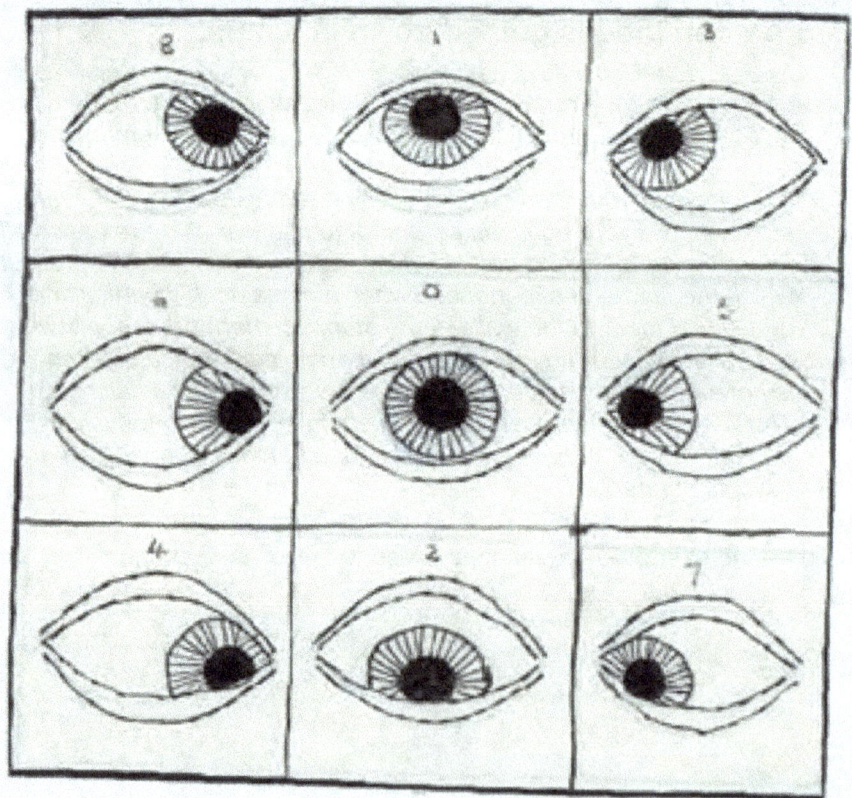

exercise **Tense Lens Muscles** The other muscular operation of the eye is the focusing of the lens inside the eyeball. People often tire their eyes by using them for long periods at a fixed focal length. If this tends to happen in your occupation, take one minute to smoothly shift your focus from near to far objects. Repeat this many times. Try to relax your eyes so that everything goes out of focus, then after a few seconds snap back into focus on something within range.

exercise Focused Observation Choose a small familiar object from your domestic surroundings that possesses detail. A matchbox, clock, radio, ornament, coin, key, postcard, brush, shoe, book, plant, identity card, mug, cushion, lamp, pencil, painting, cassette, tube of toothpaste, anything will do. Begin to observe it very closely. The exercise should last a definite time - ten minutes is a good time-span. If you cannot keep up an intense level of concentration for this long, you will find that drawing the object is a good aid. Don't worry if you can't 'draw a likeness'. Make verbal notes of every new observation you don't draw; this is an important ritual of consolidation. A new object every day will give you 360 degrees of extra texture in a year. By this time your observation will reach a magical level of efficiency.

exercise Estimating Dimensions Every time you go into a new room estimate the dimensions by eye. Note these down and then measure them with a pocket tape. How many rooms do you have to enter before you are accurate within one foot or less?

Spend five minutes going around your home estimating the dimensions of things and then checking them with a tape-measure. Continue daily for ten days, rest and assess your improvement. Continue in periods of five or ten days until you can guess dimensions including diameters within one centimetre.

Cut various random lengths from a ball of string. Each length is let fall onto a separate part of the floor. Guess the lengths and check against ruler. Take five minutes and continue daily for ten days or until required accuracy is attained. Pre-set your own goal.

exercise Colour Composition Collect objects and scraps of uniform colour. Cut areas from coloured packaging, cloth materials and plastic. Collect leaves/wood/flowers until you have filled a small cardboard box. Then arrange the pieces on a long wall, in a rainbow sequence, so that one colour will flow into the next. The scraps can then be used to make a collage or picture for which there are no formal rules.

exercise Using Peripheral Vision
   a. A group of people are asked to run in random patterns within a room; play dodgem; Use peripheral vision to avoid collisions. Walking quickly through a crowded street market we use our peripheral vision in a similar way.

b. Stand staring straight ahead. A colleague introduces objects into your cone of vision from behind. Say when you first see the object and then try to identify it without moving your head or eyeballs. Start with large brightly coloured geometric objects and move on to smaller more camouflaged objects. Assess each other's progress.

exercise **Estimating Centre of Gravity** Take an irregular shaped piece of card and guess its centre of gravity. Then suspend it with a piece of string or cotton thread as shown in the diagram. Draw the track of the suspending thread onto the card. Repeat in three directions as shown. Extending the lines of suspension will give you the centre of gravity.

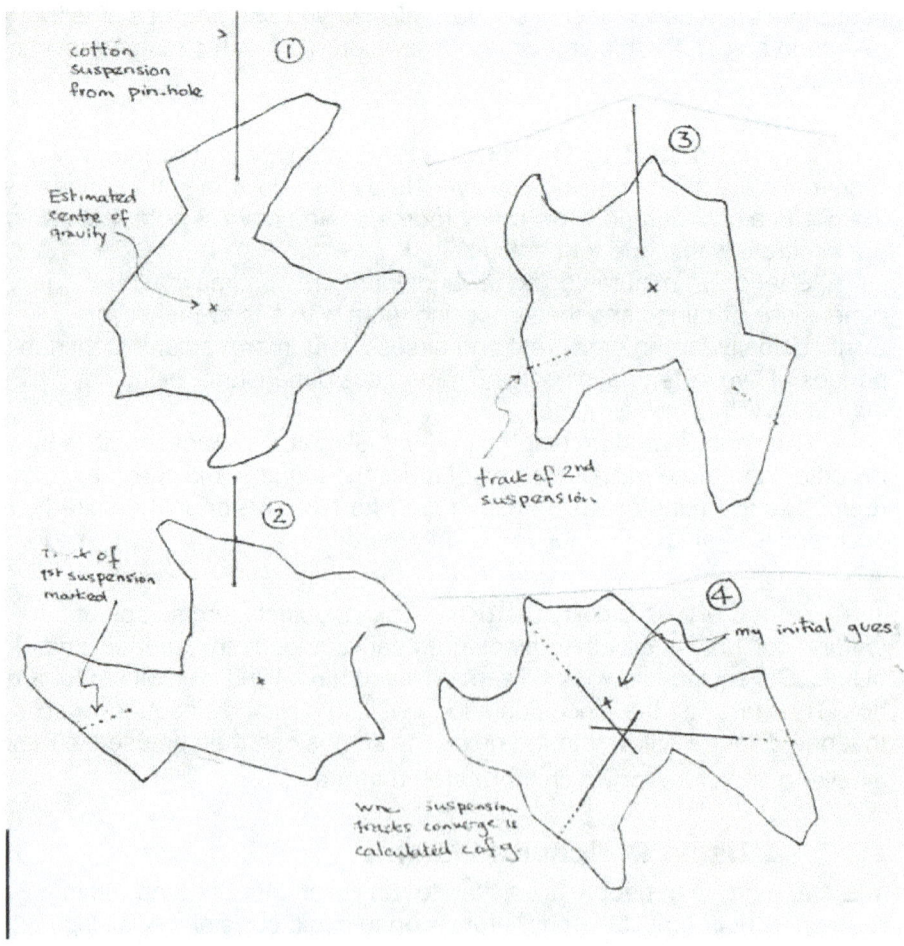

HEARING EXERCISES

exercise **Judging Direction of Sounds** You need to be blindfolded. Sit In a chair in the middle of a large room. Block one ear with a hand or an earplug. Now get a friend to move about quietly, making sharp sounds in different parts of the room. Repeat the experiment with both ears open. Which directions are the hardest to be sure of? Make a chart and check the response several times in each position.

If your sense of direction with two ears open is not excellent, repeat this as an exercise at regular intervals.

exercise **Ambient Sound Meditation**

a. How many sounds can you hear? Count them. Can you tell the direction and cause of each sound. Note differences in tone and strength; rhythmic qualities; groupings. For this exercise and each of the following developments it is suggested that you repeat it for ten days (with rest) and then note any improvements. It is essential to work gradually and methodically, or little useful progress will be achieved.

b. Select one of the most obvious sounds and list everything you can imaginably say about it. Repeat with a new sound.

c. Detect one of the faintest sounds you are hearing. List everything you can say about it.

Select a pleasant sound you are hearing. Note every reason why you feel it is pleasant.

exercise **Record Self** Audio record yourself doing some activity. You can either be conscious of the recording microphone; or forget the recorder is on by putting the recording device in a drawer. Play the recording back to yourself whilst you are doing some other activity.
Examples:

i. Record yourself having breakfast; Playback whilst watching 'Match of the Day.'

ii. Record yourself washing-up; Playback whilst having a bath.

iii: Record having a bath; Playback whilst waiting for a bus.

Don't take an excessive interest in listening. Playback unobtrusively. Keep one of the early recordings that you like. Repeat the exercise at least twice a week. After 6 months compare a recording you like with an earlier recording.

exercise **Mimicry** In front of a television, radio or audio player, tune in to something of interest and practice mimicking whatever catches your fancy. Concentrate on phrases that seem to epitomise the character of that particular sound source to which you are listening. Notice phrases that recur during the programme. Repeat these over and over to yourself making minute changes until you are able to reproduce the sound with uncanny authenticity. This can be focused on a particular category of sounds. Eg. Buy a recording of common bird sounds and learn to mimic some of them. In this way not only will you recognise birds by their sounds but you will also be able to call back to them.

exercise **Focusing on One Sound Amongst Many**

Collect together three radios and a clock. Put the radios all on at equal volume and different programmes. Shut your eyes and listen attentively to one programme only for a timed minute. Switch attention to another programme for a further minute. Every minute switch your attention.

If you find this too difficult move the radios apart and sit facing the one you are paying attention to. If you find this too easy add more radios.

Do this from three to ten minutes daily for ten days with rest.

exercise **Musical Ear Training**

A Basic Programme.

1. We must first learn to 'perceptually isolate' or identify a note without being confused by its overtones or harmonics. To make the predominant pitch of a musical note into a concrete muscular experience learn to imitate notes played on a variety of common instruments. The memory and discernment of different notes is reinforced by their vocal expression. The variety of instruments ensures that the pitch of a note is not confused with other parts of the 'overtones', which give different tonal qualities to each type of instrument.

2. The second job of appreciation is then to be able to clearly perceive the pitch of a musical sound and compare it with another to judge which is the higher. This should be continued until the 12 equal divisions of the octave (i.e. semitones) are clearly distinguishable. Two notes are played one after the other. Sing them and identify which is higher.

3. The next step is to distinguish the interval between notes. Two notes are played one after the other. Sing them and name the 'interval' or how many notes apart they are. Start with the easier intervals: the second and octave; then a third and fifth, then a fourth, sixth and seventh. Note consonant intervals, and the intervals that produce more dissonance. It is conventionally useful at this point to learn to name notes by their code letters and to know their position on the five-line stave.

4a. Move on to groups of notes. Get someone to play a few notes simultaneously. How many notes are in this chord? Learn to distinguish between two and three note chords. Above three notes will become more difficult.

4b. A chord is followed by its lowest note. Identify the other notes by singing or naming them.

4c. Distinguish between chord inversions. Root position, first inversion, and second inversion of the triad a common major chord. Inversion is the process of turning the shape of a group of notes (a chord) upside down.

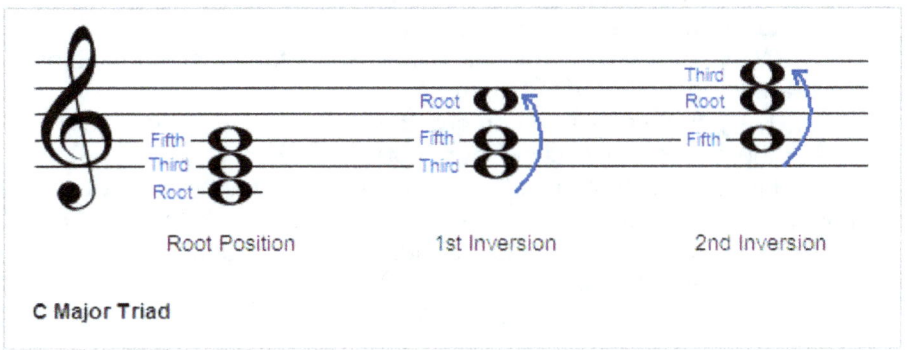

4d. Differentiate between major and minor triads of a common chord. When you've got this go on to differentiate the diminished and the augmented.

5. Listen carefully to some simple short melody, played on a piano or organ. Try to reconstruct the melody from memory. At first you may only remember a few notes; don't be discouraged; build up from whatever scraps you can remember. When you are able to reconstruct simple melodies, you may wish to increase, step by step, the complexity of the music you start with.

NOTE For those who do not possess or have access to a piano or similar instrument: Take an audio recorder to the nearest available piano and record relationships as indicated in the text above leave a space after each example and then after fifteen or twenty-seconds say what the relationship is in words. Do not memorise what you are doing. Later playback the recording and see if you can guess the correct answer.

exercise **Social Listening** There is a psycho-social aspect to listening when it is another person that you are listening to. The manner in which we listen is an important component of human caring. Creative listening can turn a dull anecdote into a fascinating story. It can bring out the beauty of someone who at first appearance seems dull and lifeless.

1. Decide that listening is going to be your main activity. Your argumentative faculties go into suspended animation.

2. Without making a cross-examination ask for the elaboration of what seem to be the important details.

3. The person may insist on giving a short version of their story at first. Ask them to retell it eliciting more detail and descriptions.

4. Listen with the motive that listening is good caring. Your own curiosity may interfere with the person's own direction. Make it clear that you are listening because you care about the person speaking rather than your own interest in the subject matter.

5. Prepare yourself beforehand to be ready for anything. Do not let yourself react in a shocked or judgmental manner by unexpected disclosures. This type of attentive listening is powerful, be prepared. Calm, alert and fearless attention is what is required. Keep listening. Keep attentive! Don't let your facial expression pass judgement. Try not to show boredom.

6. Be prepared for laughing, crying, trembling, yawning or scratching. If they come up as a reflex response to what the person is talking about they should be encouraged as natural releases of emotion. Be pleased at any such response and do not offer overweening sympathy or other distraction.

7. Don't associate from what people say. Almost anything anybody says could remind you of some experience of your own but, for the moment, keep it to yourself. Their story, however similar to your own experience it appears, is unique and special.

8. If someone is asking for suggestions get them to think for themselves. Only make suggestions, solve problems, think of improvements if necessary.

9. Be receptive to the person; rather than the story.

TOUCHING EXERCISES

exercise **Two Point Discrimination** Obtain a pair of blunt compasses. Open them so the points are about three millimetres apart. With this gap, you will probably be able to discriminate two points touching the skin of the fingertips, but if you now place the compasses on the chest you can only feel one poke. Adjust the gap until you can feel two separate points. Measure this gap. In this way, a chart may be made of the sensitivity of the skin in different parts of the body.

Having made a chart, repeat this exercise for a minimum of ten days, with rest, and see if there is any increase of sensitivity. What conditions change the sensitivity of the skin to touch? This exercise is best done if the compasses are placed on the skin by a helper, and the subject keeps their eyes closed.

exercise **Feeling Objects** Spend 15-30 minutes exploring your room blindfolded. Be sure to make a good job of the blindfold, putting cotton wool pads over the eyelids if the contours of our face make it difficult to get a good seal. Identify objects by touch alone. Estimate the weight and dimension of various chosen objects, checking your guesses later. When an object you know well surprises you with the way it feels, spend some time with it. Notice the exact position of fittings such as handles, relief design, indentations, holes, robustness, flexibility, articulation, etc. Gradually increase the speed and confidence with which you can move about the room. Repeat this exercise with rest, until you can move around your room with almost as much ease as if you were not wearing a blindfold. After a break of a week or so, move on to the bathroom or garden.

exercise **Informational Massage** We often associate touching each other as a demand for, or a move toward, having sex. This expectation can sometimes create a situation where the only time we get touched is just before sex, and sometimes we miss out on touching just for the pleasure of being touched and caressed. Reestablishing feelings of closeness, affection and trust can be done through massage that does not lead to sex.

Set aside some time to explore how and where you like to touch and be touched.

With permission from a friend or partner, spend fifteen minutes stroking her or his body solely for your own pleasure. Ask the receiver to give comments only if you cause them discomfort or pain. Respect these limits.

Take a short break and then spend fifteen minutes touching your partner or friend for his or her pleasure. Follow their instructions. Ask for a commentary on how it feels.

Is it easier for you to touch for your own pleasure or to give pleasure to another?

On another day, switch roles. Is it easier for you to give or receive?

Adapted from S.A.R. Sex Guide. With permission.

exercise **Object Identification**

1. Procure many similar sized objects covering a range of basic forms. Arrange these on a tabletop. Wearing a blindfold, examine these by touch alone. Become readily conversant with their different shapes, textures and details.

2. Ask a friend to present you with several surprise objects, which you don't see beforehand. Sit comfortably before a table, wearing a blindfold. Try to determine what the articles are by touch alone. Objects might include: a wax candle, a parsnip, a potato, a piece of clay, a light bulb, an empty box of matches, a hand torch, a toy, etc.

Repeat for ten days, with rest, and then note changes in perception.

exercise Weight Get about a dozen plastic boxes of the same size. Now add hidden weights to the boxes in pairs, so they increase gradually in weight. Two are made to weigh half-an-ounce approximately; two are made one ounce; two are one-and-a-half ounces; two are two ounces, etc. The hidden weights may be plasticine, clay or whatever dense material is to hand. The weight should be marked inconspicuously on each box.

Now place the boxes, at random, on a tabletop. Blindfolded and using only one hand, arrange the blocks into their similarly weighted pairs. Check and note results. The boxes are mixed up again, and rearranged using the other hand. Check and note results. Are both hands equally perceptive?

The boxes are mixed up again, and then rearranged into their pairs using both hands alternately. Check and note results.

The weight differences are then gradually reduced eg. Half an ounce, three quarters of an ounce, one ounce, one and a quarter ounces, etc.

Continue over ten days, with rest. Note improvement.

exercise Head & Face Massage Relax your hands. Massage and shake them out until they feel tingly. Rub them together giving attention to the fronts, backs, between the fingers and finger tips.

Begin by slapping your scalp all over with a loose wrist and limp fingers. Then massage the scalp using the fingertips. Think of tension being released in the back of the neck; as it releases the neck lengthens. Fingertip massage around the hairline. Stroke your forehead. Place the palms of the hands over the eyes and imagine the eyeballs sinking back deep into their sockets as they relax.

Massage the nose. Pinch the bridge of the nose on each out-breath for five breaths. Rest head onto thumb-tips placed under the notches that you can feel in the inner top edge of your eye sockets. Massage your gums.

Brush the skin back from centre temple around to the ears. Continue this down the face pulling the skin back from the centre line in slow rhythmic waves. Rub the palms up and down the sides of the face in opposing directions stretching the skin diagonally. Finally make wild face stretching grimaces including poking your tongue out.

This is a guide to start with. As you discover new things about your face or new things to do with your face, include them in your routine. Such simple pleasure can seem unworthy of the effort of self-discipline and not functional enough to be included in the daily rituals of self-care. Nevertheless, repeat daily for ten days with rest and note the effect.

The sequence above is derived from Tai Do practice.

exercise **Foot Massage** Use your intuition and the following diagram. Press firmly with finger and thumb tips. Concentration and sensitivity is essential.

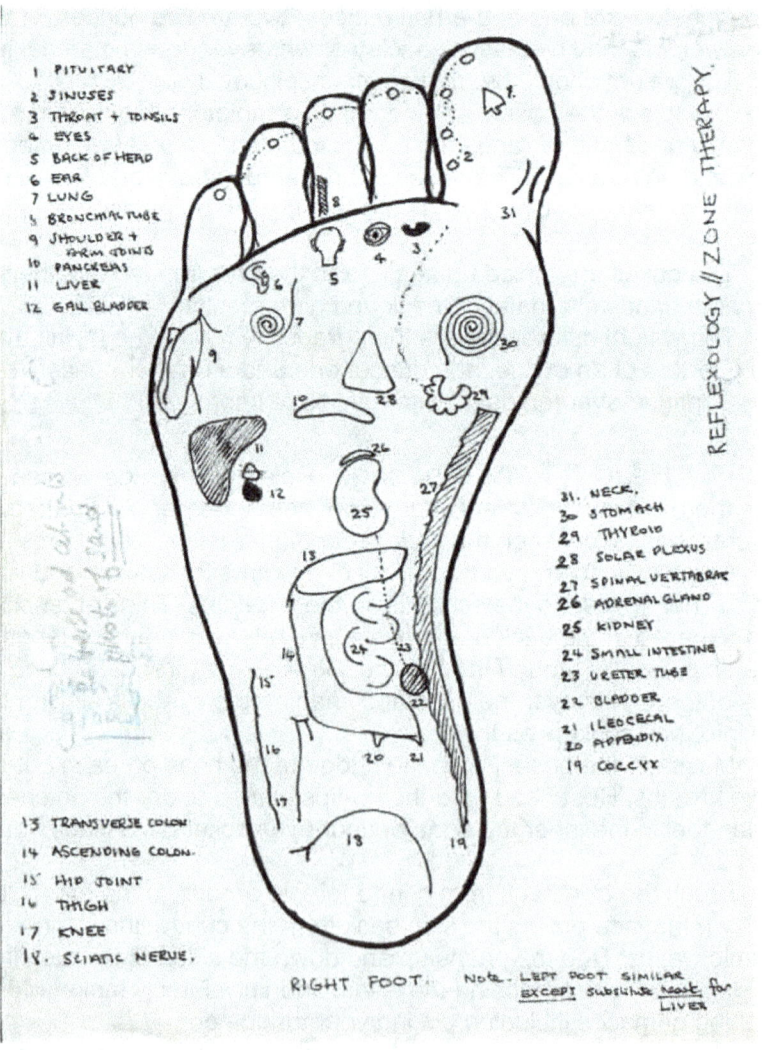

SMELLING & TASTING EXERCISES

exercise **Explore 1** Explore your room/apartment/house/hut systematically for smells. Note down 50-100 smells and describe each one in a couple of words. Can these smells be organised into groups using one of the classification systems mentioned in the introduction to smelling? This initial exploration will give you plenty of information on where to find smells for doing the following experiments. It will also give you an extraordinary odour map of your house.

exercise **Explore 2** Explore your environment.
    A. Visit a derelict lot in which a variety of plants are growing. Make a systematic map of the predominant smells using graph paper. Attempt a classification.
    B. Visit a store. Go systematically around all the counters smelling everything and taking notes. It might be a good idea to be surreptitious to avoid being escorted out. Keep it up for at least 10 minutes. What smells are intrinsic to particular commodities and which have been added?

exercise **Personal associations and mental effects** Sit with a particular smell within effective range. Meditate upon its associations and note them down. Then further involve yourself with the sensation and notice any psychic effects - does it elevate or depress you? Enter the smell and live in its world.

exercise **Touch/taste discrimination**
    A. With a small spoon drop a dollop of syrup: onto the tongue. Is it the slippery feeling or the sweet taste that is first perceived?
    B. Put a very little pepper onto the tongue. Pinch the nostrils. Is there a sensation separate from the irritation?
    C. Experiment with other edibles. List them and note the components of the sensation that they give. Repeat these exercises for 10 days, with one or two days rest. Note any improvements.

exercise **Sweetness** Two glasses of water are sweetened equally. Ask a friend to add a measured but tiny amount of Angostura Bitters to one glass. Now say which solution is changed by the addition of the bitter. The bitter may be increased until a difference in sweetness is perceived. Extra sweetness should be noticed before the solution tastes bitter.
    Repeat every day for ten days excepting a day or two off. Note improvement.

exercise Flower Smell In spite of the extensive neglect by horticulturists in maintaining the fragrance of many cultivated flowers, there is still much pleasure to be had from the aromatic garden. Wallflowers, Cottage pinks, Flowering Tobacco, Sweet William, Alyssum, Heliotrope, Violet, Rose, Acacia, Lily of the Valley and Lavender are good examples.

Put half a dozen fragrant flowers on the table before you. Pick up each flower in turn, and savor its scent. Then with your eyes closed shuffle the blooms about, and then taking each one separately, try to identify it by its smell. Afterwards reconstruct these smells in your imagination, relating each to the flower to which it belongs. Repeat for ten days, with rest.

"If you take any flower you please and look it over and turn it about and smell it and feel it and try to find out all its little secrets, not of flower only but of leaf, bud and stem as well, you will discover many wonderful things." Gertrude Jekyll

exercise Extracts Obtain a range of extracts, perfumes, essential oils or flower essences. Take two of them at random. Inhale the odour of one then do the same with the other. Then moving away from them, think of the first smell, then think of the second. In your mind compare them, noting the difference. Repeat with different pairs of extracts.

Do this for ten days, with rest.

exercise Detail Differentiation Take a particular category of taste or smell and sample five or six. If these can be sampled simultaneously, as with cheeses, note the unique characteristics of each. Then arrange it so you may sample each one without seeing it and guess which one it is. If several may not practicably be tested simultaneously, as with bottles of wine, then make notes on the taste at the time. Compare your notes and memory of one taste with the next. Later compare your own findings with those of cheese or wine writers.

exercise Sensitivity Using the essences find the smallest amount that you can detect by putting a drop into a pint of water. If you can smell it, dilute with another pint of water and throw half of the solution away. Repeat dilutions until any smell is no longer detectable. If one drop is not detectable, add more drops until you can smell it. Repeat for 10 days with rest, making a graph of your results. Why can you smell better on some days than others? Does your sensitivity increase by the tenth day? Repeat with different smells. Compare results.

exercise Comparative Analysis Arrange to be presented with a pair of smells. Attempt to identify the two individual smells. If they cannot be named, try to describe them. If the separate character of the smells cannot be discerned ask for the name and description of one of the pairs. Does this help you to guess the other? What smells are easily distinguished? What smells merge? The selection of smells for this exercise, are best selected over a range as suggested by the classification mentioned in the introduction and paired in roughly equal strengths. This is an exercise for the advanced osmologist.

exercise **Combinations** Try three smell combinations making notes of your sensations. From these notes decide which smells in the combinations are most elemental. This exercise may be combined with the process of cooking daily meals.

THERMAL SENSING EXERCISES

exercise **To Objectify Temperature Sensations** You must equip yourself with at least two air thermometers. Set up one outside, in the shade and under cover, and one in your room. If possible also have a humidity meter. Now at the same time every day for a year, keep a record in your diary. First assess the temperature by how you feel; taking into account changes of clothing, health etc. Note this guesstimate, then take the thermometer reading. At the end of every month, add your readings to a graph, made out for the year, and note the progress in the accuracy of your assessments.

exercise **Surface Temperature Variations** The simplest way of shocking the bodies heat control mechanisms out of their central heating slumber is to vary the surface temperature of the skin quickly without allowing serious heat losses. The best way to do this is to go to a shower with separate hot and cold controls. Set the heat up high, then vary the cold until you can comfortably bear it. When you are well heated step out of the shower and turn off the hot. Then dive back under the now cold shower, for as long as you can bear it, or until you are well cooled off. The first time you may only be able to bear a quick splash, but regular repeated practice makes the practice a pleasant and invigorating one. Then repeat this quickly three or four times until you feel yourself tingling all over. This tingling is the lazy old thermo-nerve endings spluttering their way back into operation. The refreshing effect initiated by the tingling will continue for as long as half an hour. I have found that regular 'hot and colds' with a bit of jogging beforehand makes me practically immune to common colds, flu and other commonplace ills.

The aerotone, sauna, Russian and Turkish baths can do a similar job, but require more time and money. Outdoor swimming in spring and autumn will be as good. Make sure you get well warmed-up between dips.

exercise **Radiant Heat Source**

a. You must be blindfolded. Get an assistant to move a lighted candle across a table towards your open hands, face, or other exposed parts of the body. Say as soon as you can feel the heat and record the distance. Then move the candle gradually away across the table. As soon as the sensation of heat fades, record the distance. Repeat daily for ten days with rest. Using the same area of body as a sensor and having the room at about the same temperature. Does having warm or cold hands make a difference to your sensitivity?

b. At the distance at which you can barely feel one candle alight.

Arrange a short ark of unlit candles. Blindfolded, get a friend to light and extinguish candles in a random order. This must be done silently using a taper. Guess how many candles are alight at any time. Repeat ten days with rest.

exercise Ice & Blood Find two small strong glass jars with smooth bottoms. Fill one with hot water bearable to the hands, the other with crushed ice. Arrange for someone to track these slowly around your body using oil or talcum powder as a lubricant. Can you always be sure which is the hot and which is the cold? Note the varying sensations in different parts of the body.

exercise Extremes What is the warmest water you can put your hand into without feeling pain? Beware! Increase the temperature gradually! What is the coldest water you can dip into? Both extremes need to be approached cautiously. Know where to stop.

    The hot extreme: Hot water from a kettle is gradually added to a bucket. Find the temperature at which you can't bear to comfortably keep your arm in for a count of five. Take the temperature of the water with a household thermometer. Record with comments. Repeat at regular intervals and compare results.

    The cold extreme: Can be done in a bath by gradually reducing the temperature of a bath by one degree each day. It is a richer experience, done at a swimming pool or in the sea during the change from summer to winter. Attendance twice per week will give your body time to adapt. This technique will improve the self-insulating properties of the body and this seems to helps guard against seasonal illnesses.

exercise Assessing Conductivity of Materials Different materials have the capacity to hold different amounts of heat. Metal hold a lot and wood holds little; this is known as the materials conductivity. So, even when it is at the same cool temperature, a metal bar will feel colder than a wooden rod. Go around your garden or your house and check out the feel of different surfaces and objects. List them in order of their conductivity. Earth, tree, grass, concrete, water, glass will all be at roughly the same temperature but will feel different because of their different thermal conductivity.

GRAVITY & MOVEMENT EXERCISES

exercise **Basic Body Imaging** Study of the skeleton and establishing an internal picture of your own skeleton is invaluable preparation. Start off any imaging session with relaxation and a general sensory focus. Sense what is there now in your body. The technical term for this sense is proprioception.

Allow your upper body weight to hang from your spinal column. Then through this experience of your mass, allow a centre line to be imagined and rise up through the torso and out of the top of the head. Finish this centre line way above your head. The line could be imagined as made of light, string, steel rod, or as an abstract line; anything that feels right.

Once you have achieved this imaginative feat standing immobile, take it into slow movement. Gradually incorporate the imaging sessions into your everyday life.

Finding your centre line or axis is of fundamental importance to many movement philosophies and posture training. For further images see the chapters on standing and running.

Movement with Image: With the centre line image established in a standing position; swing your arms around the axis turning from above the waist. Keep the hips still. Swing the arms in an easy manner. Another useful movement whilst imaging your centre line is a plié or knees bend. Let your sacrum drop just a few inches. Then imagine a movement or force sliding up the long centre line that moves your torso up.

exercise **Tendon and Muscle Stretch Receptors** S-T-R-E-T-C-H your body in all directions. Make all stretches very gentle. Do not force limbs into painful positions. Use only the weight of the body itself; relaxing the muscles as much as is possible. This can be done to music. You might find the piano music of Wim Mertens ideal for this.

exercise **Balance** A good balance means that the bones must be aligned so that weight is transferred down through the centres of your joints. Do not rely on the support of ligaments and muscles.

a) Find ten body positions in which you can balance for one minute on one leg. Five balances on the right, five on the left; ten minutes total. Continue for ten days with rest. How is your wobble?

b) Stand. Move up onto tip toe. Keep your balance. Then lower your body slowly through standing to crouching and on down. If you are comfortable to sitting on your haunches you can go that far. Then rise slowly up again. Your arms may be held in different positions each time. This is a difficult exercise. To do ten up and down without toppling may take you months of practice. Persevere. Be careful not to strain your knees.

c) Fix a beam close to the floor. Ideally this would be a piece of timber 4" x 4" and about 10' long lying on the floor and fixed to a wall at one end. Walk along it forwards without looking. Walk backwards keeping you eyes to the front. Balance on one leg. Become confident on this 'line'. Advanced skills might be turns, hops and skips. This is an advanced exercise!

exercise **Centre of Gravity** With a light stretch to the whole body find the place that your body will balance horizontally over a supportive and cushioned box. This can be over the back of another person on their hands and knees. Then begin to slowly move arms and legs and notice how the centre of gravity changes position depending on the shape you are making. Try to pinpoint this dynamic centre in your body and notice how it shifts with changes in body shape. Don't 'worry' about it; just *play* around in an aware frame of mind. You will gradually internalise an awareness of your centre of gravity.

As you get the hang of this exercise reduce the size and speed of movements until they are very slow and small. The most important information will be found on this microscopic level of perception.

exercise **Experiencing Gravity** We experience gravity in two ways, through the receptor in the inner ear, and by the weight it gives our limbs and body.

a) Falling - Most of us are so used to having our heads upright all the time it can be disorientating to feel gravity in a different direction. Stand relaxed on a carpeted floor. Close your eyes. Bend your knees and slowly lower yourself as low as possible. When you can do this confidently without falling over, repeat the process with your head tilted forwards or to the side. As you begin to go down you will probably fall. If you do fall; roll softly onto the floor. With your eyes closed roll around on the floor, gently, deliberately, holding your head in different positions. Then open your eyes and slowly get up to standing. Take care that there are no hard objects to fall onto. Repeat for ten days, with rest.

b) Rolling - Lay on a warm floor in any comfortable way. Become aware of the weight of each part of your body as it presses against the floor. Imagine that your weight is gathered in the part of your body nearest the floor whilst the upper part of your body is light and airy. If you want a more exotic image think of your body as hollow containing an amount of mercury that evenly covers the lower surfaces of your body shell like a silver lake. Then, very, very gradually, begin to roll onto your side. Imagine the sensation of mercury flowing to the new area of floor contact. The upper surfaces are light and porous. Continue to roll, very slowly, from side to front to side to back, keeping relaxed and with your attention on the area in contact with the floor.

exercise **Labyrinthine Receptors** These sense acceleration and change of direction of the head or whole body.

a) Spin slowly and evenly around. Gently get faster then slower again. Do not allow yourself to become dizzy. Repeat this exercise daily for up to five minutes. At first you should only turn very slowly. The aim is to experience acceleration and small changes of direction, not whirling. Dervish like whirling is an ecstatic mode you may get into later.

b) Whilst standing or sitting upright allow your head to fall forward and hang with a little residual muscle tension. Feel its weight. Then, very slowly and carefully, without pulling it up, roll it around to the side. Rest again and feel its weight; then roll to the back so your face is slightly tilted upwards and on to the other side, completing a full circle. This is a neck stretch, but become more aware mainly of the movement and position of your head. Repeat daily. Avoid if you have any neck pain.

c) With your head hanging forward, gently swing the torso from side to side, using the weight of the head as a sort of pendulum, allow this weight to pull you off into a turn. Using the free-swinging weight of the head as a momentum engage in a short movement improvisation. Concentrate your attention on how to reestablish stability after each swing.

exercise **Learning New Movements**

1. Learning a new movement sequence is a mental process. If the idea of the movement is well formed in the mind then the actual practice will follow relatively easily.

2. However, to create the movement in the mind or transfer it from the visual sense, having only seen a demonstration, is an advanced skill. The sequence must normally be marked out, in sections, several times. This means that you go through the movements slowly, bit by bit, and become familiar with the vocabulary of flexures, turns and changes involved.

3. After 'marking out' a sequence of movement, go over it in your mind. It is best to be able to imagine the sequence in detail in your mind if you are going to remember it. When you have marked it out a section several times go over the whole thing in your mind without moving.

4. This is only possible if you are fluent with the movement vocabulary used. If elements of the sequence are new, you may have to spend hours learning how to do them comfortably. However, a sequence can nearly always be simplified so it may be expressed within a vocabulary closer to everyday movements.

MEMORY EXERCISES

exercise **Short Term Memory Testing** Someone reads a set of random digits aloud to you. The set consist of from two to ten digits. You repeat them immediately following the reading. The reader increases the readout size until forgetting is consistent. Before starting, the reader says this standard instruction: *'I am going to read numbers and when I have finished, I want you to repeat the numbers in the same order'*.

A similar experiment may also be arranged using consonants, different coloured cards, nouns, simple geometrical shapes or short phrases.

Note: Unusually high scores in short term memory are only possible if the sets are mentally organised into subgroups and are then given their own label or code. See the techniques listed below.

exercise **Memory: Criteria of Retention 1. Primacy and Recency** The beginning of an event, lecture, film, journey or list is more likely to be remembered than other parts (all other things being equal!). This is also true of the final scene or conclusion. This characteristic of memory can be used to advantage by introducing the main points or characters early on and summarising your conclusions at the end. This principle will even work for periods of several years as it will for short lists of objects or a lecture. It is also true for life as a whole in that early events are most influential and recent events most easily remembered in detail.

Application: Think of ways that first and last things seen can be designed to envelop the whole. With an essay, this may be a first paragraph that summarises your argument and a final paragraph that summarises your main points. Or you may wish to simply grab your audience's attention with a dramatic quote or description.

exercise **Memory: Criteria of Retention 2. Categories** When a number of things have something in common they can more easily be remembered by grouping them under their shared feature. Instead of naming the individuals of a company or team, they are given a name. Perhaps the things fit into a natural series such as 1 2 3, or mountains/plains/seas. If the things needing to be remembered are completely disparate they may be artificially made into a linked set. One way of doing this is to include the things as part of a story that you make up for this purpose. The story, as a rich set of linked ideas in which the things are integral elements, is more easily remembered than a disparate list.

Application: Take what you wish to remember and list what the material has in common. If this seems unhelpful create an artificially linking structure like an imagined house in which each fact or object to be remembered is visualised in a particular location.

exercise **Memory: Criteria of Retention 3. Difference**

A foreign or exotic word might stand out from a passage of normal prose. A flower might stand out in a muddy battlefield. A sparrow would stand out in an aviary of finches. The weird, unexpected, unusually strident or out of context, will be remembered. Exaggerations of SIZE seem to be especially effective.

Application: To memorise a common name, use a ludicrous or exaggerated metaphor that will make it stick in the mind.

exercise **Memory: Criteria of Retention 4. Sensual Power**

The more enjoyable the sensation, the more likely it will be remembered, all other things being equal. For some senses, this means an increase in strength in others it is a matter of timing. On a mundane practical level, reading material is more likely to be remembered visually if it has key words in colour and is as brightly lit as possible without glare.

A message in several media, where different senses are stimulated, is more powerful than in one. It follows then, that an idea expressed through a story, will have more effect on our memory than a straightforward statement. The more fantastic, evocative or powerfully illustrated a story is, the stronger the memory of it will be. However, best of all is to directly express the idea in actions. Sometimes this may be done as an experiment, sometimes as an exercise and sometimes it can be a less specific action in the world at large. Sexual or sexually linked data will probably be easily remembered because of our pervasive taboo on sex and because sex has a high level of sensory power. Anything vulgar, horrific, obscene or repulsive will also be easily remembered. Anything associated with fear which is not threatening in itself like the story of a murder, will be more easily remembered. This will vary depending on your personality. *Vivid perception is the best aid to retention.*

Application: To get people to remember what you say or write make sure it appeals to a range of the senses either directly or by association. A subject that is dull can be associated with one that is bright. A dull black and white plan will draw attention to itself simply by being pasted onto a coloured background.

exercise **Memory Criteria of Retention 5. Repetition and Review**

Repetition is essential for the retention of any low key or complex information. Each time a particular object, process or condition is perceived, the memory trace is etched deeper.

This principle can be used in two ways. First, in learning a passage of prose or collection of objects, the passage or collection must be gone over and over, until it is learnt. Second, if the thing needs to be learnt so that it is permanently ready for recall, then it must be reviewed at intervals. Review is recommended ten minutes after first learning; the next day; the next week; the next month; in four months. After four or five reviews, separated in time, the item enters the long-term memory from which it is never lost.

Repetition is most effective if it is active. If one speaks the words, with gestures or if the facts are made into a model, sculpture, poster or conversation topic. Passive repetition needs more cycles to gain an equivalent retention. This is the main ploy of advertising, where essentially unimportant material is absorbed by passive but repeated exposure. Passive absorption has the advantage of avoiding the reactive filters of the conscious mind.

As a mental faculty, memory cannot be improved by repetitive practice. By remembering more telephone numbers, you are not improving your memory as such. What you may be doing, if your retention of numbers gets better, is developing and improving techniques with which to remember.

If a thing is worth repeating it is worth repeating at least three times. Rub it in.

exercise Memory: Criteria of Retention 6. Personal Interest or Use Value

Retention improves with increased motivation. This may be due to an increase in the intensity of perception. Whatever the reason, motivation is an important factor. If an action, object or item of knowledge can be seen to be of use then motivation increases. A perception that is irrelevant to our survival, or whose use is obscure, won't generate much interest and so will not be easily remembered.

Application: In setting up material to be memorised it helps to make its use value clear. This seems an obvious point and yet in much school work the reason it is useful to learn the facts presented is not given. An interest may also be achieved by firing questions at the material until a link with personal experience is found.

Artificial motivation may be generated by mystical or fictitious reasons of use, or by associating a 'useless' fact or object with one that is more fecund. This is one of the most common strategies used in advertising.

exercise Criteria of Retention 7. Attention and Concentration

A basic perceptual ability is to be able to shift attention from the general to the specific. In this way, the power of cognition is focused in a very small area. Other sensations and irrelevant thoughts are rigorously excluded to achieve this specialisation.

A one-point focus is difficult to keep steady for very long. Apart from mental interference from wandering thoughts and chains of association there is the perceptual phenomenon of adaptation. In practice attention is available for periods of 10-45 minutes depending on the material. Between these periods of concentration there should be five minutes breaks for rest and assimilation. Consecutive periods of study should provide a variety of stimuli. Its a good idea if similar subjects and media are not revised one after the other.

<u>Application</u>: An environment free from distraction is essential. This is a personal thing but it is often useful to get out of your own house. Go to a library or get a studio. Difficult material, like heavy technical information, will generally require shorter, sharper periods of attention. Take regular breaks for physical exercise.

exercise **Memory Criteria of Retention 8. Preparedness**
Are you in the right frame of mind? If your mind is elsewhere you will not be able to key into a subject as quickly as if you had 'warmed up' beforehand.

<u>Application</u>: You will do better in an interview if you have mentally reviewed your CV beforehand. Reviewing memories of a subject before a lecture will facilitate your retention of new facts and ideas. Things with which the new ideas can be linked are then fresh in your mind.

exercise **Memory: Remembering a Name**
Relate the name of the person to the person in some way. Make a connection; any connection! You may have to be wildly imaginative. Repeat the name to yourself sub-vocally whilst looking at the person's face. Go on to study the face for distinctive features whilst repeating the name in your mind.

"*John John JOhn JoHn JohN John John John*". "*Hmm, wart on forehead, grey eyes, grey hairs, unshaven, high cheekbones...*" Now make the imaginative leap: Imagine a golf ball between his teeth which suggests a John Player golf tournament. He couldn't smoke with a golf ball between his teeth; suggesting John Players cigarettes. This absurd sequence of imagined associations will make it easy to remember his name when you meet again.

This means making quite a creative effort when you are introduced to people. It may not be easy if there is shyness involved when meeting new people or you have other urgent business to attend to.

Repeat the name of the person you have met in conversation as soon as possible. Repeat the name as often as conversation permits without giving an impression of over familiarity. Other people you know with the same name, if the name isn't as common as 'John', may be used as a conversational gambit. Linking the name to an occupation as they do in

Wales with something like 'David the piano', can be helpful. It takes quite a bit of practice before a dozen new introductions at a party can be retained, but it is possible with practice and ingenuity to compress the technique into very few seconds.

exercise **Remembering Words and Sentences** Select a succinct and simple piece of prose to develop your technique. Ideally also, a passage that is important to you. Half of the task is done if there is a very clear conception of what each word means; and how its position in the sentence qualifies its meaning; and how each sentence embodies a meaning of its own. Further, in exactly how the meaning of the sentence is expanded by the following sentences.

A good dictionary is essential. No words should be doubtful or ambiguous. New words should be noted.

Having thoroughly understood the passage to be memorised, repeat the first few words keeping the meaning alive in your mind. Repeat them, until they are easily repeated without view of the source material. Then go on with the remaining words in the sentence. When these are implanted repeat the whole sentence, keeping the meaning of what you are saying to the front of your mind. Go on in this way, sentence by sentence, adding small units to the whole, until you have acquired a modest part of the passage you want to know by heart.

In any spare moments in subsequent days make sure you review the passage aloud. Further periods of learning should be planned on a regular basis until the passage is learnt. You will soon get to know the amount of time you need to set aside for any memory task.

Many young people around the world learn to recite the whole of the Koran by heart. I noticed that those who excel at this feat have a musical intonation to their sentences.

exercise **Remembering New Vocabulary** When reading note down any new words and collect them on the left hand page of a large exercise book. When the page has two columns of new words get out a dictionary and make minimal notes or thumbnail sketches to describe the meaning along side each word.

Then write out an imaginative passage making use of all the words. The words dictate what happens next. Just allow yourself to associate wildly between the different words.

This piece of writing is then reread a few times in the next few days. It is surprising how naturally interested you will be in reading what you have created, however nonsensical it appears. You are reminded of the meaning of the words by the context that you have made for them. Example below:

The Story of Philosophy
*The broadsheet was a **paragon** of clarity. Netiara held the disquisition at arms length and admired the sharply rectilinear pulp wafer. Within its four corners the **nasute** iconoclast, feet planted firmly in **illabile** stance, roars challenge to the **mendacious teleologic** professors; a gowned and chalk dusted **congerie** of learned manhood. The proud **chanticleers** of humanities cerebral **pandects**, staring at the yellowed reflections of their own **noumenal** condition.*

*The vandal approaches within the distance that she may be certain of an **expectorant** bulls-eye. The excreted phlegm lands before them like an offering. A **jejune** master of **approbation** separates himself from the heap with a **sedulous** effort. He staggers forward with his head thrown back, a gurgling coming from his gaping mouth. As he approaches the pool of spit he lifts his arms and cloak and steps into the dance of the **chimeric** avatar with a concomitant **persiflage** directed up to a plaster relief of the **Portola**. His **raillery** becomes more agitated and gradually breaks into an airless **ululation** out of which the avatar would spring **auguries** damning the impatient appetite of the street-fighter.*

*At last, spent, he slid to the floor like a black bag of bones. The warrior spoke in deeply flowing tones. "You, where all is perspective and reflection... The Library cannot tell you of each **nascent** moment, an **approbation** of the crystal."*

---

exercise **Remembering Ideas from Books & Reading**
Paraphrase the essential ideas to yourself at the end of each reading session. If the situation allows read these notes aloud.

Then read the crucial passages again and paraphrase afresh. As you are doing this note down the most important points; as if you were relating them to someone else. As you go on through the book describe to yourself the connections between the essential ideas. Relate each new idea to the preceding material. If the 'argument' or 'structure' is complex you may find it helps to use a keyword note diagram (see below).

After each chapter or other substantial amount of text, summarise the argument so far. These summaries may be taped and played back when the whole book has been read.

Having made a summary; criticise and question the ideas so far. Again, think out aloud if possible. Aim to make this succinct.

It is a real 'effort' to start to use this technique when one has been used to reading being a passive, quiet activity. The extra effort will be rewarded by a much stronger and clearer conceptual life.

exercise Memory: Keyword Note Diagram Go through any previous longhand notes that might be worth reviewing and underline the key words and phrases.

a) Put a name for the subject area in the centre of a sheet of paper. If possible this should be represented graphically as a symbol or little drawing.

b) Branching from this are the main features to be considered - The primary key words or phrases. Draw a line out from the centre and print a relevant key word along this line. Do not worry about 'organising' the structure; it is better to work fast. PRINTING THE KEY WORDS might be slower but the extra clarity is worth it.

c) Extend these initial branches out with an unfolding of details of main features. Secondary keys are those subordinate to the main categories.

d) Think of the keyword diagram as a picture. Make creative use of colour, code marks, arrows, simple geometrical shapes, symbols. The first version can be quite messy and wild. The point is to make it lively, unique and memorable.

e) Review after 10 - 30 minutes, next day, next week, next month. The next day review should be a redrafting of the diagram. Emphasize any geometrical forms or other patterns that suggest themselves. Rearrange things to make corrections clearer. Encircle important areas with colour

f) When taking notes of keywords keep an adjacent page for lists, diagrams, formulas, quotes and other stuff worth keeping as it stands.

g) The key word format may also be used to plan things as in preparing a talk, clarifying thinking in some area or making a complex process clearer.

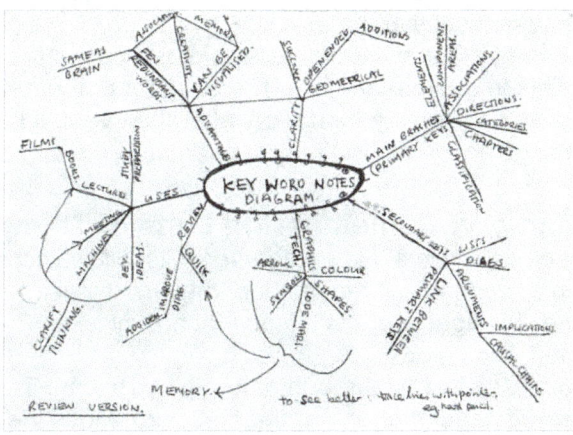

exercise **Memory: Stories & Gossip** When things are passed on by word of mouth, certain changes occur. It is useful to be aware of these 'weak' points in the fidelity of reported information.

Passing on a story many times: Choose a short story of around 300 words. Record yourself reading it. Play the recording to a friend and when the story has ended ask them to retell the story to you and record this. This second version is then played to another person who, in turn, records their version. In this way, the story can be heard and retold several times. Transcribe the last of these stories and note how they have evolved. If transcription is too difficult compare the last version with the first by listening to one then the next. It should be interesting to:

1. Compare what you see happening with the eight criteria of retention (see above). This experiment should illustrate the principles of memory. The results will vary with the type of story used and the personal experience of participants.
2. See what sort of process seems to occur as people reconstruct the story. It is said that errors of reporting are most common with colour, then position, then size and last of all shape.
3. Think about or discuss how does this process effects the dissemination of ideas in everyday life?

exercise **Memory: Remembering Verbal Material** In situations where you are unable to refer to visual material for review, recapping is a useful technique. Recapping also does away with the need to take immediate notes.

What you do is to interrupt the speaker, at a suitable moment, and say you would like to ensure that you have understood what has been said so far. You then express in your own words the main points made and ask for correction if necessary. This ensures communication is fully understood. It is also a powerful memory aid and helps concentration, especially on boring or unpleasant subject matter.

At the end of the presentation do a major recap of the material as a whole (if possible in groups) and ask questions for further clarification. This recapping can be done with a third party after the event. It can also be used with books or films and video material.

exercise **Memory: Remembering Lists of Things** The making of lists is in itself an external aid to memory. A list allows items to be reorganised in a manner that the memory may more easily absorb. The structure of the list might suggest things that are missing. Priorities may then be decided.

Basic method: Read the list through at a regular rhythm. Then covering the list with a sheet of paper, remember the first word. Move the paper down to reveal the first word - look, check, memorise. Try to remember the second word, whilst it is still covered. Move the paper down to reveal the second word - look, check, memorise. Repeat for the third word - and continue through the list. Keep going through the list in this way until each item is anticipated correctly. Repeat a few more times. Now run through the list several times out aloud, faster and without the copy.

Review after 20 minutes,
Review in 6 - 10 hours,
1 day,
1 week
1 month

The list is now installed in your memory for life

exercise **Memory: Remembering Lists of Words by Imaging**
This exercise relies on the principle that if two simple events are brought into vivid relationship with one another then the subsequent occurrence of one of these events will lead to recall to the other. The relationship formed for this purpose may be quite arbitrary as long as it is vivid

1. The first word of the list is read out aloud. Simultaneously make a strong visualisation of the word.

2. The second word is then read out aloud and visualised. Make the images exaggerated and fantastic.

3. Now imagine an active relationship between the two images.

4. Having made this connection vividly, dismiss it from the mind and read aloud the third word and visualise it. It is important that the visualisations are separated and not allowed to become welded in a stream of fantasy. This selective attention may require some considerable practice.

5. Now relate the third image to the second.

Dismiss from the mind, read aloud the fourth word, visualise it, e

Using this process, you can remember a list of words. By simply remembering the first word the second is recalled, and so on in a chain of associations.

Example: Bread, Pegs, Nails, Disinfectant.

a. Bread - Visualised as a hot, delicious smelling loaf.

b. Pegs - Visualise large coloured pegs on your own clothesline.

c. Bread & Pegs - Visualise bread pegged out on the line to cool. Dismiss this unlikely relationship from your mind.

d. Nails - Visualise six-inch nails.

e. Pegs & Nails - Visualise wearing a peg on your nose because of the smell of the animal pelt you are nailing out to dry. Dismiss this relationship from your mind.

f. Disinfectant - Visualise disinfectant going milky as you pour it into the toilet bowl.

g. Nails & Disinfectant - visualise having accidentally banged a rusty nail through your hand and you put disinfectant on the wound.

Examples are of limited use as it is largely a process that relates to your own personal preferences and experience.

Practice learning a different list of 10-20 items each day for a week. Each day test yourself by running through the previous lists. You may find the process laborious at first but after practice the visualised connections may be made at great speed. After the initial week, practice as the chance comes along on such things as shopping lists or key words from reading.

exercise **Memory: Imaging Numbered Lists (advanced)**

Think of a rhyming image to fit the numbers one to ten.

   One - sun
   Two - sky blue
   Three - tree
   Four - door
   Five - beehive
   Six - kicks
   Seven - tavern
   Eight - plate
   Nine - line
   Ten - pen

Become really fluent with these set associations so that the number sequence and the images can be reeled off spontaneously and in any order. Take the list of words that you want to memorise, and number them 1 to 10 eg.

   1. Bread
   2. Pegs
   3. Nails
   4. Disinfectant
   5. Etc.

Make an image relationship between sun and bread, blue and pegs and so on. In this way, the list of words can be memorised. The advantage of this method is that if someone asks you for the seventh item on the list you can remember it without having to go through the whole list.

Note: The Visualisation of Objects in Lists: It is found that when coming to remember lists by visualising, people often use their own methods of linking which are often not a definite system but a flexible and creative approach. Each object spontaneously suggests its own best possible method. For instance, if I visualise to remember numbered objects, I arrange or transform the object to link with the number. Thus, for the number 6 I imagine a bed with 6 legs. For the number 5 I imagine five oranges, in a pentangle on a lawn. Sometimes the connections are not easy to describe but are personally felt quite strongly.

exercise Memorising Numbers using Herdsons Mnemonic

Visual associations with numbers may also be used to remember abstract numerical relationships. This may be done in several ways. Here is one method:

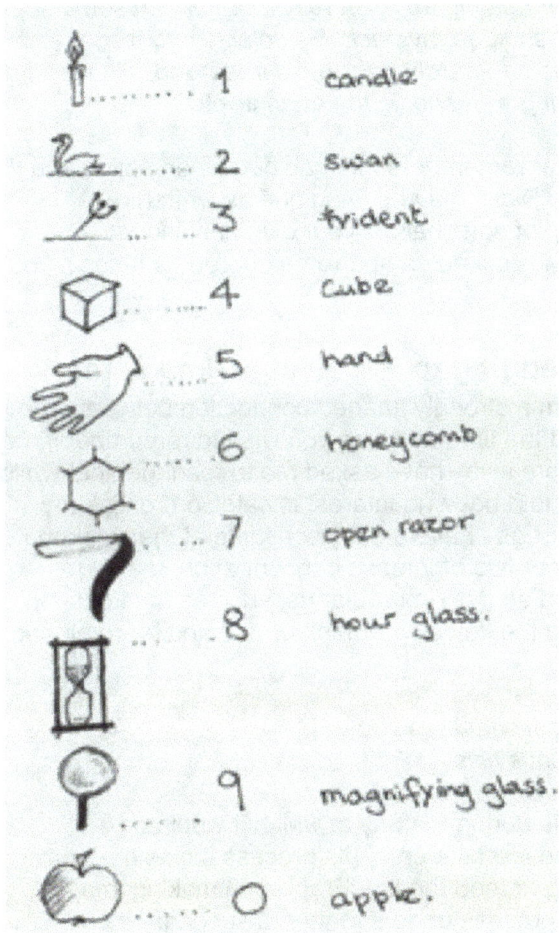

Make up a story which links the number symbols into a sequence. The richer and more surreal this story, the better.

> To remember the number 7 3 1 8 0 3 5: **Shaving** *over a deep pool, I was surprised by a* **trident** *coming out of the water with a single lighted* **candle** *on its left barb, an* **hourglass** *on its centre, and an* **apple** *impaled on its right barb. The* **trident** *disappeared again in a*

swirl of wave. I found myself waving my **hand** *to signal goodbye'.*

This takes less time and is more entertaining and lasting than rote learning of the numbers. If you find difficulty in beginning a story imagine yourself on a walk.

> To remember the number 6 7 4 8 8 5 0: *'I am walking down a lane, I look down and see a* **hexagon** *marked on the path, looking up I am confronted by a robber holding an open* **razor**. *I offer him some sugar* **cube**s *but he demands to see my pack. He selects* **two large hourglasses** *which he can hardly hold in his free* **hand**. *He walks off and I sit down, quivering with shock, to eat an* **apple**.*'*

Numbers are otherwise better remembered if imagined as an active and sensually interesting activity. Digits may be imagined as written on a blackboard with a large lump of soft chalk in your own handwriting. Numbers may be linked to musical notes and remembered as tunes if you have the necessary tonal skill.

exercise **Memory: Arranging to Recall at a Time in the Future**

What we do is form a strongly imaged connection between, the item to be remembered, and the time at which you wish to remember it. For instance, the people two doors away have asked me to feed their cat whilst they are away at the weekend. I have no interest in cats so I realise my mind will not easily remember as I have a busy schedule at the weekend. What I do is spend a minute or two of intense concentration, making connections between cat and an item in regular us, such as the kettle. In this way, every time I pick up the kettle I will think of 'cat' and be reminded of my task.

> *Cat – kat – ket - kettle*
> *Spout of kettle like a cat's tail*
> *Steaming hiss like a cat's hiss*

The kettle is used at intervals during the day at which it would be convenient to go around, and feed the cat. This process saves me from worrying about remembering to feed the cat. Practice in making imaged connections can speed this process up to a matter of seconds.

It is worth noting that the mind seems to have its own time clock. We can decide to wake up at a particular time by deciding to before we go to asleep. If there is no set schedule to the day we can use this 'sense' of time to remind us to do something, like making a phone call at a particular time. Notice when you already using this faculty without being aware of it.

ASSOCIATION EXERCISES

exercise **On the Process of Association** Make a random collection of about 50 small objects. Put them in a cake tin or small cardboard box.

Pick out any object. What does it suggest to you? Keep that suggestion, preferably the first thought, in your mind. Look through the objects and connect this suggestion to another object. What new suggestion does this second object offer you? Connect this suggestion with a third object and go on like this until all the objects are connected. As you connect them take the objects out of the box and place them in line on a table top. Repeat 3 times with the same objects, but in different orders and making different connections.

exercise **To Understand How Association Works** Take a word, thing or process. The thing or process should be represented in a single word, symbol or even photograph. Write, draw or stick this in the centre of a large sheet of paper. Then using the word or picture as a focus, write around it as many associations as you can jot down in 5 minutes. This in itself may be revealing.

It is interesting to see someone else's associations and thoughts around a subject as a reference point from which to judge your own.

Another stage to which you can take this is to do another version in which you allow more structured thinking around the subject. Represent this thinking by key word notes which branch out to follow different sequences of thought. This process may be found useful when entering upon a new subject of study. The extensive associations give you a clear sense of what surrounds the subject in your mind. Successful learning is all about connecting new things to things you already know in a meaningful way.

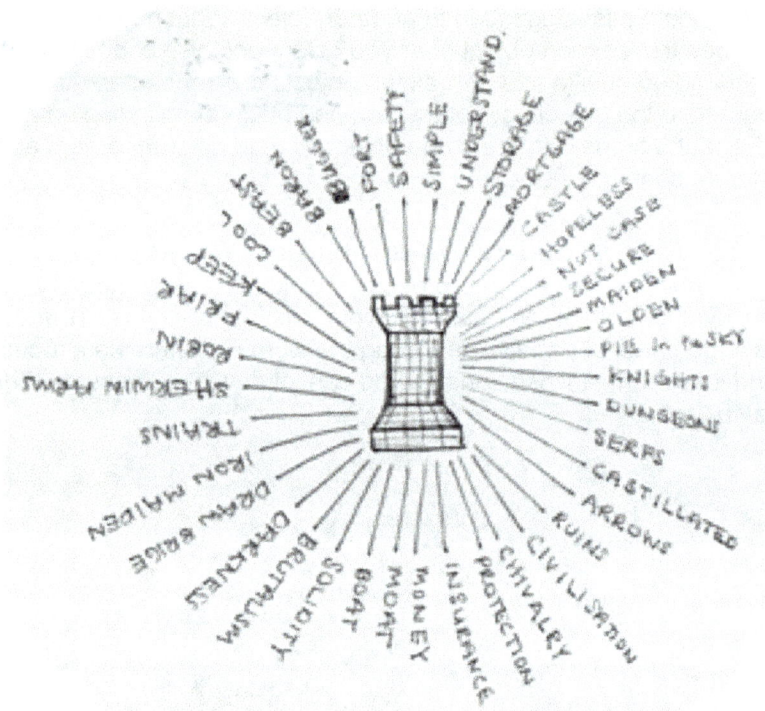

exercise **Collecting** Collect a miscellany of about 200 small objects, (such as: pencils, coins, cards, mechanical bits, containers, clips, buttons, etc.) in a cardboard box. When you've got a lot, tip them out onto the floor and examine them. Decide on some way of arranging them according to some principle – shape, size, colour, frequency of use, value or whatever you fancy. Take a photo.

    Arrange them in at least five different ways. How many ways can you think of arranging the objects in a meaningful way? What preferences have you got? When is contrast preferable to graduation? When is disorder more agreeable? How do the things you observe relate to bigger issues such as the arrangement of furniture in your room?

exercise How Association Links Casual Thoughts Sit and daydream. Allow your mind to wander. Have a notebook by your side and every half-a-minute make a one-word note of the thought that you are having. Jot this down in such a way as not to disturb your reflections. In this way you can keep track of your wandering thoughts.

After 10 or 15 minutes stop and look at your notes. See if you can identify the connections by which they lead one from the other. Often the link is not 'rational' but simply a quite arbitrary association.

Repeat this exercise daily for a week. This is a study of how your mind's uncontrolled action finds continuity. Similar mechanisms operate in dreams.

exercise Associating Real with Abstract It is worthwhile taking the time to make symbolic connections between material reality and abstract ideas. The smell of freshly turned soil might be connected with the fertility of the earth and its potential bounty. In this way, a simple perception brings to mind an abstract idea. An experience is enriched by such consciously intended associations. A single flower can bring to mind the 'productive power of nature'. Smell seems to be a potent sense with which to make such associations.

1. An inspiring poem, thought or whatever is recited in the presence of a strong, clear sense impression. Repeat until the association is imprinted on the mind. This may be done with a bunch of fragrant flowers obtained with this in mind.
2. Having come across a heady sensation, make the decision to give yourself up to it. Do not rush on, but pause, absorb the experience and allow the mind to fall into reverie. Find the most worthy thought that comes to mind and explore it in this time.
3. Create a ritual around the idea.

exercise Sartorial Associations The clothes we choose to wear always communicate particular attitudes even if you think; *'I don't care about my appearance'* or, *'You can't label me'*. They also identify us with social groups. You can tell a lot about a person by the way s/he dresses. The clothing conventions of particular groups are quite particular.

Try adopting a particular style of dress for a week and note the differences in the way people react to you. Then change to something different for a week. Continue this chameleon existence for a month. Even in this short time you will be able to make enough observations to considerably develop your sartorial skill.

You can try more subtle changes. Sometimes these can get just as dramatic a reaction as complete changes of costume. Odd socks can cause excited comment and laughter. An extra shirt button undone can make difference between casual and sexy. A different hat everyday can get people talking about you.

exercise **Associations in the Environment**

a) Select about ten objects from your room that you like. Note your own associations with each of the objects. Then arrange to present them one at a time to a 'panel' of friends. Each member of the panel is asked to write down the associations that occur to them and then their opinion of the objects.

b) Change the colour of your front door every month for a year, and keep a diary record of the different reactions you get.

c) What do people associate with you? Put a photograph of yourself, taken outside your home, in the middle of a clear sheet of paper. Ask a variety of people who know and don't know you to spend fifteen minutes writing down all their associations; be brave, encourage people to be uninhibited.

What do you learn about how you appear to other people from this exercise?

exercise **Drift**
Association can generate ideas. If we enter a fresh situation with an open-ended direction in mind, the random connections provided by the environment will spark novel relationship and thoughts.

The fresh situation, can be an 'I Ching' reading or a random selection from a novel like 'Finnegan's Wake', by James Joyce, but in my experience, nothing can beat a real journey.

The journey should not be too tightly planned. Give your intuition the reins. Routing may arbitrary. Aimless drifting is good. Make decisions as opportunities arise. Stop following your usual routes. Be open to changes. Jump at the chance to talk to that stranger. Take up an unexpected invitation to look around a local temple.

Journeys of this 'aimless' sort can be used at critical times in life as a major catalyst of creative reorientation.

MEDITATION EXERCISES

exercise Meditation Gaze at the secondhand of a clock without the slightest wavering of your attention. When your mind wanders note the time. As you repeat this exercise you will notice your attention span increasing.

Some gurus claim that if you can keep full attention, without wavering, or being mesmerised, for thirty minutes then you have achieved enlightenment.

Satori is only half an hour away.

exercise Meditation The basic principles

1. Sit comfortably in a quiet, safe, calm, place where you will not be interrupted. Do not lean or slouch but gently hold the body erect. The head should feel as if held up by a thread attached to the top of the skull.

2. Close your eyes.

3. Relax the whole body gradually, part by part, up from the feet. Instructions from an audio recording or another person may help concentration here.

4. On each out-breath visualise an infinity symbol or any non-distracting symbol of your choice.

5. This symbol is used as a fix to steady the mind. When a meditative 'frame of mind' has been achieved, after many weeks of daily practice, allow other perceptions and thoughts to intrude into your field of concentration. Watch them in a detached way; try not to get caught up in them; return to your symbol when you get distracted.

6. Do this for a set period each day. End of meditation may be signaled with an alarm or gong. I recommend starting with ten minutes and building up to one hour.

Note: Before and after sleep are considered the best times to practice.

exercise Meditation Guidelines

Breathing
/\/\/\/\/\/\/\/\/\/\/\/\/\
Watch the mind wandering and finally;
Return to breathing
/\/\/\/\/\/\/\/\

Perhaps sexual or other distracting thoughts arise ... here they are obliterating all else ... watch your sinking into them ... watch your enjoyment of them ... watch your struggle with the thoughts ... watch how powerful they are ... how they tighten muscles, pull on sinews ... watch now, how your memory comes into action, reminding you of your meditation ... watch

your will power coming into play r e t u r n i n g your attention to breathing.
/\/\/\/\/\/\/\/\/\/\/\/

Did your will power interfere brutally with your sexual fantasy? Did you see exactly how the thoughts faded, how the body changed, how the breathing altered. Oh yes, b r e a t h i n g
/\/\/\/\/\/\/\/\/\/\/\/\

Suddenly you realise money is on your mind. Where did that other fiver that you thought you had in your pocket disappear? You worry about your bank imbalance. Let all these superficial thoughts be absorbed by the deepening breath. Rising and f a l l i n g like the waves of an incoming tide breaking onto a beach.
/\/\/\/\/\/\/\/\/\/

The meditator is a hunter, catching the nuances, the connections, beginnings, mixings, changes and endings in our stream of consciousness. If you can see how a thought arises, how it persists and how it fades, it is said that the thought can then have no negative power over you.

INTUITION EXERCISES

exercise **Positive Frame of Mind A**

Spend a week pushing yourself to notice the positive aspects of people and places you would not normally exude enthusiasm towards. Each day go up to someone and fearlessly compliment them on some positive quality you have noticed. Repeat this 'seeing positive' week occasionally until the practice becomes a permanent habit. Once you have the knack of always taking a positive direction or viewpoint it won't seem an effort.

exercise **Positive Frame of Mind B**

Write out a testimonial to some quality you have enjoyed in yourself in the last week. Having difficulty? OK try this: write down something positive about yourself, the smallest thing will do. Expand it with examples and anecdotes. If you get stuck not remembering anything, don't stop - make up some qualities you aspire to! It's better to have a positive fantasy than to be stuck feeling down about yourself, and it may even make you laugh. Repeat weekly at a set time until your notebook, and your head, is filled with positive self-reflections. When everything you have had to deal with is taken into account, you have always been doing 'your best'.

exercise **Positive Frame of mind C**

Negative events must be seen as learning experiences. Choose a negative event and see all its constructive aspects. Take a sheet of paper and at the top write a title for a bad event. Then below make a list of all possible positive aspects that ensued or might ensue. Let your imagination run riot.

There is always something to be learnt from the troublesome. It is of prime importance that this is brought to the fore if intuition is to work well.

exercise **Positive Frame of Mind D**

Each evening as you go to bed prepare some positive thought with which to begin the next day. Make a collection of such pleasant and inspiring thoughts. Keep it as a direction through the day. Any suspicion of melancholy should be combated with reference to these thoughts. Such positive directions can be associated with an amulet or 'charm' which will act as a constant reminder of your reasons to be cheerful.

exercise **Positive Frame of Mind E**

On meeting another person be sure to point out something worthy of notice. Ideally notice something you like about them. Then go on to tell them something pleasing that happened to you recently and encourage them to do the same.

As I have noted in the Memory section it is the first impressions and parting shots that are most memorable in meeting people. Starting a meeting on such a positive note will effect the subsequent pattern of events out of all proportion to the effort that it requires.

exercise **Positive Frame of Mind F**

Stand back and take a panoramic view of your life. Take a day off. Write the story of the last year in the third person. Be a ruthless, but not negative or pessimistic, documenter. Reread it and then write it again in a more positive, insightful or useful way. Then leave it for a week or so and coming back to it read it as if you were a critic out to review and analyse the performance of a dear friend.

exercise **Information Saturation**

The area in which you need intuitive insight must be looked at from all angles and with all senses. Interact as fully as you are able with the subject.

Select a defined area of wall or pin-board as your centre of operation. Pin up a list of approaches to your area of interest. Make a timetable. Find illustrations and put them up. Decorate the 'centre of operations' for its own sake. Concentrate on making this area lively rather than trying to hard to solve problems.

Take any excuses to make visits. Arrange to meet old codgers who 'did it first'. Ask museum curators, and continue to amass relevant data and other things that take your fancy at the centre of operation. Sometimes let yourself wander off the subject. Look through a magazine. This light focus with good attention is just what intuition needs to come up with unforeseen ideas.

exercise **Identification of Your Own Subjective Position**

It is a matter of getting to know yourself and the origin of your opinions and feelings in the events of your past. Becoming aware of your own history and the conditions in which you developed.

Look at your life story in detail to notice areas in which emotion is stirred. What strong views do you hold that have never been carefully thought through? How do they relate to your biography? The best way to investigate this difficult area is to make a pact with someone to exchange life stories in detail with and understanding of mutual confidentiality. Keep to one person's life story for at least half an hour. The person not telling their story should ask questions and be supportive but refrain from interrupting with similar stories from her own life.

If this isn't possible write or draw a cartoon-strip of your story illustrated with photo-snaps and other evidences. Be sure to answer the following key questions and all their implications. Having identified your peer groups it is a good strategy to spend time lightly reviewing what you like and then what you dislike about them.

Key Questions:

What class are your parents? What jobs did they do? How well off were they?

What class or life-style were you brought up and schooled in, in the first seven years of your life?

What was your schooling like after age seven?

What race(s) or ethnicity are your parents (or guardians)? What part did different cultures play in your upbringing?

How has your gender influenced you? How do you relate or identify with any gender stereotypes?

How did your emerging sexuality affect your experience?

Did you identify able-bodied or disabled?

Were you considered good-looking or physically ugly for any reason?

How did religion play a part in your upbringing?

How were you treated by the adults around you?

Did you experience any traumatic or life changing events not covered by the above questions?

What subcultures did you take part in as you grew up? What music were you into?

Each identity group has particular stereotypes leveled at it as well as values and culture to be proud of.

exercise **Improvisation with Visuals** Conventional 'artistic' materials are not allowed. What can you find around and about that can be used to make a picture or a sculpture or an item of costume? Rubbish is a good source and readily available. Industrial waste material can be especially good. Get an assortment of things from the jumble sale or charity shop if there is nothing at home.

If you have an idea it will help your search for materials. If you have no ideas then collect things first and the materials will suggest ideas. Be messy with clean materials. Be meticulous with filth. Draw local scenes on scrap paper with burnt sticks. Make an impromptu public exhibition on an unused wall or noticeboard. Dream up or copy a design for a head-dress. Then make it with materials that are to hand. Leaves can be feathers. Milk bottle tops can be medals.

Visit the local rubbish tip or raid factory dustbins. Look through skips in middle class areas. Pile up your scavenged materials in the middle of your room in a topsy turvy heap. Set to work immediately to fill the walls with your creations. The secret is to get stuck in quickly. Its no-good holding back looking puzzled: bend things; turn them over; fit them together; play around; tie things together. Suddenly an idea will form or you'll get a sense of direction. The junk materials take on a new sense of purpose. Photograph the results.

exercise **Visual improvisation with Objects**   Collect a dozen or so objects or materials that you like but that have been thrown away or are conventionally valueless.

Bring these objects together in a box or on a table top and consider them together. This consideration might include listing all the associations these objects have for you. Observe them all closely from every angle. *'What does it remind you of from this angle?*

How could you put several of them together to make a unified whole? Play with the many possibilities of arranging them in relationship to each other. Pleasing effects should be noted but do not be satisfied with the first hint of cohesion. Aim to make an aesthetically pleasing conglomerate after a pre-decided amount of time. This may be a sculptural or fantasy object or anything. Additional colour may be added with paint to make the finished product.

Intuition holds the key to our aesthetic judgement and ideas of creativity.

exercise **Drawing Improvisation**   You need a wad of blank paper and a good drawing implement.

Allow your hand to draw some ambiguous and perhaps amorphous shape of its own. Don't think about it. Then start casually moulding the shape on impulse. Don't care a fig about results. Work quickly giving full responsibility to the hand. When the sheet bores or frustrates you, persist through the boredom or start a new sheet.

If after five minutes or five sheets, nothing of any interest has occurred postpone the exercise and do something else. You may have to do several sessions like this before something happens. Some may recognise this technique as a form of the much-maligned activity of doodling.

exercise Sounds Improvisation Without any instruments, unless you call a pair of shoes an instrument, spend an hour or more compiling a vocabulary of sounds. Try for range and variety. Find out what's possible.

Begin playing with these sounds with a real sense of the importance of what you are doing. Every moment of your life is important! Stay open to ambient sounds. Produce only what is needed. Repeat sounds if you want to. Remember what you are doing. Forget yourself. Be ruthless. Once you are into it record what you are doing for a few minutes.

This may be difficult to do because letting yourself go lays you open to ridicule and abuse. Find trusted company to do this with. And people who can listen without expectations. On this level of doing there are no aesthetic scales or standards. All that is necessary is to open yourself up. Letting go whilst remaining sensitive.

exercise Intuitive Massage Everything is allowed: except the recipients discomfort! Don't allow them to get cold. Don't tickle, dig, punch or pinch.

'Listen' to the person you are massaging. This is not just listening to what they are saying; listen to their body with your fingers and palms. Then you should tune in to the persons psychic state and do whatever seems right. Invent the strokes and finger presses and knuckle kneading as an empathic response. Keep in touch with your subject.

Much emphasis should be given to the reassuring placement of hands on the body. Don't underestimate the beneficial effect of simply touching with the palms of hands. The experience may be varied by changing: rhythm and speed; using different aromatic oils; having hot water bottles and pillows for support. Different textures of cloth and glove can make such a massage as rich an experience as a piece of music.

Music is a good accompaniment.

exercise Mime and Movement Improvisation Split up into pairs. One person in each pair talks to her partner for five minutes. Decide beforehand what is going to be the topic. Choose something like: *'What happened from the time you got up this morning until now'*. The other person says nothing but gives attention. Change over after five minutes.

Once both of you have taken a turn the second stage is the same process but miming or acting out the experience instead of talking. Take about five minutes each again.

The third stage is to take the essence of the experience picking from things that have come up the previous two times, and to improvise in movement and sound for up to ten minutes each. The person giving attention acts as an external focus for the people working.

Discuss afterwards.

Adapted from Emilyn Claid's article 'Improvisation', New Dance #6. Spring 1978

exercise **Automatic Writing** Write the first phrase that comes into your head. Then stop; look out the window. Read the phrase you have written, however absurd, then write the first thing that comes into your head. When you pause to think and consider – stop; look away. Reread and continue.

If you have prepared yourself sufficiently, so that this process happens unselfconsciously, the result may be weird and seem dissociated from your own self.

Even better done with two people each with laptops or typewriters; both people simultaneously type out a sentence or paragraph about anything that comes into their heads. They then exchange writing machines, read each other's and continue typing on from where the other person left off.

In this way stories grow in unpredictable and exciting ways. The previous paragraph will usually spark off an immediate and original response.

exercise **Story Telling** The essence of good story telling is rich and detailed descriptions and strong characterisations within a succession of events.

Explanation is not necessary and can be supplied by the listener. The way to start is just to say whatever comes to mind however clichéd and witless it may sound at first.

Practice regularly every day.

A young child is an ideal audience as most children love stories told to them face-to-face, however ridiculous and disjointed. Topics may suggest themselves in a preliminary conversation with your audience.

The stories will be more effective if they find ways to involve the listeners. This is much more important than beginning, middle and end. Regularity of practice will develop a style and probably some themes you will enjoy repeating and embellishing, probably on demand from your audience.

exercise **Taste and Smell** You have been too busy to get food in. Some friends arrive. This is the perfect setting in which to do this exercise. A meal can usually be made with scraps and bits not normally considered in routine cuisine. In the larder find those few dried beans and the quarter full bag of flour, all those things you don't get around to finishing. Those few vegetables in the garden of that empty house down the road; Sorrel from the wasteland; Nasturtium leaves make a tangy salad.

Scour your house and neighbourhood for anything edible. Put all your findings onto a table. Choose some items that need cooking longest and start to prepare them. When you start ideas for combinations of ingredients will start coming to you. Style and presentation are as important as taste and smell so don't let them be forgotten. Continue step by step carefully tasting at each juncture, to ensure you are taking a wise direction.

It might be an idea to draw on the knowledge and tastes of your guests!

exercise **Feed Ritual** Select an aim in your life that requires a degree of randomness or luck for it to occur. Things like getting a job, meeting the right person, finding money in the street.

Spend ten minutes or so in a garden or local park selecting a twig and a leaf. This is a meditative preparation so give full attention to the selection of the twig and leaf.

Now, thinking of your aim, break the twig and then drop the leaf. Walk away and get on with your business. This may require a belief in the interrelatedness of all things and the subtlety which the intuition is capable.

exercise **Tapping Group Intuition - 'Brainstorming'**

> *"Synectics (meaning the joining together of different and apparently irrelevant elements) aimed at stimulating the rate and complexity of combination of ideas through use of metaphor, symbol and fantasy."*
> Frank Barron 1958 p144

A group technique in which a problem or question is agreed by all as the subject. The group then throws in ideas all around the subject area. Lunacy is encouraged as it is often in the wake of an absurdity that the most original ideas arise. During the 'madness' seemingly irrelevant material should not be suppressed. The aim should be to, drop inhibitions and conventions that will normally keep our thoughts to the straight and narrow. Group trust is essential. Do not expect fantastic results from your first sessions.

Everything that comes up can be recorded on audio or video. Before the group meets again a concise typescript is made of the results and duplicated so each person can have a copy. The original is kept for reference. Discussion of the transcript takes place, new ideas arise and a more serious critical appraisal of any useful material that has arisen takes place.

IMAGINATION EXERCISES

exercise **Basic Visual Imaging** Prepare a series of colour squares with a dimension of 1.5" to 3" and find a range of coloured backgrounds covering the colours of the spectrum.

Study a white square on a black background for several seconds. Then shutting the eyes, try holding this picture in the minds eye for a count of 30 ....

Do this with different colour combinations, practicing in a systematic way until you can conjure up any colour square against any other colour background. Having achieved the basic skill, get a friend to call out combinations whilst you sit with eyes closed imaging them as they are called. Go for clarity and steadiness of image.

The next stage is to image using triangles and circles as well as squares. When these shapes have been successfully imaged try the purely mental exercise of switching a red square into a red circle into a red triangle, red triangle into blue triangle into blue square into blue circle and so on. Continue systematically.

exercise **Face Imaging** Practice imaging faces until you can see them in your minds eye - large and detailed. Do this by studying a face on a bus or in a magazine then shutting your eyes and reconstructing the face with your imaging faculty.

Then when you can do this, have a five-minute session with your eyes shut, bringing to mind a series of faces. Each face should be 'held' for several seconds as a clear image, and may even talk or make different expressions. Try to make one face merge with the next. The series may be chosen from different situations such as friends, relations, business acquaintances, film stars, bus drivers and so on.

As an advanced experiment try imagining a series of faces you have never seen. Hold each new face for several minutes and examine it in detail.

This exercise may be more fundamental to our imaging ability than the 'basic' exercise with coloured squares, as the first pattern we looked for after birth was a human face.

exercise **Picture Imaging** Go to an art gallery and stand before a well-known painting. Study the painting for not less than five minutes until you are familiar with all its details. Now, sit on the nearest chair and imagine the painting with your eyes shut. Return to the painting to fill in details that escape you. Return to the painting repeatedly until the painting lives as vividly in your imagination as it does on the canvas.

When the picture is established allow it to come to life. Figures move; leaves rustle; water twinkles. Notice how the impression changes and the picture evolves. Can you now regain the original image a few minutes later whilst having a drink in the museum cafe?

exercise The Effect of Imagination on the Body

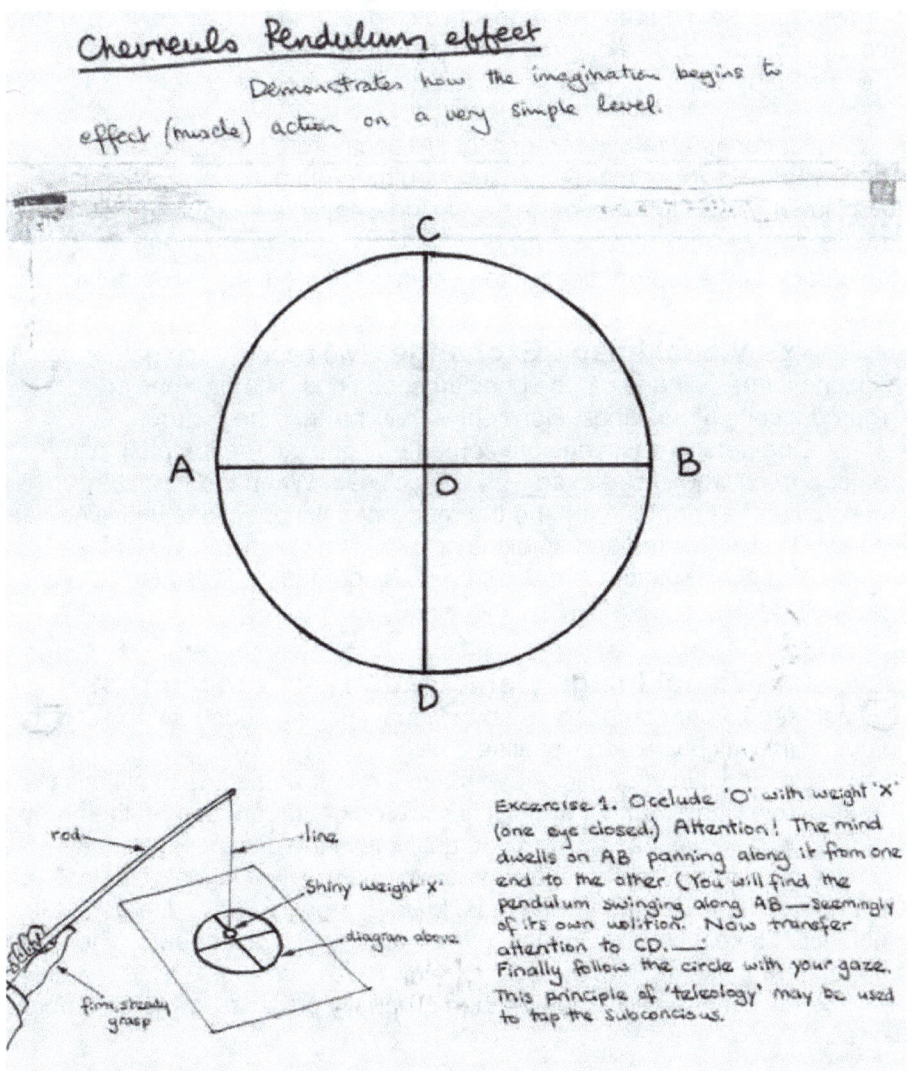

Chevreul's Pendulum effect

Demonstrates how the imagination begins to effect (muscle) action on a very simple level.

Exercise 1. Occlude 'O' with weight 'X' (one eye closed.) Attention! The mind dwells on AB panning along it from one end to the other (You will find the pendulum swinging along AB — seemingly of its own volition. Now transfer attention to CD.—
Finally follow the circle with your gaze. This principle of 'teleology' may be used to tap the subconscious.

Occlude 'O' with weight X (one eye closed). Attention! Let your mind dwell on the A/B axis panning along it from one end to the other. The weight swings on the same axis. Now transfer attention to the C/D axis. Finally follow the circle with your gaze. This principle of apparent teleology may be used to tap the unconscious.

exercise **Visual Imaging Game** Two people sit facing each other over a table equipped with paper and coloured crayons. Each person draws a simple diagram using only two colours and then holds it up for the count of 10 .... The diagrams are placed on the table face down. Both people then attempt to reconstruct the diagram they have seen.

The original and the transcript are compared. If high fidelity has been achieved the partner makes the first step more complex with, say, an additional colour. If however, reproduction is inaccurate then the diagram is made simpler until accurate reproduction is possible. The judge of 'accuracy' is the reproducer not the originator. This is not a competition.

exercise **Visual Image Exchange** Two people each gather about a dozen pictures. These can be postcards, cuttings, photographs or reproductions of paintings. Don't show your partner the pictures.

One person describes the contents of one picture in detail to the other person who sits relaxed with eyes closed. When the verbal description has come to an end the recipient asks questions until s/he has established a detailed and stable image.

The actual picture is then offered as comparison. Discuss before swapping roles.

exercise **Visual Image Manipulation - Advanced Control** As a final test of your complete grasp of visual imaging chose an object from your room which you can visualise clearly.

Holding it in your minds eye make it rotate and come to stillness. Imagine walking around it whilst it is still. Look at it from above, then from underneath. Move it away from you until it is in the distance. Gradually bring it closer until you are looking at just one detail of it. Make the colour change once, twice and three times. Make it grow larger and larger. Make it gigantic. Make it shrink. Continue shrinking it until it disappears. Then make it reappear in its original form.

Use simple objects at first then gradually progress to more complex ones.

exercise **Articulating Imaginary Mechanisms** Obtain a simple mechanism or puzzle which dismantles into four or five parts. Study it carefully from all angles. Dismantle it slowly considering each part and its relationship to the whole.

Put the thing away and sit with eyes closed and bring the mechanism to mind. If this is not possible with great clarity, go back to studying it again. In your mind dismantle it and put it back together again. As you do this be aware of the functions of each part.

Repeat this process of studying the reality and then reconstructing the visual memory of that study mentally.

Continue this exercise with mechanisms of increasing complexity.

exercise **Sounds Story** Write a story or draw a comic which comprises a sequence of events having a sound as their main quality. It may be a story that makes narrative sense or just an abstract sequence of sounds represented by words or drawings. The story may be read out or looked at. Pauses should be made so listeners can give full reign to their sound imaging faculties.

Another method is to collect a scrapbook of acoustic images. Look at each picture and imagine the sound it suggests.

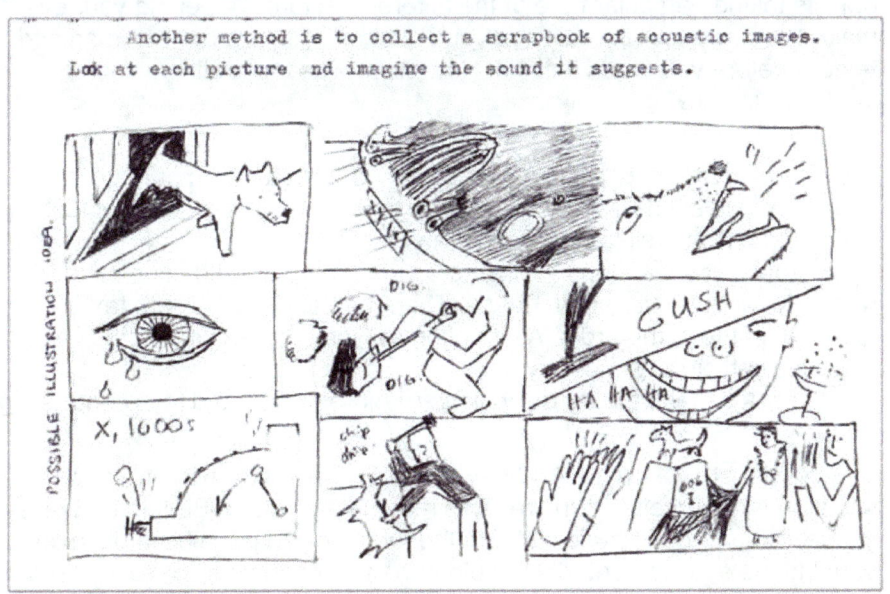

exercise **Sound Imaging Tunes** We can all 'hear' tunes going around in your head. There always seems to be a handy tune to whistle as you saunter along.

Using this phenomenon, think of a tune but don't sing it out aloud. Allow it to go around in your head for a while. Then follow it with another. Pause. Now sing, whistle or hum the first tune you thought of, followed by the second.

When you can do this try thinking of three consecutive tunes before you pause and sing them aloud. Gradually increase the number of tunes you can bring to mind and then sing.

exercise **Imaging Sound Environment** At first choose an environment with a complex but steady sound character such as a busy road, bus, bottling factory. Listen carefully to all the component sounds; mimicry to be encouraged. Finally, listen to the overall effect.

Away from the sound source, preferably in a very quiet place, conjure up the sounds you heard, in your own head. Are you able to imagine each component sound plus the general effect?

When you can do this try it with sound environments in which sounds are less repetitive.

exercise **Touch Imaging** Sit in an armchair with eyes closed and take an imaginary blindfold tour of your house touching surfaces and objects taking particular note of the different textures. Opening your eyes, make the same tour in reality as you imagined. Remember the imagined texture before you touch for real. How close was the reality to your imagined texture?

exercise **Touch Imaging Texture** Collect a range of material squares of widely differing textures. Try to include a wide range of textures such as; PVC, fur, silk, hessian, net and wool.

Touch them and then imagine an action replay with your 'minds hand.' Touch three in a row. Pause. Then mentally replay each texture you touched, in the same order. As it becomes easier to re-experience each texture clearly in the mind, try four, five and six in a row.

Try a series of textures, which are more similar and less contrasting.

exercise **Touching Fantasy** Create a fantasy environment or situation for yourself to explore. This may be a castle, a Beduin tent, a spacecraft or a penthouse suite. In the fantasy, you put a blindfold over your 'minds eye' and set, of to explore the tactile qualities of your imagined environment.

exercise **Taste/Smell Imaging** Select the name of a food or flower. Write down your choice. Shut your eyes and imagine the smell and taste. If the sensation imaged floods the mind with piquant detail and your mouth waters, then tick your choice and write down another. If, however, you are unable to imagine the appropriate sensation put a cross by your choice and continue. Later seek out the actual objects whose names are marked by a cross in your list. Re-experience the taste and smell sensations with a mind to capturing them.

exercise **Hot and Cold Imaging** Put on an imaginary blindfold and imagine walking around your house or flat. Touch things as you go and notice the temperature of things. Notice how wood feels warmer than metal; notice how it feels when you walk open into a patch of sunlight; or open the 'fridge door; or go close to a light bulb. Imagine picking up fresh toast; or opening a window; or getting under a duvet. Find the line of the hot water pipe under the plaster by running your hand over the wall.

If you cannot imagine such experiences vividly, do the actual walk and then sit down and run through it in your mind. Repeat this recent sensory memory until the sensations become a part of your imaging vocabulary.

exercise **Kinaesthetic Imaging - Muscles and Balance** When watching an exciting dance performance or sports match we respond to what we are seeing with tiny muscular movements in sympathy with the movements of the players. This phenomenon is called a kinaesthetic response and will give us an exhilaration which is the shared pleasure of balletomanes and football fans.

Allow this kinaesthetic response full reign next time you are a spectator at some exposition of movement. Allow yourself to identify with a player you like and flow along with their movement. Be right THERE with every balance, swivel and collision! Identify with every leap, fall, kick and glance.

After the event find some time in which you can spend a few minutes alone. Close your eyes and relive the highlights of the game. Try to FEEL the main actions vividly. Allow your body the freedom to identify with the movements that have been seen and even to reproduce them in miniature. You may remember only vague impressions at first but if you persist the details will come.

Aim to gradually increase the possibility of transferring yourself into the body of a performer. With a repeated performance like choreographed dance you can image all the movements in your mind as you watch the performance.

exercise **Moving Imaging - Muscles and Balance** Sit, relax and close your eyes. Imagine yourself doing some physical activity. It might be a job around the house, like fixing the gutter, or it might be a sequence of Yoga or Tai Chi. Concentrate on what the movements feel like.

Start off with short, simple sequences and work up to long, complex tasks. Feel the effort required to do different actions. Be aware of any counterbalance necessary.

Physical tasks may be practiced in the imagination before doing anything. Dancers will often learn to image a sequence before they do it.

Try thirty imagined press-ups or a jog around the park.

When this movement imaging faculty is working well you can even imagine doing things that would not be physically possible!

exercise **Transformations - Complex Imaging Control**

Decide on a scene and think about a change that could be made within it. Imagine the scene again with the planned changes. A couple of examples will make things clear;

1. You imagine an empty street. It gradually fills with parked cars. You see and hear each car approach; manoeuvre into a parking place; and the driver leaves and closes the car door. Notice the colour, make and model of the vehicle. What is the weather like? Can you deal with two or three motors arriving at once? You'll have to be relaxed to do that or rather let it happen.

2. You vividly imagine a face. Watch the hair change; a beard might grow or be cut back and finally be trimmed into a small moustache. The hair might grow very long, be tied, cut and permed into ringlets or brushed into a bouffant. It can be dyed a different colour, lacquered, tied in a pony tail and then cut short or shaved off

The face can be felt and smelled as well as seen.

Now write your own scenario.

exercise **Surreal Creations**

Imagine objects relating to each other as they never do in reality. Defy social conventions and physical laws. Allow objects qualities and powers that are in reality alien to them. Make a list of these objects. Illustrate the list with drawings or collages. Make your own surreal ideas book. Don't get put-off by all the old surrealist cliches and awkward juxtapositions that may come up at first.

Persist for original results.

DREAMING EXERCISES

exercise Remembering Dreams
  1. Put a notebook and pen by your bedside.
  2. On awakening do not open your eyes and lie perfectly still. Any quick motor movement may throw your dream into oblivion.
  3. Ask yourself, '*What has been dreamt?*', but do not search for an answer or try to remember. The dream will come flowing back of its own accord.
  4. When you have run through the dream again in remembering it, open your eyes and note it all down. For therapeutic purposes, it is important to describe your feelings than the facts of what occurred, so be generous with your adjectives. Paint or draw if this comes more easily.
  5. Persevere with this method. At first you may get nothing or just remember snatches of a story or just a vague feeling. Put it all down and your recall will gradually improve.

exercise Control of Sleep dreams To direct your night dreams you must immerse yourself in the subject you wish to dream about. You must be fully concerned with the subject and seriously desire to dream about it. Sit in a quiet place and think of your dream topic. Decide what you want to dream about and say it out loud at intervals throughout the day and just before you go to bed.

You must fall asleep with the quiet confidence that your mental dream machine will be working for you through the night. Morning will come, you will awake and things will be much clearer. As you fall asleep you can say; '*I'll leave it to the dream machine to solve that problem.*'

Your dreams reflect some of your deepest innermost fears and anxieties so that mundane problem solving my not take priority.

exercise Technique for Day Dream Generation
The generally accepted preparation is relaxation. However, this is not essential as some people will see images when tense or frightened. Another method is to create some rite of entry,

Baron du Potet, the C19th mesmerist, would draw a white chalk circle in the middle of a black floor and ask his patients to stare into it until they experienced visions or hallucinations (Mary Watkins, Waking Dreams 1977). Sigmund Freud would press his hand onto the client's forehead to elicit any image, emotion or memory. Of course, gazing into a crystal ball or dark pools of water has been a traditional device.

Apart from the physical relaxation that is usually necessary, the routine concerns of the consciousness must also be encouraged to subside. This is possible through doing a mental concentration exercise. It may also be done by using an image; you may think of becoming like water. Play Beethoven's Moonlight Sonata first movement and think of water.

> Pretend this water is you.
>
> Your routine pre-occupations create waves and ripples, currents and whirlpools.
>
> Gradually allow the water to become still. The ripples become smaller and less frequent and the water becomes clear and still.

Initially this can be read to you slowly by another person or made into an audio recording. It may be repeated until you are in a good space to receive a dream. The point to be made, is that you must experiment to find the rite of entry into dreamland that is most appropriate to you as an individual.

exercise **Daydream Direction and Control** If your daydreams are irrelevant, erratic, unfocused, confusing and generally not getting anywhere it may be useful to start off by 'entering' an imagined archetypal scene.

The scene should be emotionally neutral in itself so that the dream activity that evolves out of this scene relates to current feelings in your mind rather than associations with the scene. A meadow, hill or brook are usually suitable. Check that the scene you chose doesn't have any strong associations for you. The procedure is to do the preparation and then conjure up the entry into it for yourself. Exercises in the section on imagination could be helpful here especially concerning 'entry.' Then once you have got yourself into the fantasy let it take over and develop as it will.

It is helpful if you can tell the dream to someone else soon after having it. This will get your attention back onto present time reality so you do not get partly 'lost' in the fantasy. This relating can be done in any media: eg. dancing, painting or words.

Used in this way daydreaming can allow you to discover the character of your own subconscious - invaluable in the development of all your thinking. Ideally done with an experienced dream guide.

Carl Leuner's Ten Themes for Directed Fantasy.

1. Plains, prairies and open country.
2. Progression from a plain up a mountain.
3. Descent following the course of a river.

4. A house discovered and visited from top to bottom.

5. Pick a name then describe a person who fits this name. Not a person known to you.

6. Imagine a person you know, describe them in detail.

7. Meeting a driver on a lonely road.

8. An exploration of a cave.

9. Images from your own scrapbook

10. A potpourri from the above.

---

exercise **St George Slays the Dragon** Daydreams may be used in a more aggressive way to change yourself.

Working from themes or symbols that have occurred in your own sleeping dreams is often most productive here. Refer to your dream notebook. As before, imagine the consciously chosen starting situation realistically. Then, you enter the dream and allow things to happen.

Your will probably find some images that appear threatening. Keeping in mind that the images are only mental fabrications and are only to be taken metaphorically. Try to allow things to happen without imposing your will.

Any difficulty you have whilst in the fantasy is known as a 'resistance.' These resistances represent real impediments, blocks or fears that you may have. Working on these resistances can lead to resolutions of real mental disfunctions and a deeper understanding of yourself.

However, dissolving or combating heavy resistances should be done with the help of a supportive guide or counselor, who has experience in these things, as the emotional catharsis that may result might be disorienting.

exercise **Inventions** Invent something new. The new thing can be functional or it can be purely for fun. Don't take your results too seriously at first. Do it 'for a laugh.' The majority of inventions that are patented are fairly silly things so don't worry if your first attempts are quite ridiculous.

Two types of invention may be usefully differentiated. The first is the open ended creative design such as grotesque new animal, mysterious monument or entrancing garden in which we use our life experience to produce something original and unique. The second has very particular goals and usually a very specific function. eg. a new tool for peeling potatoes, frightening off burglars, making beds or washing dishes.

First Type: Method - Allow your imagination to produce images associating from the basic idea. Note these images down and be on the lookout for an appropriate structure around which to organise the best of these images; then image purposefully to fill in gaps. You decide to design a garden sculpture. Wildly list your first thoughts picturing them vividly in your mind. For a structure, you might decide on something as simple as the four points of the compass. You then pick images from your list that illustrate west, east and north but there is nothing appropriate for south. You then image purposively around the idea of 'south' until an appropriate image emerges.

Second Type: Method - Intensive study is usually necessary in the area chosen, unless we already have great knowledge in this area. Methodical thinking goes hand in hand with vivid association of imagery. How would you make traffic lights more responsive to local traffic conditions? Before attempting to think of an actual design think of at least ten completely crazy ideas for achieving this end. You might have to research to find out exactly how traffic lights work at present and possibly the criteria which designers work with. Other research into traffic control might be useful but quite often it is the technology from another discipline that will provide the key innovation.

If you are designing a potato peeler you might be able to use knowledge from your own domestic experience. It is perhaps better to choose such a subject for your first exercise as the required information can be obtained from direct observations.

exercise **Self Imaging - Situations** Conscious imagination facilitates the achievements of real effects through catalysing the intuition. Goaded into action in a willed and worried way the mind routinely operates in a linear and often clumsy manner. Stimulated by an image, the multidimensional and roundabout ways of the mind are exploited to their fullest. Results may be achieved in subtle ways.

1. Interview. The aim is to be self-assured socially. Imagine yourself at an interview. You are completely in control. The interviewers have expressions of amazement as you tell them your capabilities. They are extremely friendly and seem genuinely interested in everything you say. You ask several questions and are in control.

2. Redecorating the House. This is about getting something done rather than procrastinating. You come home from work, change into painting clothes, and get the ladder straight away. You chip the old paint off whistling merrily until it gets too dark to continue. Getting up early the next morning you just have time to put on a coat of primer whilst listening to 7 o'clock news before going off to work. That evening the undercoat goes on followed by a topcoat the next morning.

3. Confidence in the face of intimidating power structures. Imagine seeing the Mayor about your housing situation. He can't help but the chief

housing officer is impressed and even a little apprehensive at your air of authority. He quickly assures you he could perhaps provide property for your Housing Coop. You leave and make an appointment to see your boss later in the day. She can only see you for a few minutes but says she has enjoyed listening to your suggestions. You return to your office and call a quick meeting to put everybody in the picture.

4. Write five or six outline scenarios, perhaps a bit longer than the ones above, about areas in which you would like to change or get things done. Scenarios, which are just one step away from reality, may produce better results than impractical dreams. A powerfully trained imagination can achieve surprising feats of self-redirection.

exercise **Self Imaging - Generalised** Assumption: We are all fundamentally self-confident, highly and flexibly talented, and capable of learning efficiently; it is only negative conditioning and past obstacles that have obscured our power to learn new things.

We may use imaging to regain a picture of how we are and by-pass or contradict the negative self-images. The more strongly can entertain an affirmative image of ourselves, the more effectively will we counter the pressure of incorrect conditioning.

Possible Directions for Personal Self-imaging

- I am pleased to be me, to consider my life gives me a warm glow of satisfaction.
- I find no fundamental conflict between myself as an autonomous and as a co-operative being.
- The hurts and mistakes of the past are finished and I bear no grudges to interfere with my future progress.
- I am a creative power - I make things happen.
- I am a caring, loving, sensual being.
- I will get all the support I require if I think clearly and ask questions.
- My days are filling with sensual pleasure and stimulating thought.
- I have all the time in the world.
- Nothing diverts me from what needs to be done.
- Fear cannot stop me doing what is right. I shake fear off like water off a duck's back.
- As I breathe easily my body maintains my wellbeing.
- I do my best at any moment if everything is taken into account. I can ask for remarks to the contrary to be rephrased in a constructive manner.
- My actions are effective in the world.

- My thoughts get straight to the point.
- Not a moment of my life is wasted.
- No problems in my life are insurmountable.
- There is always at least one elegant solution to a problem.
- Limitations of cultural or gender stereotypes will not stand in the way of me claiming my full potential.
- I am not intimidated by attitudes and values that I do not agree with.
- I value the respect of people attained through sticking with the truth rather than the collusions of timid people.
- Crying is a sign of strength not weakness.

These things are true of all humans but sometimes we can lose sight of them. This does not imply that to reclaim your full power you would act alone!

You must design your own individually tailored affirmative imaging guide. Write your directions in your own language to contradict the particular conditioning that you have suffered.

Repeat them 10-20 times with a minute or so between each repetition. Note down your mental responses or imaginative effects that arise. The imagery may then itself be repeated or translated into a picture or song.

exercise **Materialisation** Vividly imagined desire motivates mental processes which seem to produce concrete results, in a roundabout and often difficult to follow way.

Method

1. A firm decision must be made about what you want. The object or condition is then imagined as already there.

2. You must be clear about your motivations.

3. Set a scene in the imagination. Be in it.

4. Imagine your desired object or activity as being present in this scene and in active use.

5. Imagine the wish is fulfilled. There is a feeling of inner contentment.

6. Release the whole scene like a bubble. Let it 'float away.'

7. Rest or sleep if possible. Don't 'disturb the seeds'.

8. Have faith that you will get a result. Continue to work for your objective in rational ways as best you can. Be alert but not constantly expectant. The result might finally be a realisation that your 'desire' might not be for the best!

exercise **Moving from Dreaming to Imagination** It is useful to be able to move from a wild daydream to a controlled articulation of imagery.

Prepare as for day-dreaming. Set an alarm clock or egg timer to go off in two or three minutes. When the timer goes off select the current subject of your dreaming and explore it imaginatively. Make it as 'real' as possible. If it is an abstract image or feeling, bring to mind a range of image associations.

Being able to snap out of a day-dream and consciously consider a topic that has arisen is of great use. After some practice forgo the alarm and 'snap out' spontaneously. Note down the subject and map associated images.

Advanced skill: The reverse process may also be useful. To be able to daydream for controlled periods, at appropriate points, in a conscious thought process can be useful. 'Appropriate points' are places where a complex muddle or lack of ideas has made issues unclear or solutions not forthcoming.

exercise **Distancing - Ants Eye / Bird's Eye** An exercise to practice the imaginative capacity to see the world from different vantage points. This exercise is best done in a group. Select a well-known place in your town; the market square, town hall, park or an office block. Each person describes the place spontaneously from the points of view of:

1. A baby in a pram
2. A balloonist
3. A truck driver
4. A newspaper seller
5. A police officer
6. A young child of 3
7. An ant
8. A merchant banker
9. A councillor

Take no more than one or two minutes on each viewpoint. The number of viewpoints may be reduced if there are several people in the group or time is limited. The group also needs to be relaxed and unhurried to get the kind of insights this exercise can immediately produce.

exercise **Inner Guardian** A realistic persona may be created by your own mind who may then be asked for advice or guidance when your own judgement needs 'support' or can't see the wood for the trees. It seems that such a construct can bypass certain types of mental block, confusion or lack of confidence, and produce valid thoughts not available to direct self-enquiry. Seemingly supernatural guardians may be demonstrating how much of our total power is occluded by a previously maltreated consciousness; or harbour a dangerous unreality!

To make a guardian for yourself build up a conceptual model in great detail. First choose a guardian type you like and can hold in your imagination easily. Wizard, angel, fairy, genie, are possible but you may prefer something more ordinary. Then elaborate the details of this helpful character over time. The appearance of the guardian should be developed as 'realistically' as possible. The character should be chosen as one that you can trust and may be modelled on a real person or fictional hero.

exercise **Inner Guardians and Guides** Rather than build up your guide with a conscious imaginal effort it is also possible to create a ritual situation so the 'guru' appears fully grown from the unconscious.

Go to a lonely abyss or cave. Rub one small stone over a large one in the direction of the sun. Continue for 3 days. After the third day, a spirit you can talk to will emerge from the rock. (Naranjo in M.Watkins 1977).

exercise **Getting into Your Imaginary body** With eyes closed. Stretch out your imaginary hand and you see it before you as you would in reality. Raise your head and imagine that you see the front of your body, your clothing and shoes. Describe the landscape you see in front of you in your waking dream and then turn your imaginary body around and describe the one to the back of you. (Freligny & Vivel, in M.Watkins 1977).

Developing your imaginary body is a conceptual tool that allows you to get emotionally involved with your imaginal environment. This imaginal ego may have a different appearance to your physical body. The differences may be slight or you may find yourself in the guise of a different species of being. It is good to make a detailed drawing of this imaginal body.

More advanced work with an imaginary body.

The imaginary body or vehicle for travel in imaginal space may be given a home base and put to work in various ways. For instance, it may be put in charge of the 'life programs console' in the cranial control centre.

Be sure that any fantastic extensions of this fantasy are symbolic of realistic expansions of your own power and control. These can take the form that most excites you, but are best kept simple. Not recommended for people who are feeling mentally ungrounded, under stress or suffering from trauma.

exercise **Creative Play - Invention** Pair off with a young person; ideally someone eighteen months or younger. Gather a few harmless objects from the corners of the miscellaneous drawer. Forget any original specific function those objects may have had. Watch each other play with the objects and reflect actions. How many different ways will the objects fit together, bang down, balance, be sucked, spin, drop, open up, make noise, take apart or roll across the floor.

Much play uses the imagination alongside present perception. An egg on the table grows horns and becomes the head of a Viking warrior. We are not hallucinating but possibilities can become vividly evident to us.

REASONING EXERCISES

exercise **Key Checklist of Thinking Errors**
An annotated list of 15 common sources of reasoning error are listed below; followed by four exercises showing ways the list may be put to work.

thinking error 1. DEFINITION If we are to reason using everyday language we must be clear about exactly what the words we are using refer to. Everyone attaches slightly different meanings to the words they use depending on their particular experience. This is not so much of a problem with concrete nouns, but is commonly a source of confusion with more abstract ideas. As ideas become more abstract the connection to our experienced knowledge becomes more distant. Words like 'freedom' and 'democracy' are almost worthless unless brought down to earth with a tangible definition. Other descriptive words, like progressive, beautiful, bad or nice, require qualification if they are not to be too vague.

thinking error 2. AMBIGUITY Referring only to a 'dark brown table' can be worthless if the object is being offered for sale. Does brown indicate mahogany or thick paint covering shoddy construction? This shows ambiguity caused by using a word that is not precise enough for the context. In other cases, and especially in English, we find a single word that has two quite different meanings. These meanings can even be contradictory as in 'to go fast' or 'to stand fast'. In this type of example definition is often provided by the context. Other cases of ambiguity may be subtler, and these are more likely to cause errors in argument. If a word is causing confusion it is best to reconstruct the statement in different words.

thinking error 3. INCORRECT BASIC IDEAS It is useful to think of this on two levels; that of our assumptions and that of our basic propositions in a particular piece of thinking.

    A. Assumptions - These are the unproven intuitions, beliefs and so-called instincts that underlie our thought structure as a whole. Most people are not aware of the assumptions upon which they act. Assumptions are usually tied up with our early experiences or inherited traditions. Philosophers have identified fundamental assumptions that we can all share such as the consistency of the universe and the principle of induction. Seemingly clever thinking on unchecked assumptions can lead to disaster.

    B. Basic Propositions - Any rational thought process starts from certain basic propositions and from these we may deduce an outcome.

This outcome will vary from a definite conclusion to the formulation of more questions. To make this process clear we must first articulate our basic propositions in full. Then we should check they are factually correct, or to what extent they are supported. Are the supportive references reliable? On what authority are they based? What interests might the authority be acting on behalf of? We must try to work back from any opinion to find the propositions on which it is based. We check these and sort out the factual from the emotional, the intuitive from knowledge based on experience. Are the facts reliable or verifiable? What real conditions are behind the emotional feeling? We need to be clear what parts of our thinking rely on intuitive judgements.

This process is invaluable in any area in which you are working or otherwise involved. It allows you to become articulate and clear and will make any subsequent programme of action much more effective.

thinking error 4. CAUSE OR ANTECEDENT Sometimes cause is separated from effect by considerable space or time. The connection between the two may not be obvious. In such cases another factor that is closer in space or time may appear to be the cause. Sometimes causal connections are implied in speech: "*After I had taken the medicine my pain went way.*" From this information alone we cannot be certain that the chemical properties of the medicine were the cause of the pain ending. The point is that the cause is not always the most obvious factor. Apparent causes need to be investigated until actual concrete relations are ascertained.

thinking error 5. REAL ATTRIBUTE OR ASSOCIATION? It is important to be clear about the real characteristics of an object or event as distinct from its associations. Stereotypes are bad enough simply because they generalise about people who are individually different. They are even more absurd when it is likely that the stereotype has little factual basis. Unwarranted associations that appear as real characteristics are most pernicious. Working class people are said to be dirty and thick. Although put so blatantly it is clearly absurd, this stereotype appears in many more subtle guises and plays an important part in maintaining class divisions. Sometimes we are interested in the associations of an object or event rather than its real characteristics. It is the associations of a Star of David medallion that are important rather than its physical characteristics.

thinking error 6. SPURIOUS GENERALISATION Sweeping generalisations are one of the most common weaknesses of everyday reasoning. Incorrect generalisations are usually made on the grounds of inadequate evidence. Observation of a few cases, however vivid, does not mean the rest of the cases that comprise the category are similar. On entering a port, in a country you have never before visited, you may 'get an impression of the country'. You may see many cars for instance. Then on another trip you travel further inland and find a completely different scenario with very few cars. Other generalisations are misleading in that they do not give any idea of the number of exceptions to be expected. Generalisations that are not truly all-encompassing should be qualified.

Test for Spurious Generalisation

    a. Were there enough observations made from different viewpoints in sufficient locations?

    b. Are the instances recorded representative?

    c. Were they recorded objectively?

    d. Was a thorough search for exceptions made?

Note: It is possible to make the opposite mistake; assuming a single case when there are more than one. Thinking you are the only person feeling so-and-so whereas there are usually many others feeling the same, but not communicating about it. Common in areas of taboo: such as men talking to each other about their emotional life or health concerns.

thinking error 7. CLASSIFICATION Classification systems will attempt to make a universal division of the world but this is rarely possible from one place in space and time. Particular classification systems always highlight some aspects of the set more clearly than others. Essentially classification is a reductive simplification of the world in which individual things are likely to share a range of similarities with other things. However, classification is useful because it provides an organised summary allowing us to find things, and because it helps us understand underlying structure and pattern.

    Some classifications become more real than the world they are dealing with. Classification is only ever a temporary device for us to understand the world not a grid through which we should live. When we look for something in a library index we must remember we are looking through a classification grid devised by fallible human with specific viewpoint and set of interests. A disadvantage of classification can be seen on the most basic level in the verbal classifications of polar opposites: Good/bad; middle-class/working-class; normal/abnormal; clever/stupid; sane/mad. These polarities simplify a reality that is spread out on a multidimensional continuum and not in reality divided into two separate categories.

    The most complete and flexible classification system is of course language and yet language itself will reflect the bias of those who are most culturally dominant. So, published English has, in the main, reflected a male, middle class, middle aged, white, able-bodied view of the world.

thinking error 8. EMOTION There is a very strong tendency to formalise one's early emotional experience in later conscious philosophical beliefs or ideology. We will try to use reason to create a plausible justification of our irrational feelings and the values they give rise to. This is important because it is such an insidious and profound process and it is difficult to be aware of such subconscious steering. Our whole life will have been arranged according to our emotional requirements so our vested interest in this not being challenged is high. In more particular ways emotion plays a part in confusing rational thought processes. We may coolly use emotive terms, 'my country, right or wrong' to move people emotionally. We may also be dramatically emotional and say something like; 'I'd like to kill you', without having any intent to commit an act of violence.

Learning to differentiate between feelings and rational thought, and responding to each separately in an appropriate way, is one of the most useful things we can do to think more clearly. Rational thought will almost certainly bring us up against our emotions and those of others. This is particularly true in trying to think of how to reduce humans harming humans. A change of opinion might threaten the loss of friends or a secure job. Unless we know how to deal with our feelings separately we will only find the 'easy' options in life open to us. We are likely to 'rationalise' our choices rather than admit to our fears and face realities. A common emotional block for middle class people is *fear of failure.* They are conditioned to success being the only acceptable outcome and to fail is equated with humiliation of oneself and one's family. The reality is that trial and error is a necessary part of the learning process. Only if we overcome *fear of failure* can we innovate and move onto new ground.

thinking error 9. PERSONAL EXPERIENCE Personal experience is more influential on our thinking than secondhand knowledge from books or other sources. It is perhaps not surprising that we can give knowledge gained from direct experience a status of law. Personal experience is certainly the most vivid and rich form of knowledge. At the same time it must be accepted as unreliable whilst unsubstantiated from other sources. Perceptual errors of magnitude and recognition are common. A generalisation that is based on too small a sample is the usual error made when using personal experience as our main source on which to base a decision. We may think street violence is on the increase but studies of widespread data can show it is in fact decreasing.

Personal experience is of great value but should be checked against third party sources. On the other hand, a knowledge gained from books and reliable media is greatly enriched by personal investigation.

thinking error 10. VALUE AND OPINION We must be clear how our values are formed. There is the judgement based on objective evidences and measurements and then there is the intuitive evaluation. The latter may be based on personal experience, associations and emotional bonds. If we are to be sure of our opinions we must be confident that our values are formed from reliable sources. A common way to check opinions based on experience is by extensive sharing with your peer group. Hearing many other people express a similar feeling can turn what seemed like personal idiosyncrasy or neurosis into a political demand. However, this peer group might, for instance, be irrationally xenophobic. The appeal of racism to provide a scapegoat often diverts thinking from the rational analysis of other grievances. Widely held group opinions have been held in error. A few hundred years ago the majority of people believed the world was flat. If many people share a strong feeling or opinion you can be sure there is a reason for that opinion, even if the opinion is incorrect.

thinking error 11. CONTEXT It is well accepted now that many personal problems that people suffer have larger social causes. By examining the person as an individual there may be a limitation to what we can discover. It is only by looking at a wider social context that we can discover the root cause of the problem. Ecology has demonstrated the interrelation of small events with the larger world. If a problem cannot be solved as it presents itself, perhaps you have not fully appreciated the implications of its context. Getting this wider view may not be more difficult than reading a carefully chosen book, taking a walk or listening to someone with inside information for an hour or two.

thinking error 12. VIEWPOINT A single viewpoint is inevitably limited. In thinking about complex phenomena, it is most important to consider one's viewpoint most carefully. The more viewpoints from which we study any phenomenon the more aspects will be revealed. When we get stuck thinking about a 'problem', taking another viewpoint is always a good move. Disagreement is often caused by differences in viewpoint, which may make the same perceptions lead to radically different conclusions. It is important to start any debate by stating your point of view, or *where you are coming from*, with as much detail and passion as possible and to listen well to other people's points of view. Then, if it seems useful, you may need to think about developing bridging ideas.

thinking error 13. THE PURITY OF SCIENCE An absurdity is built into our society and its knowledge production through the artificial division of people into manual and intellectual and then into the separate intellectual fields of arts or science. These divisions are artificial and should not be treated as if they represent real differences. A car mechanic will go through a perfect model of rational analysis when finding the cause of a fault in a vehicle. A good mechanic must have as logical a mind as a scientist. The practical confirms the abstract and intuition and imagination complement reason and scientific logic. Rationality is not healthy when it is raised up as an isolated and elite ability. Its integration with the senses, intuition, imagination, emotion and action should be accepted.

thinking error 14. FALSE VALIDITY Fallacy: Any argument, which deceives us by seeming to prove what it does not really prove. Logic: Rules underlying arguments which, when followed, will ensure that only true conclusions are drawn from true premises.

a. A logically valid argument is used to imply the truth of one of its premises.
> "The validity of a syllogism is quite independent of the truth of its premises. *'I have sent for you my dear ducks,'* said the worthy Mrs Bond, *'to enquire with what sauce you would like to be eaten?'*
> *'But we don't want to be killed.'* Cried the Ducks.
> *'You are wandering from the point.'* Was Mrs Bond's perfectly logical reply.
> From Lewis Carroll's preface to the third edition of 'Euclid and His Modern Rivals' 1879

b. True premises are used to suggest a false conclusion: eg. 'I saw it in the newspaper'. 'All newspapers tell lies'. The false conclusion suggested is that 'It' was a lie. The true conclusion is that it *might* be a lie. eg. 'Some ties are not artistic. I admire anything artistic. A false conclusion would be that there are some ties I do not admire. This may be expressed as a formula. If A is C and B is C, then it is a false conclusion that A = B. A and B share the same characteristic but are equal only in that respect.

c. Conclusions that are self-evidently true can suggest a valid argument: eg. 'No thieves are honest. Some dishonest people are found out'. The false conclusion is that some thieves are found out. Although it happens to be true that some thieves are found out, it cannot be deduced from the stated premises.

d. False causality: If B follows A, then A is often taken as the cause of B. If you go to Harley Street to find a cure for your disease and afterwards get better this may suggest, but does not prove, that your recovery was due to the specialist's ministration.

e. Irrelevant application: Validly drawn conclusions are often then reapplied to material, which is not part of the original premises. The reaction of guinea pigs to different coloured light might be used to imply that there is a similar human response.

f. False induction: By giving a plethora of substantive detail and avoiding the mention of contradictory instances. Attacks on Western medicine will instance the times it goes wrong without providing the same space to mention its considerable successes.

thinking error 15. ANALOGY

An analogy is used to describe or explain something unknown by reference to something known that has similar characteristics.

> "Presumptive reasoning is based on the assumption that if things have some similar attributes their other attributes will be similar."
> Shorter Oxford Dictionary

Analogies tend to run away with themselves. They are interesting as poetry or illustrative imagery but can begin to imply much more than their limited purpose. This is commonly noted in religions where helpful analogies tend to become blind articles of faith. The limits of any analogy should be made clear. If we learn that atoms are 'like billiard balls' it should be made clear exactly in what ways they are to be imaged as 'like billiard balls'. The temptation to overuse a rich analogy should be avoided. There tends to be a confusing transference of properties between analogy and subject. As analogies develop always check with reality that all attributes compared are equivalent and there is no implication of further equivalences.

The perfect analogy: The ratio 2:4 is equivalent to 50: X; therefore $X = 100$. But expressed more loosely as 2 is to 4 as 50 is to X, we can derive the result $X = 52$.

Analogy is a powerful mode because of the minds propensity to match up similar patterns.

'Below are four exercises suggesting formal uses of the list of 15 errors of thinking given above':

exercise Errors of Thinking Checklist 1.

Without too much consideration write a few pages on your current beliefs, values or whatever and the reasons you have for holding these positions. Then using any of the checklists comment upon your thinking and reasoning. Conclude by summarising the strong and weak points of your opinions.

exercise **Errors of Thinking Checklist 2.** Obtain an introductory pamphlet in which some group introduces their ideas or other written material that concisely argues a case. This type of thing is sometimes provided in a newspaper editorial or feature. Using the checklist criticise the reasoning. What strengths and what weakness does it have? Do you notice weaknesses not mentioned in the checklist? Summarise the argument as stated and make your own evaluation of it.

exercise **Errors of Thinking Checklist 3.** Visit a court of law whilst a case is being defended. Follow the argument making notes of underlying assumptions, strengths and weaknesses. Do you agree with the ruling of the court? Could you have added extra dimensions to the case? Where was the reasoning lucid and where was there more room for doubt, or even logical error. Other visits could be made to the Houses of Parliament or to the local Council chambers.

exercise **Errors of Thinking Checklist 4.** Collect newspaper articles on some controversial issue like European Union democracy, arms trading, capital punishment or immigration. What opinions and assumptions can you read between the lines. Are people trying to imply something they simply dare not say? What is your own likely bias in each case? What view might you hold if you were unbiased?

exercise **Problem Solving Procedure**

    1. Select a problem and express it clearly. Write out several different descriptions of the problem from different viewpoints. Put it in a wider context. Note any solutions that arise whilst doing this.

    When a problem is clearly understood scan your memory for all previous experiences in similar and related matters. Note any solutions that arise.

    Rest. Treat yourself to a day outing. Note any solutions that arise whilst resting.

    'Brainstorm' solutions. If stuck ask yourself; 'What might the answer look like?'

    List the solutions thought of so far. Make a shortlist of the best. Evaluate these in conversation with friends. If a few solutions stand out as equally possible, list points for and against. Discuss pros and cons separately. Give time to think through each side of a contradiction. Ask yourself; 'What is the implication of this idea?' Enter into each solution imaginatively as if it is already fulfilled. Rest. Later, review process and make decisions as necessary.

    If there are still no adequate solutions refer to expert advice.

    Test any solutions in practice.

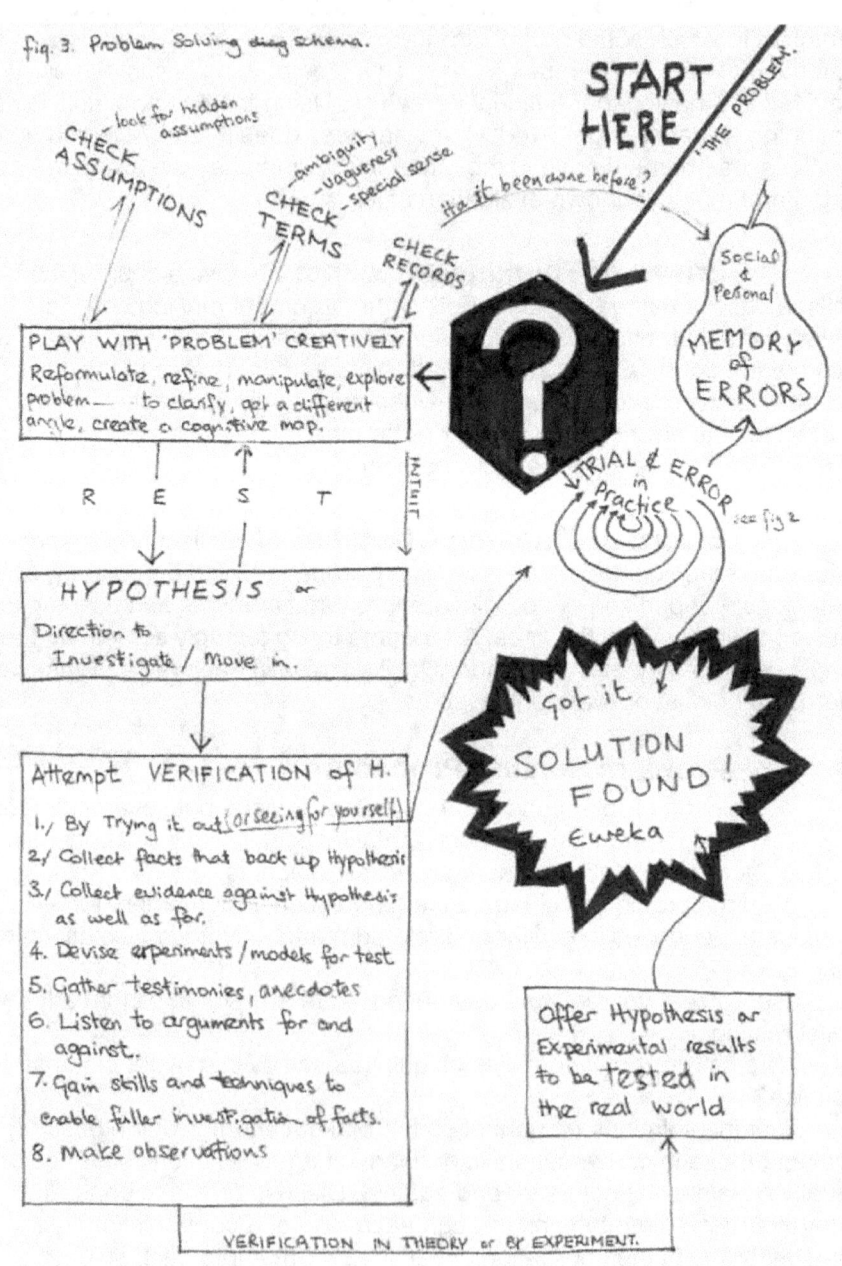

fig. 3. Problem Solving schema.

exercise Key Questions It has been said that the central task of all rational enquiry is to formulate significant questions and design ways to answer them. Bombard the area of interest with questions.

HOW? The manner in which, operation, process, measure.

WHY? Reasons, motivation, purpose.

WHERE? Spatial, geographical, direction, context.

WHICH? Definitions, names, specification, connections.

WHOSE? Personalities, ownership, benefit.

WHAT? Is to be done, nature of it, name, classify.

WHEN? Relations to time and sequence examined.

When a subject is complex separate underlying structure from illustration, decoration and detail. Try subdividing the structure and asking questions of each part.
Arrange answers in groups. Arrange groups in sequence.
We usually have a purpose that directs the course of our questioning; this purpose forefronts key questions that seem to require answers at all cost. However, asking 'all' questions opens the subject up and may present fresh and previously unimagined possibilities.

exercise Focusing Ritual The figure drawn below signifies the mind turning in on itself, excluding irrelevancies and getting to the heart of the matter. Draw your own version of this diagram on a clear sheet of paper. Imagine yourself excluding irrelevancies, focusing your whole interest on one subject of attention.
When you have instilled this idea in your whole being turn to the work at hand; forgetting the exercise.

exercise **Focusing Attention** Choose three subjects, which you could do with thinking about. Sit down in your favorite chair or position. Using an egg timer or alarm clock to measure periods of 3 - 5 minutes. Think of the first subject intensely for three minutes. Switch to the second subject. Switch to the third subject for three minutes. Rest for three minutes. Don't worry about 'getting anywhere' in each three minute period. Results may not be conscious and may only be evident later.

exercise **Fundamental Questions** It was natural for us as children to ponder such philosophical questions as:

    Where do we come from?

    Why is there famine and war on earth?

    How can I grasp the infinity of space and time?

    To what purpose am I here on earth?

Answers to such questions are often awesomely inconclusive or have implications that bring us up against disturbing feelings of powerlessness or mortality. Adults who are aware of this and wishing to avoid discomfort, will often give children facile nonsense in answer. One of the most useful and exciting of the fundamental questions is to examine the value of human life and of our own life. It is only possible to do this and see the implications clearly if we can deal with the feelings that inevitably arise. If we do not, the feelings will cause the shut down of our thinking before many of the implications even come into our consciousness. Difficult as this path appears to be, it is the direction in which human evolution lies and is the highest application of human mental endeavor.

    What use are the main actions in your life?

    To what end or purpose are they designed?

    Is this end or purpose a desirable component of a further end?

Follow the chain along which such questions lead you until you come to that which has value of its own account. Are your actions useful to some end that you truly value?

exercise **Assumptions** The project of identifying the assumptions upon which we act is a lifelong one. We will find that our assumptions are based on feelings and personal experience as well some fundamental self-evident and common-sense truths.

    Buy the most expensive hardback exercise book that you can afford. On the first pages try to write down the assumptions that you make. If it is difficult to start to identify your assumptions answer some of the following questions to start you off.

- What assumption do you have to make to believe the definition of a word in a dictionary?
- What assumptions do you make when the lights fail in your car?
- What assumptions do you make when you believe today's news headlines?
- What assumptions do you make when you see a black woman driving a Rolls Royce?
- What assumptions do you make when you meet white men in isolated jungle?
- What assumptions do you make when you see a parent slapping their child?
- What assumptions do you make when you cast your vote in the General Election?
- What assumptions do you make when you see a man pushing a pram?
- What assumptions do you make each time you telephone someone?
- What assumption do you make when you read about St George slaying the dragon?

Subject each assumption that you write in your book to intense scrutiny. Are there further assumptions upon which this assumption is based?

Review your list of assumptions every six months. How has the last year or so changed your values or viewpoint? Add to or amend your list as appropriate. Check the mutual consistency of your assumptions. Do some contradict each other? If they do, ask yourself why?

exercise **Trial and Error** Most new thinking comes from a process of trial and error. Failure is almost essential to find new solutions. See the following diagram:

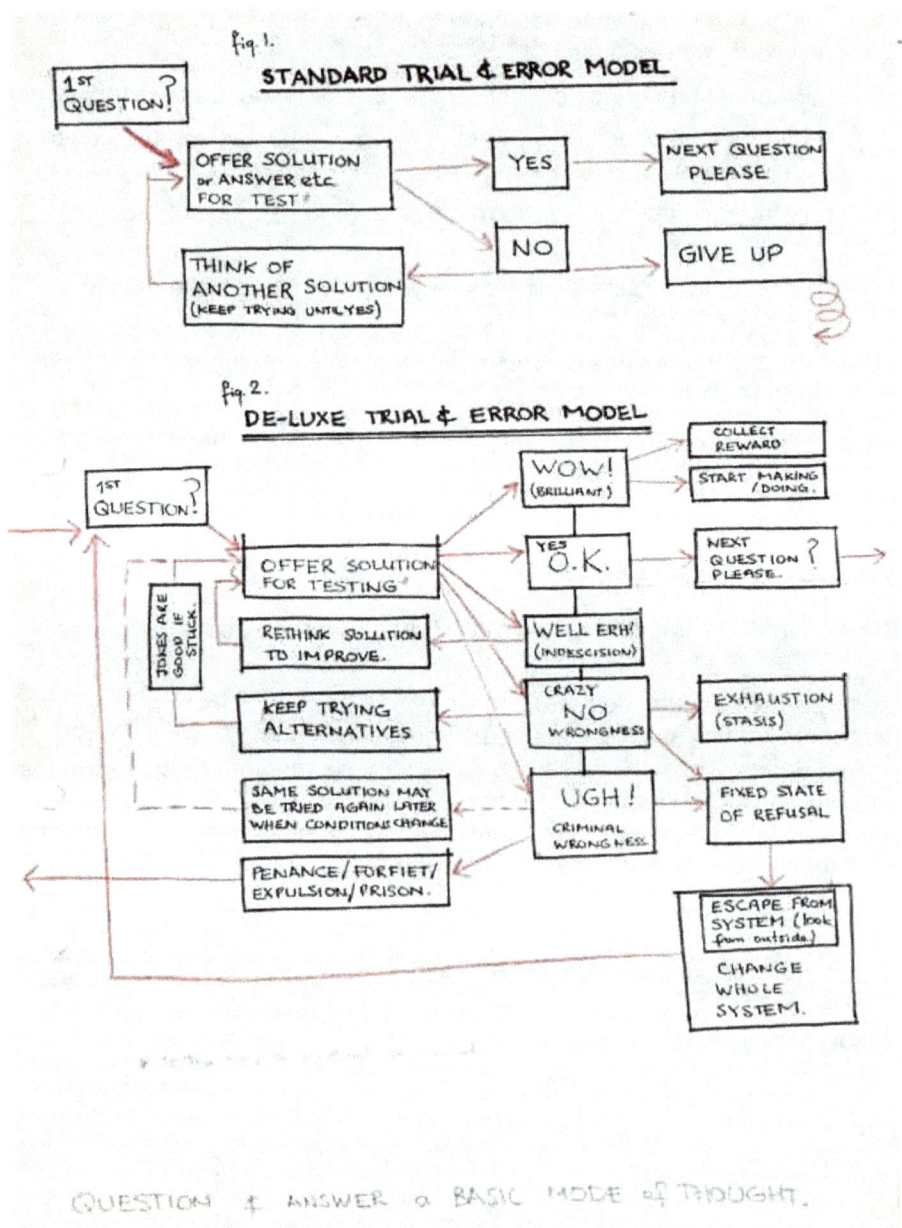

QUESTION & ANSWER a BASIC MODE of THOUGHT.

exercise **Thinking Practice** Think aloud into an audio recorder. At first ramble on about anything at all until you become familiar enough with the situation to lose self-consciousness about thinking aloud or recording yourself. This in itself may take several sessions. Having worked through initial embarrassments it is possible to focus in various ways.

1. Choose a challenging rather than a mundane topic. Don't spend time recycling old worries. Develop your thoughts about this topic over several sessions.

2. Choose a different topic each session.

3. Leave it completely free to include spontaneous stories, fantasy, images and flashes of insight.

Talk for half an hour. Play back for half an hour. To start each session, blurt out anything about the topic that comes into your head. Then assess what you really think. It may help to imagine that you are addressing an enraptured or infinitely benign audience for whom you can do no wrong.

Mark recordings worth keeping to playback later. Thinking aloud forces the mind to reveal its rational processes. By recording our thinking, we can become more aware of our rationality and this will also improve self-confidence.

exercise **René Descarte's Method of Systematic Doubt**

1. Doubt everything until you find the reason for not doubting it.

2. Believe nothing which you cannot see quite clearly and distinctly to be true.

3. The only thing that is absolutely certain is the experience of your own existence.

René Descartes 1637

If you go far enough asking questions about the truth and validity of any piece of knowledge you will come to a level on which doubt exists. When I was doing my 'A' level physics it took a prolonged interrogation over many weeks before the teacher admitted that he really had no idea in any absolute sense, what matter or energy, or more specifically electricity, was. I realised that science only provided a relative rather than absolute answer to questions of essence.

A. Make a list of things you have your doubts about. What are these doubts? Can you put words to them? Are they justified by any evidence you can find?

B. Make a list of things you feel certain about and things that you have never doubted? Think about these things and find the area where some doubt at least exists.

A doubting frame of mind slows us down and makes us think more, investigate, be skeptical and ask questions. Doubt brings up alternatives, generates ideas and is creative. Feeling we are right allows us to act immediately, generates action, be decisive, grow and get results. On the other hand, always feeling right is susceptible to mental rigidity.

Both attitudes are useful at different times. Can you switch between these modes? Any thinking should be effective in a particular situation. Righteousness may not allow space for broad considerations of effectiveness. On the other hand, constant doubt can makes it difficult to act.

exercise **Reading Facts Fast**

1. OVERVIEW: Make an initial survey at speed. Using a pointer scan through everything but the main text. Look at the contents page, pictures, back cover blurbs, summaries, conclusions, graphics, margin notes, italics, bold type, capitals, subheadings, quotes, tables, dates, statistics, graphs, footnotes, etc. Be especially careful to use the pointer around the outlines of diagrams and other illustrations. Aim to understand the overall structure. Is it worth reading from cover to cover? No? Then are some parts worth reading in detail? With most books, this initial survey can be done in ten minutes.

2. PREVIEW: Now read the beginnings and ends of each chapter and scan the rest of the prose. Aim to get the gist of the argument but leapfrog the difficult or verbose bits. Draw a keyword diagram from your notes if the structure is complex. Examine the index to see what is included and what is not. The index can give you key words and the weight given to different topics. The bibliography will give you the key references. You can now begin to select what is useful to study further. Criticise the content and reject parts.

3. INVIEW: Reread what you have decided will be most useful. Rescan the difficult bits but still don't get bogged down. If its not clear move on regardless. Few authors will not summarise their key points clearly at some stage! It is important to find these summaries and definitions. Mark key text and obscure passages with a light soft pencil. Make your own index on the rear fly leaf.

4. REVIEW: Reread key text and obscure passages. Scan to make key notes. For a heavy book or area of study make a large general diagram of the overall structure and sub-diagrams for each section or topic.

5. SECOND REVIEW: Read notes next day and then in one week and in a month. In the first review redraw the initial key word diagram to clarify the overall pattern or 'argument'. The subsequent reviews can be quick; a matter of 5 minutes.

Note. The above is not a rigid formula but can be varied to satisfy the needs of different material. Break the conditioning that books should be read properly or not at all. Using these methods, you can cut study time by at least 50 per cent.

exercise **Writing**

1. The best way to improve is to practice. You will need to arrange to get a response to your efforts from *a reader*. A sympathetic but knowledgeable friend may give you criticism and encouragement. Otherwise it's all down to an evening class or otherwise paying someone to give you considered comments.

2. Study writers noted for their clarity in English like Samuel Butler, George Orwell, Adrienne Rich and Pat Barker. Notice how their sentences are constructed and how they are limited. Look at writing in your own dialect, ethnic patois or language. Use this in preference to Oxford English wherever possible.

3. Vocabulary. As you read always note words you don't know. Look them up in a dictionary. In the next few days use them in a bit of your own writing from your own imagination. The writing may be directed by the words themselves. Writing spontaneous pieces from random vocabulary increases the interconnectivity of the brain. This means an increased level of creativity. Avoid the use of overused words and obscure words. (Unless they are key terms in what you are trying to say.) Examine your writing and make a list of words that you use too often or vaguely. The next few times you write avoid using these words. Make a short collection of popular clichés from the local press.

Before tackling a new subject, it is worth glancing at a glossary of terms commonly used in writing on that subject. You won't then have to stop every few paragraphs to look up new terms. If you use dialect or colloquial terms that your audience may not understand, provide them with your own glossary. Be proud of the language that is yours, without hiding behind it.

4. Keep sentences short. Use the full stop. Keep to eight syllables per sentence in comics or about 20 syllables per sentence in prose. Usually make just one assertion per sentence. See the sentence from the reader's point of view. Could it be read in a way that would make it ambiguous? Ask this question of each sentence until you correct any habits of vagueness.

For details of how to structure your writing to have the effect intended see the eight criteria of retention in the Memory section. The 'sense' should run fluently from sentence to sentence. Again, try to see the writing from the point of view of someone reading it. Extra connecting sentences may need to be inserted. Paragraphs form natural units; see them as bundles of sentences. Try to cut down on the use of commas and use them only when necessary.

5. Organisation: Write an outline of your idea first; having organised your notes or other data. Check the ideas to see there is no confusion and you have sufficient information. The outline may be rewritten many times and data studied until you are quite sure about the clarity of your ideas. Decide on subheadings and even on paragraph contents. Although it is

often a good idea to leave the outline open-ended as ideas are generated in the process of writing.

Depending on your skill, the subject matter and the soundness of your outline it may only be necessary to write one draft. It is more common, however, to write at least two or three drafts. The first draft will often spark off new thoughts to evolve and refine your ideas. Especially when you come back to it after a few days or after discussion with a friend or reader.

The Art of Becoming an Original Writer in Three Days!

> *"Here follows the practical prescription that I promised. Take a few sheets of paper and for three days in succession write down, without falsification of hypocrisy, everything that comes into your head. Write what you think of yourself, of your women, of the Turkish war, of Goethe, of the Font criminal case, of the Last Judgement, of those senior to you in authority - and when the three days are over you will be amazed at what novel and startling thoughts have welled up in you. That is the art of becoming an original writer in three days."*
>
> Ludwig Borne 1923

EMOTION EXERCISES

exercise **Chronic Bad Feelings** Many of our emotional feelings play a recurrent part in our lives, that is they make us feel less than brilliant about ourselves almost all the time. One tactic with such negative feelings is to DECIDE to pay no heed to them and to instead put our attention onto our present time life.

The mental phenomenon of decision plays the major part in the direction and control of our attention. We need therefore to repeatedly make a decision that our nervousness, fear, embarrassment, self-deprecation or whatever, is superficial and will not effect our intelligent choices of action or intrinsic worth. Written and daily repeated decisions will probably be necessary. They may be focused on particular feelings or be general:

'I will not get depressed after contacting my (father) - I lead my own life now.'

'The (manager) will not intimidate me with his innuendos - I will speak my own mind confidently.'

'From this moment on I will always be my true self.'

'From this moment on, I decide not to repeatedly dwell on negative thoughts and feelings; instead I will put my attention on present time and other worthwhile matters. This means ……'

As well as this decision making it is useful to review what is good in your life and what you want out of life, on a regular basis. This is best done as an oral exchange with a friend but writing a list is a good second best.

If a friend is depressed or otherwise sunk into negative feeling a good technique is to get them to review happy memories. This can be done in person, by phone, email or letter. You may have to ask questions about a range of subject areas that are likely to have happy memories about. The beach, sea, countryside, flowers, games and holidays are good topics for most people. It is useful if you know the person's special interests and even more useful if you know their life story.

exercise **Dealing with Sudden Strong Feelings** Other feelings come up suddenly and unexpectedly. You get angry and fly of the handle or you feel dominated and go quiet and submissive. These situations can reoccur quite often and it can still be surprising how strong and even overwhelming the emotion feels.

A useful technique here is to temporarily exit the situation. Leave the cause of the upset. Leave the room and walk into the garden. Go out the back gate and up a nearby hill. Take a cab to the airport. Go where you need to go to escape the imposing feeling. Take some time to think about what is real and what is unreal about the situation you are in. Emotions often carry a sense of drama and false importance but if you can detach from them they can be seen as superficial or temporary; and even sometimes illusory!

Before returning, decide what your most powerful reentry, into the situation, which caused the upset, might be. Entertain yourself with this thought. It may help to decide aloud to not get snagged or brought down by what was that was getting to you.

exercise **Basic Peer Counseling** It is useful to be able to separate emotion from thinking and acting in everyday life. The way this can be done is to set up a special time and space to look at our emotions; a space in which negative emotions can be expressed without any adverse consequences.

The simplest way this can be done is to set up a listening exchange with a friend. The roles of listening and speaking about how you feel are clearly agreed. The person listening should just listen and not proffer her opinions, advice, experiences, 'helpful' stories or otherwise interrupt. The listener should also *decide* to be non-judgmental. The length of time you are going to do the session for is agreed beforehand. The place chosen is ideally a space where you will not be interrupted. You might also like to agree that the content of what each of you says is to be treated as strictly confidential. This allows the person speaking to say emotive expressions like *'I could kill him when he does that...'* without fear it could get back to the person in question.

The longer you can set aside for this and the more regularly you do it, the more profound the results can be. However, even a ten-minute session, can be very useful at the right time. It is surprising how few people have experienced ten minutes of uninterrupted attention and how powerful it can be.

exercise **Intermediate Level Peer Counseling** Having set up the basic relationship of exchange of listening time a few dynamics are worth knowing. It is useful to start and end on an up note. So, before the timed session, both of you would start by relating something good that has happened and end with something you are looking forward to. Even simply pointing to things in the immediate environment or asking questions about things in the room can provide all that is needed. If a session has not been going well and one person is still sunk in negative emotion then a prolonged series of such questions may be necessary. Leave the time to do this.

- One of the commonest negative emotions is caused by the lack of appreciation in people's lives. Providing plenty of appreciation within the counseling session can do wonders. You can also encourage the person to spend a few moments appreciating themselves.

- The expression of emotions should be encouraged, calmly accepted and validated. People sometimes fear they could get 'lost' if they begin crying heavily, but in my experience in the last 35 years this has never been the case.
- A certain degree of physical closeness can help a lot. If the two people have the sort of relationship in which a hug is normal then this can be useful. A well-timed reassuring hand on a shoulder can be powerful. The details of this will vary depending on cultural norms. Respect is important.
- If a person speaks for some time without any emotional expression or colour in her voice you may have to go back to pointing out mundane positives. Where an emotional situation is going around in circles then thinking about the opposite to the situation can be useful. If there were few happy or safe times in your childhood a request to make up a story in which a child is safe and happy may bring floods of tears and a huge sense of relief.

Finally, it's all down to a caring attitude, time and trying different things out.

Note: There is no advanced exercise because I think that advanced counseling needs the guidance of an experienced teacher.

exercise **Acceptance** Self-appreciation can be a good strategy to survive a stressful or frustrating situation and find creative new directions. Particularly when your best efforts at life do not achieve your goals. Things are all going wrong and you may seem to be losing control. There are too many demands on you.

Our attempts to overcome the limitations we inherited and grew up with, and to make the most of what abilities were left intact can be a joyful struggle. It is often when we can appreciate just how well we having been doing, when the whole picture of our situation is taken into account, that we can come to a self-acceptance that allows us to progress step by step. We might need to appreciate how we have survived the difficulties in our lives. What struggles have you faced? Make a list if needs be. You will probably find that it is indeed remarkable you are doing as well as you are doing!

Achieving a degree of self-appreciation is often the ground from which we can progress and find happiness.

exercise **Attention**

> *"It is more than looking someone in the eye whilst they talk, although that helps. It is a really deep, dynamic form of concentration, bringing to bear all you know about the person you are focusing on, plus holding in mind everything else which might be relevant, whilst keeping yourself mostly quiet. It is about having respect for, expectations of and curiosity about, the other person. It is about creating a safe space for the focus person to express their own thoughts and feelings without fear of criticism or judgement."*
>
> Micheline Mason & Alan Sprung, 2015

Apply what you can get from this quote to key relationships in your life. If a person is going through a particularly difficult time several friends can get together and decide to make that person the focus of their attention. Get the supportive friends together to talk about this quote beforehand.

POSTURE EXERCISES

exercise **Correct Use of Body - a checklist** It is difficult to assess your own wrong habits accurately or in detail due to the fact we have become habituated to our posture. To assess our posture you really need the help of an expert, however here are some useful images to try:

- Imagine the weight of your head held up by an invisible thread. The neck muscles are released and the head balances on the spine with the minimum of help from neck muscles.
- Feel breathing as an activity of the middle back and sides of the abdomen as well as to the front of the chest where rib cage movement is more obvious.
- As you exhale release tension in the upper chest, shoulders and neck. Imagine that air is being pumped into the spine.
- As you inhale feel the trunk expansion as a full and even increase of girth and length. Notice how the back widens and spine elongates. Relax and allow it to happen as fully as it will.
- As you breathe out check that the genitals and buttocks are relaxed.
- To check the flexibility of the lower ribs, which is most important for the full use of the lungs, rest the wrists against the sides of the ribs just below the breasts. As you breathe in it is common to find the chest rising instead of the sides of the ribs expanding. To remedy this place your fists against the lower ribs and press hard as you exhale. Then feel the ribs swing out as the breath comes in. Repeat this rhythmically several times.

exercise **Postural Imagery** Lie on your back with knees up and arms to the side. Have a small cushion or book supporting your head; breathe normally; relax and choose one of the following images to hold in your minds eye:

- See your own diaphragm as a piston that moves up a few inches during exhalation and down during inhalation.
- Imagine a long thermometer in the central axis of your trunk. The red mercury moves up towards the head in exhalation and down towards the pelvis with inhalation.
- Inhaled air is imagined flowing down channels in the back to fill balloons in the pelvis; which extend down the legs towards the heels. Hiss out the used air without effort.

exercise **Release of Shoulders** To increase the flexibility of the shoulder girdle and rib cage.

<u>Rest Position Method:</u> Lie down with knees up and arms extended beyond your head. Exhale forcefully with a prolonged sibilant sssssssssssssssss. Hiss for as long as you can without bending your spine. Repeat four or more times resting between each attempt.

<u>Standing Method:</u> Lift shoulders and then let them drop. How easily do they fall back into place? Raise arms above head and hold them up there. Exhale, hissing, as long as you can on a single breath. Then whilst inhaling allow the arms to swing down and hang loosely. Shrug your shoulders again and compare the ease with which they drop with your previous attempt. Repeat four or more times. Be sure your neck stays relaxed.

exercise **Core Strength** Enable the Transversus Abdominis muscles to do their stabilising work by bringing them into conscious control. The aim is to strengthen the muscles your inner pelvis and lower back. This work should help you avoid sciatic and vertebral disc problems.

First, find the neutral position of the lower back. Not too arched and not too straight. Second, lie in the critical rest position (on your back with knees up) and breathe normally. On an out breath tense your pelvic floor muscles; gripping your anal sphincter will activate this set of muscles; and then at the end of the out breath make a 'hummm' noise. You can feel the Transversus Abdominus muscles contracting by placing a finger inside the front of your pelvic girdle. Contract them about 20% and hold for a count of ten.

Repeat ten times daily.

During this exercise, it is important that the spine remains still, that the upper abs and neck are not tensed and that breathing continues in a relaxed way.

This exercise may be taken into sitting and standing.

exercise **Postural Imagery 2** The most fundamental image for breathing is that of the long 'spine'. Imaging a long centre line through the torso will help us to relax the eyes, nostrils, jaw, neck, shoulders, and to breathe easily. Touch these parts of the body as you 'let go' or 'release' and relax; thinking of the long centre line.

You head must be seen as an extension of this centre line, as the spinal cord is an extension of the brain. This image and the resulting improved balance of the head on top of the spine makes the head feel lighter.

On exhalation feel your weight dropping down the back of the spinal column.

Having achieved the above mixture of perception and imagery do the following: inhale and feel the spine lengthening and the space between each vertebra increasing. This relieves the intervertebral disc pads of undue pressure. Allow yawns or sighs if they arise.

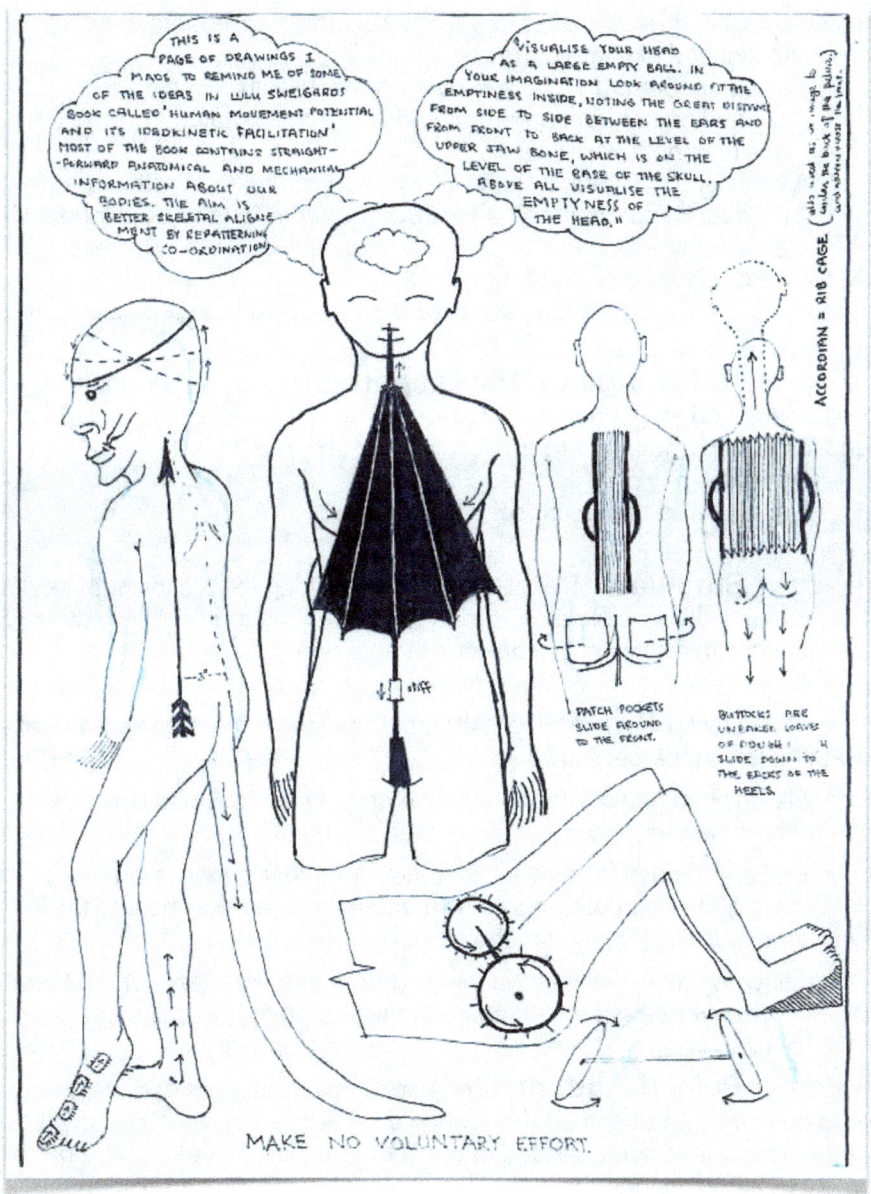

Notes in diagram from Lulu Sweigaard 1974

BREATHING EXERCISES

exercise **Buteyko Breathing** Although this is a breathing exercise system designed to alleviate the condition of asthma, a simple form of it may be used to strengthen the lungs and breathing apparatus. It also clears the sinuses to some degree.
- Take a deep breath followed by a normal breath. On the second exhalation hold the breath at end of natural exhalation. Time your ability to hold your breath.
- After letting go of the held breath, avoid starting to breathe again with a gasp. Keep the breaths shallow and rapid for a while. Repeat two or three times.
- Repeat daily before eating.

More advanced Buteyko guidance may be found online.

exercise **To Strengthen the Diaphragm** Without tensing the throat make and long staccato exhalation; a series of little puffs out. Allow deep inhalation and then breath normally for six breaths.
Repeat.
Don't overdo this exercise.

exercise **Stimulate the Lungs** Finish a long exhalation with several puffs out, until all possible air is evacuated from the lungs. Repeat two or three times with a few normal breaths in between.

exercise **Deep Breathing** Attempt to perceive the motions of relaxed breathing low in the pelvic region.
- Lie down in a comfortable position on your back. Close eyes and breathe naturally.
- Place a hand on the lower abdomen. Notice the movement there. Image the air going right down into the pelvis, beyond into the genitals and down into the thighs.
- Allow the movement in the lower abdomen to increase. Try to keep your awareness on letting go in this region for five minutes.

exercise **Belly Breathing** The expiration should not exhaust the lungs completely, but some breath should be retained; enough to say a few words. Attention is concentrated in the 'Tanden', which is the centre of gravity of the body in the lower belly. Inhalation is short but sufficient air enters for a hearty exhalation.

Sit quite still, breathing gently, giving out long breaths, the strength in the lower belly. Pull the chin in slightly, open the floor of Hara (belly) wide and expel the air fully and strongly. This exhalation must, when nearing its end become thicker, like a club. If the floor of Hara is devoid of strength, exhalation is superficial and wheezy, but if one really breathes from it the breathing becomes powerful and flowing.

During inhalation, the lower belly gathers strength by itself so the changeover to a slow smooth exhalation, which it powers and controls, is smooth and easy. Although the practice here is breathing the aim is to make the tanden the centre of strength and control for all activity.

exercise **The Complete Breath** This exercise strengthens the lungs and does not attempt to improve the process of normal breathing. As a basic exercise, it can be allied to various movements to increase the range, capacity and strength of the breathing apparatus.

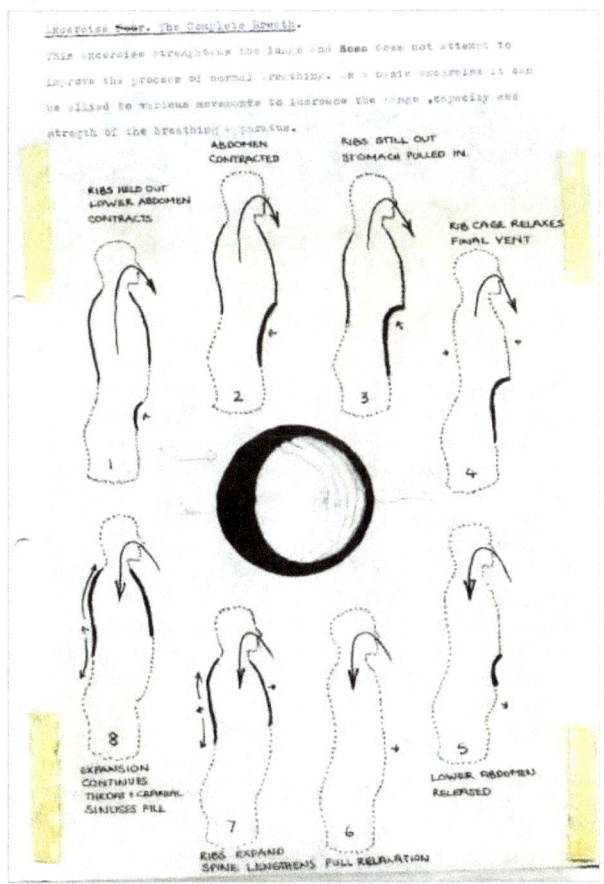

exercise **Complete Breath Gymnastic** The complete breath exercise it is best practiced with simple arm and head movements.

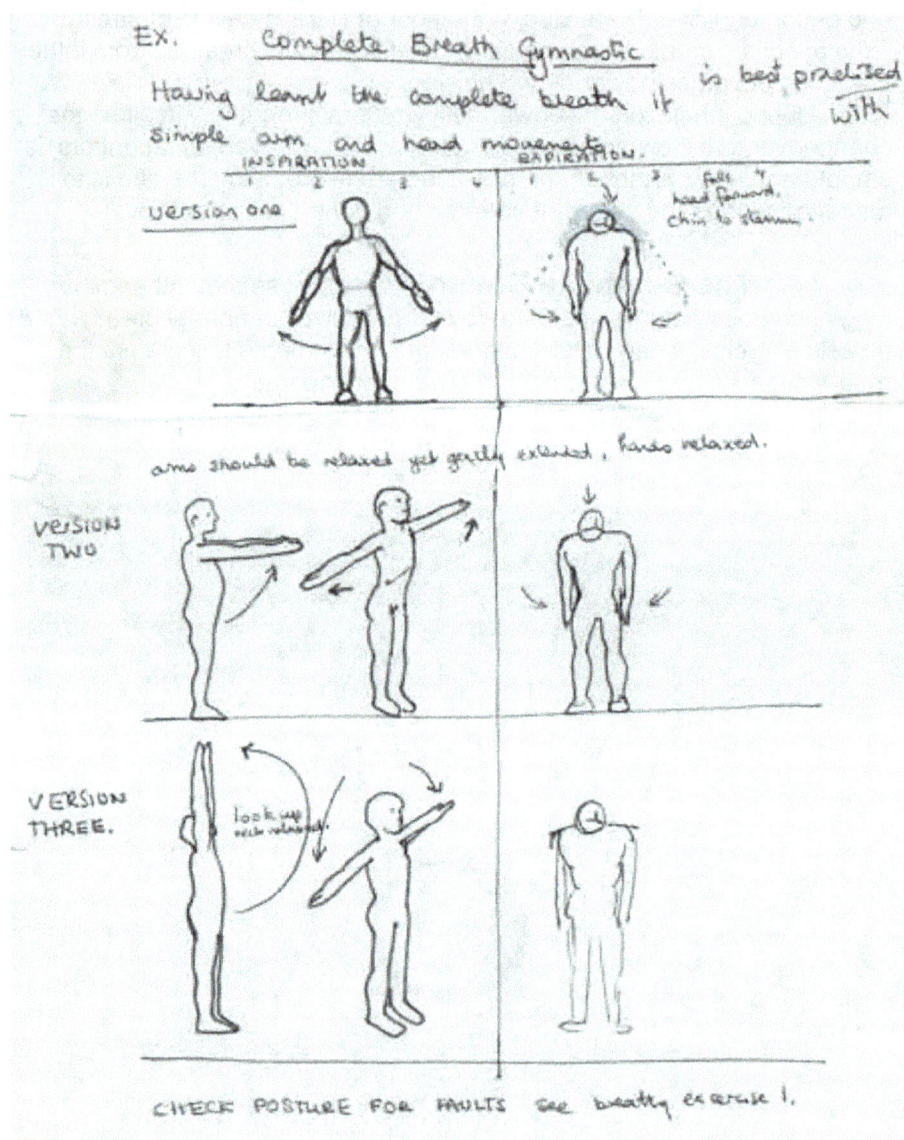

exercise **The Ten Treasures** These exercises are adapted from exercises from a Shinto Temple and were originally called the 'Reeling of Silk' which gives one a clue to the quality of movement required. They were taught to me by a Tai Chi student.

The movements should all be done slowly and smoothly except for the punches which can be done both slowly or fast.

exercise **Abdominal Retention** This is an advanced exercise adapted from Yoga. It is only suitable for those who are fairly fit and in good health. Sit in a comfortable upright position that does not restrict the stomach. The head is bowed forward with the chin resting on top of the sternum or breast bone. The forearms or backs of hands are supported on the thighs. Eyes are closed.

- Exhale fully.
- Now with a slow steady in-breath make a quiet whistling sound.
- Your attention is on the incoming air as it gradually enters the nose... throat... larynx... lungs...
- Unlike previous exercises the abdominal area is gently pulled back towards the spine. It is held in during inhalation. The full breath is held for a second or two. If you have high blood pressure or coronary trouble do <u>not</u> hold this breath.
- Breathe out steadily and evenly through the nose. The rushing of air past the roof of the mouth should be heard as a light rushing sound. The abdomen is released but pulled beck against the spine to evacuate the final portion of air.
- Now wait for a second before inhaling again.
- Repeat this cycle for five minutes if you feel it is no strain.
- Rest for ten minutes or so afterwards. Preferably take up the position known in Yoga as Savasana or The Corpse.

exercise **Alternate Lung Breathing** Each lung is exercised separately as far as it is possible by means of a simple gymnastic. The

stretch to either side flares the ribs and stretches the intercostal muscles between the ribs giving the lungs greater elasticity. To achieve this the elbows should be kept well up and back. This exercise will improve general health by toning the entire torso by alternate stretching and compression

exercise **Alternate Nostril Breathing** Sit with back relaxed but upright. The body should feel supple. The head should feel as if it is lightly suspended from a wire. By relaxing allow the chin to tuck in slightly.

- Place right thumb on right nostril; index and middle finger rest on forehead. Thumb closes right nostril, index and middle fingers rest on forehead. Inhale through left nostril until lungs are full (Apnea).
- Close left nostril with remaining fingers. Release right nostril. Breath out until exhalation is complete (Dyspnea).
- Inhale through right nostril. Change sides. Repeat seven times but only once a day.

exercise **How Much Air You Breathe** Fill a demijohn glass cider jar with water. Sealing the jar tightly with the palm of one hand, hold it upside down with the neck immersed in a bowl of water. Get someone to hold it in that position while you insert a rubber tube into the jar.

For one minute breathe in through your nose and out through the tube at your normal rate. By taping a ruler to the side of the jar, or marking it with a chinagraph pencil, you can measure how much water has been displaced. The volume of water displaced roughly equals the volume of air you have exhaled. Displacement x surface area of water = volume of air per minute. Multiply by 1440 to calculate the amount of air used in 24 hours.

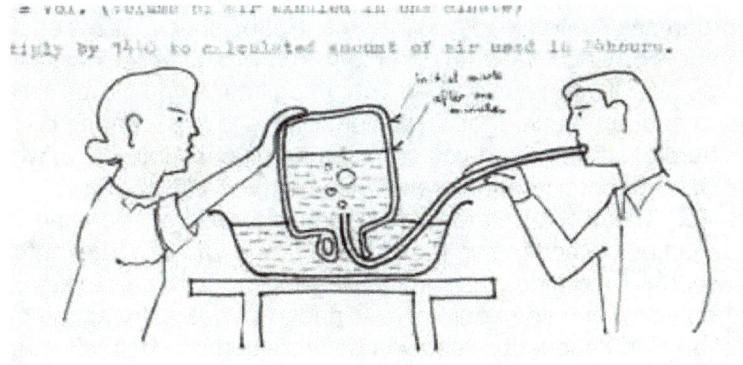

SLEEPING EXERCISES

exercise **Pre-Sleep Prescriptions** Physical fatigue is useful. With many modern occupations people do not get physically tired during their workday. Instead they get tense and mentally tired but this may hinder rather than help sleep. Relaxation happens more easily following physical exertion. An evening dance, jog or game of football will do the trick nicely. After lunch rest, after supper walk a mile.

1. Warmth: A warm aromatic bath, shower or massage are good after exercise. Infrared heat used in conjunction with massage can break up chronic tensions which interfere with proper sleep. Massage does not have to be skilled to produce marked results. A sympathetic and attentive stroking of the spine for five minutes before retiring for the night can produce excellent results. Heat is most efficacious especially if applied to the feet.

Method: You will require two bowls of water. One is hot the other cool. Put both feet in the hot bowl for three minutes then into the cold for half a minute. Repeat this, three times. This simple process improves circulation, relaxes the whole body and draws blood away from the head. Hot bed socks can have a similar, if less marked, effect. Traditionally warmed on the evening hearth.

2. Lovemaking is also an excellent preparation for sleep especially if preceded by long sensual massages and reassuring verbal exchanges. Do not discuss home economics or current problematics.

3. Meditation before sleep will help to slow the mind and reduce the time necessary for full recuperation. Reading a book is a similar and more popular technique.

4. Mental images, of almost any sort, aid sleep and are the most natural vehicle for entering sleep. Relaxation is a prerequisite of having these waking dreams. Once you are involved in the images there is a sliding progression into sleep and dreams. Relax; shut your eyes; stop thinking and worrying. Make an effort to watch whatever appears before your minds eye. If you have trained your imagination you will be able to conjure up appropriate images. Traditionally this is supposed to be sheep jumping hurdles. If untrained you can take a detached interest in whatever appears. If the mental images are worrisome try reading.

5. Fears about sleep are more common than might be imagined. Do not be ashamed of mentioning these to someone you can trust not to react embarrassedly. Emotional crisis in the evening can have a devastating effect upon sleep and so should be avoided at all costs. In fact emotional unrest of any kind should be resolved before sleep can be really refreshing. Talking to a friend is a useful pre-sleep routine to alleviate worries. Tell them the secret fears and upsets that you would otherwise carry as a

disturbing burden into the Land of Nod. Be sure to avoid repetitive moaning and end on a good note. If you haven't got anything pressing to 'get off your chest' it is a good idea to do one of the following:

- Remember good things that happened that day or in childhood.
- Think of things you are looking forward to.
- Appreciate your good qualities.
- If you are alone before bed you can still think along positive lines. A pre-sleep scrapbook of happy memories, favorite images or poems will help to focus the mind in the right direction.
- If a disturbing or fearful feeling persists it may help to adopt a defensive attitude. Cross hands and feet or lie in a foetal position.

Further: you can try performing a ritual of protection to induce the psychic protection necessary to achieve rest.

Ritual of protection: Solemnly draw a circle around your bed. Invoke a power you can trust to make this circle an invulnerable defense during slumber. Make this invocation as serious and ceremonious as possible. Fear of dying whilst asleep is common amongst teenagers and older people. If you have this fear it may be helpful to review recent achievements, however insignificant they may feel.

Ingested aids:

A. Pills, Alcohol, Cannabis. Many people achieve sleep by sedation. Such sedation is likely to reduce the effective restorative qualities of sleep. However, it may be better to fall sleep after a glass of whisky or a small grass joint than to lie awake or sleep fitfully. There is no strong but harmless herbal sedative but herbal potions and hot milk drinks can ease the stomach; should it be in an acidic condition. Try Lime Blossom tisane with a teaspoon of honey or a Slippery Elm Bark drink. Kelp, also known as Laverbread or Dulse, is said to be a good pre-sleep food.

B. Foods like cheese, beans, red meat and any fried food should not be consumed in the four hours before retiring. This is roughly the period of active digestion. The process of digestion requires a higher level of metabolism than the low level of body functioning that is best for sleep.

exercise **Environmental Conditions for Best Sleep** A room temperature of around 14C is ideal, with enough ventilation to prevent a buildup of stagnant air. A mattress on the floor has a kind of beatnik simplicity but should be avoided due to the likelihood of condensation. During sleep the human body gives off a considerable amount of water vapour, which is likely to condense on the floor if it is cold. Check under your mattress for any sign of damp or mildew. If it is not possible to buy or make a bed frame air the mattress regularly on its side.

Hot water bottles are cosy and help you relax more quickly but an electric under-blanket cannot be beaten to provide a welcoming bed in the winter. This is especially useful if the room is damp, the bed used irregularly, the bedroom has no heating or the mattress is laid on the floor.

In cold or drafty rooms a nightcap may be useful to keep an exposed head warm. If blood needs to go to the head for warmth it may also make the brain active and disturb sleep.

Blankets: Insulation below is as important as above. You may find that you are warmer putting one of your blankets under the bed sheet especially if you have a cheap mattress. A good system for over blankets is to alternate plain and cellular knitted blankets. This sandwich method provides excellent insulation as it is the entrapped air that gives good insulation rather than the fibre itself.

Duvet: Lighter weight covers are claimed to stimulate our touch sense, which remains relatively alert during sleep, less than heavier blankets. The duvet also settles around the sleeper moulding gently into her profile. Of course, it is also very warm relative to weight and it is easy to 'make the bed.'

Feng Shui: Consideration should be given to the atmosphere of the bedroom. Noise, bright lights or startling colours that will jar the senses should be excluded. At the same time, it should not be drab and depressing. Pictures on the wall may be carefully chosen to reinforce feelings of safety. The simple arrangement of having the room in darkness with a small bedside reading light may be most pleasant. If you have discovered a reassuring smell in your olfactory explorations this may be introduced.

Make a plan of how you can improve your environmental sleeping conditions.

exercise **Correct Support for Good Sleep** Check your bed with a long straight edge. There should be no sag in mattress or base. Sag will result in backache and undue body movement during sleep resulting in exhaustion. Uneven spinal support may not be noticeably painful or uncomfortable but can result in accumulating postural damage and poor rest.

New beds: The general advice is to pay as much as you can to get a long-lasting bed and take time trying out different mattresses so you get one that is most comfortable. Do lie down and rest on each mattress for a few minutes. It is not enough to push it with a fist.

Mattress: The distance between your elbows with hands on hips is the width you need. There should be six inches from your heels to the end of the bed. Clearly the width dimensions should be increased with two large partners. Partners of different weights should get a split double each half of which is designed for their weight. If one person moves a lot in the night and the other is a light sleeper you will need a mattress with individual pocket springs. It is a false economy to buy a bed less than five feet wide. The bed should be evenly supportive and the top layer of upholstery should be soft. It must have an adequate insulation value. Softer beds can seem deceptively comfortable in quick bed tests.

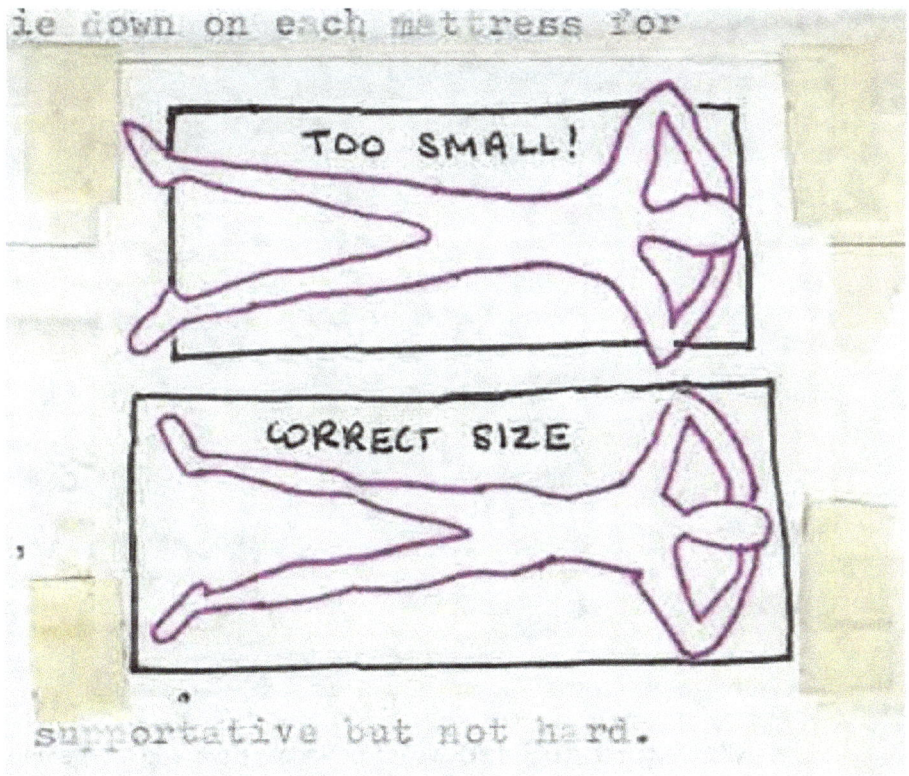

lie down on each mattress for

supportative but not hard.

Secondhand beds are usually worthless. A ten-year old mattress with have clocked up 30 to 40,000 hours of use. A decent mattress is a prime investment. A futon is probably a better choice than a mattress of the same price.

Posture: It is agreed by experts on posture and Zen masters that lying in a side position is best for sleep. Allow the shoulders to sag forward and use a pillow to maintain correct head position. Lying on the back or face pulls the pelvis downwards due to the ligament on the front of the thigh joint which prevents full relaxation.

Pillows: They should fill the gap between the shoulders and face so that the neck is aligned correctly. You can judge pillows with similar fillings by weight - lighter and plumper pillows are usually better quality. Pillows can be breed micro organisms and so should be regularly aired and changed or laundered every year at least. A regular steam clean may be more effective. Diffusions of Eucalyptus, Orange or Sandalwood may help.

Pillow test 1. Shake it out. Then bash it down in the middle. It should respond immediately by recovering its original shape when the pressure is withdrawn.

Pillow test 2. If a pillow is held up on one hand it should maintain its shape and not collapse.

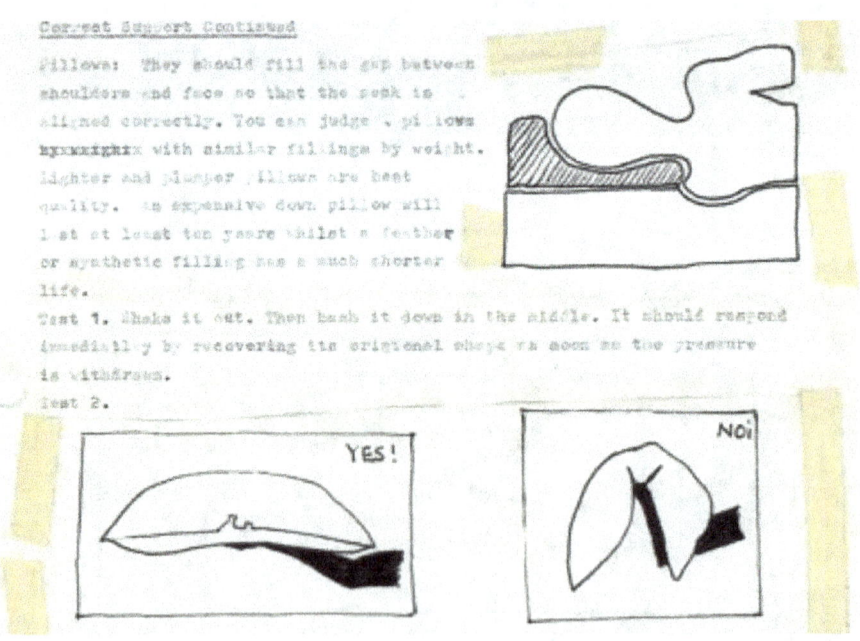

exercise **Waking from Sleep** In the periods before and after sleep we are most open to suggestion. The duration of this period of semi-trance varies with individuals. Information received during this time are most influential on the whole being. We should look carefully at the quality of our mental intake during such times.

Some people will turn on the radio when they wake up. The professional cheery tones of the D.J. divert them from any cloudy thoughts that might gather. However random DJ drivel may not be the best early morning brain fodder. It might be better to consider choosing your own audio selection. This might be music chosen for its uplifting associations.

It is useful to review what you are looking forward to in the coming day. Even if it is a day you dread an effort to look at what enjoyment might be gleaned from it will be invaluable.

Another technique is to cut the semi-comatose period to a minimum by leaping out of bed the moment you awake. The very effort of will power that this requires proves beyond doubt that you are still your own person.

Prayers, meditations or a non-religious equivalent are a possibility if you can bear to keep from breakfast and the days action.

The newspapers or news are not often a good way to start the day. They are too full of irrelevant bad news. Experienced paper readers are able to scan a newspaper for current information which catalyses their own activity; even then they may have to read between the lines of a bland or sensationalist report.

Remembering your dreams and jotting them down is another useful morning ritual which, even if you don't go to the trouble of interpreting them, can provide an interesting collection and can serve as an ideas pool for creative writing.

Choose the clothes you are going to wear the night before. In the winter warm them in front of a radiator or heater before you arise. The principle is to think of making your passage from sleep to a brand spanking new day of your precious life, enjoyable.

These minutes in which we awake to a new day are important. Beginnings and endings are important. A day is perhaps the most important unit of our life. We should aim to start and end it as well as we can.

RELAXING EXERCISES

exercise **Basic Relaxation** Position: Lying on a bed with cushions supporting the head, knees and forearms. Legs slightly apart knees bent so that the hips are relaxed. It is essential to keep very warm so cover yourself with a quilt if necessary.

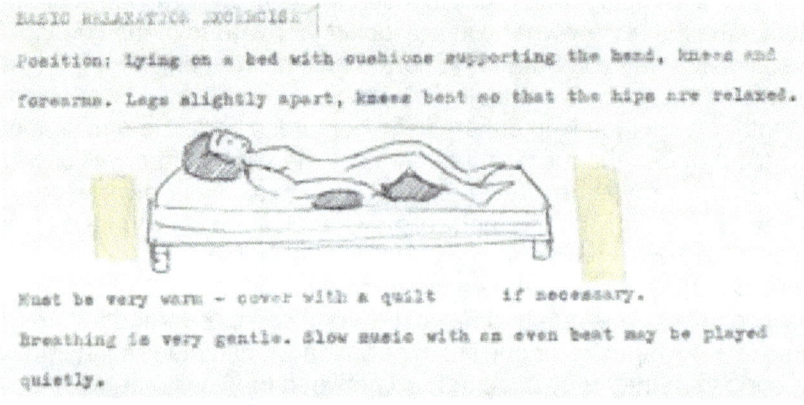

- Breathing is very gentle. Slow music with an even beat may be played quietly.
- Instructions: Breathe in for a very slow count of four. Gently and consciously stretch the whole body. Feel a slight tension in the neck, back, hands, buttocks, legs and feet.
- Breathe out for a slow count of four. Now 'let go' of the stretch and feel the body weight sinking into the couch.

Repeat this cycle of eight counts four times. Gradually let the stretch become gentler, deepening the relaxation.

Then change to shorter gentle natural even breathing: two counts in and two counts out.

If you are worried about falling asleep, set an alarm clock. You can repeat the whole thing if you haven't fallen into a restful slumber.

exercise **Autogenic Relaxation** Lie down, or if you think you might fall asleep, sit on a chair. Shut your eyes. Notice where your back or buttocks come into contact the chair. Feel the weight of your body pressing down onto the support and then imagine the feeling as if the support were pushing up.

Lift each arm and leg in turn and let it fall back by its own weight. Do the same with your head. Quietly or sub-vocally give yourself the following instructions:

'My right arm is heavy and I have let go'

'My left arm is heavy and I have let go'

'My arms are heavy and I have let go'

'My right leg is heavy and I have let go'

'My left leg is heavy, and I have let go'

'My legs are heavy: and I have let go'

'My arms and legs are heavy and I have let go'

'My head is heavy and I have let go'

'My right arm is warm and I am at peace'

'My arms and legs are warm and I am at peace'

'My whole body breathes'

'My belly is warm'

'My brow is cool'

'My face is like a limp warm flannel draped over my skull'

'My throat is relaxed and hollow and I have let go'

'My eyeballs are floating in their sockets and I have let go'

'I let go of the back of my neck, it elongates and I let go'

                Adapted from Schultz and Luthe's system of autogenic therapy (1969)

This could all be recorded in a low relaxed voice and played back.

exercise Critical Rest Position
The most successful method of easing muscles and improving posture is the daily practice of the critical rest position or 'CRP'. The body is supported on a solid level warm surface.

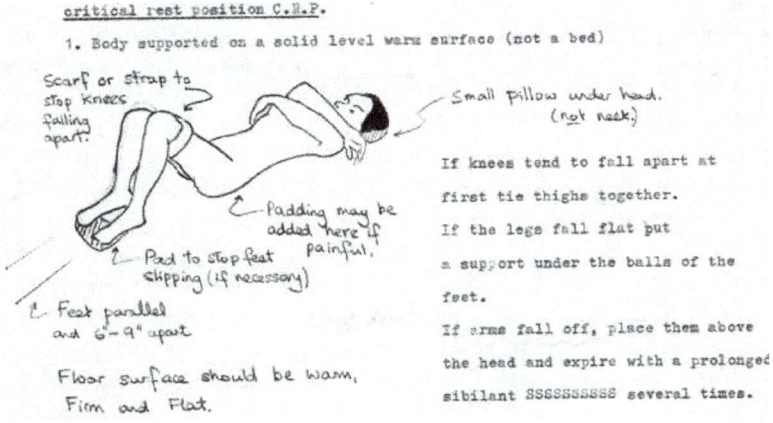

Lay on back with knees up or rest calves on a chair. If knees fall apart at first tie the thighs together. If the feet tend to slide, put a support under the balls of the feet. Place both arms over the torso. If they fall off, place them above the head and exhale with a prolonged sibilant sssssssssss several times. Do not force any part of the body into a position.

CRP is best practiced before an evening meal and before retiring. Try to do about twenty minutes, although as little as five or ten may be sufficient to make a difference.

To get up; first turn slowly and roll onto your side.

CRP is from Lulu Sweigaard's posture laboratory.

exercise **Relaxation Image**
Lie comfortably and breath easily. Let your eyelids close. Check through your body from head to toes to see if you can feel any tension. Don't forget eyes, nose, mouth, chin, throat, neck, chest, diaphragm, pit of stomach, genitals, anus, hips, knees, ankles, feet and toes.

Once you are aware of an area of tension imagine it as a shape or colour. When you can do this; let the shape or colour fade or float away. If you don't get on with imaging then gently articulate that part of the body until tension begins to drain away.

Check through the body again in stages from head to toe. Do you notice any areas of tension that you didn't before?

Then take in what it feels like for your body to be in a relaxed state. Create a vivid mental image of what it is like. Resolve to take this feeling with you as you get up.

exercise **Quick Relaxation In Twenty Breaths**
Are you sitting comfortably?

Count each exhalation and on each exhalation... R E L A X.

Every breath you take and number you count you become more, and more, and more relaxed.

This simple technique is useful in almost any situation in which you might feel tense.

SITTING EXERCISES

exercise **Getting Up from Sitting** To avoid wobble when sitting down or getting up imagine you are naked between two rough walls. Imagine the supporting chair is on a slippery floor although your feet are on a dry surface. When sitting down or getting up, take care not to move the chair or loose your balance. It's all about heightened awareness!

Weight is transferred onto both feet equally and simultaneously.

exercise **Sitting Imaging** Sit on a firm chair that is low enough to make your knees slightly higher than your thigh or hip crease. Rest palms on thighs. Establish the centre line image and balanced head. Feel or image your weight falling down the centre line of your body. At the same time drop your shoulders and release your buttocks.

As the idea of your weight reaches the pelvis the body weight is transferred laterally, through the buttresses of the pelvic girdle, down to the two sitting bones. Feel or image these. To do this it may help to locate the two sitting bones with your fingertips.

Rock very slightly from one sitting bone to the other.

Then, sitting still, imagine the spine dropping through the pelvic area of the spine to form a stabilising third prop.

REST ON YOUR SITTING BONES with the weight balanced around your centre line.

exercise **Zen Sitting**

Sit steady!
Don't wobble!

exercise **Sitting Down and Getting Up 1** The action of sitting down is an unfinished movement; it is really a half squat. The squatting action, being a fully completed movement brings more muscles into play. Try doing a squat and see how it lowers your body through your centre line if you allow your thigh and knee joints to fold sufficiently.

This experiment demonstrates the need of keeping the thigh joints flexible. It forces you to get more action into the upper part of your legs. You are unconsciously thinking of too short a distance in sitting down onto a chair in contrast to your thinking when you are dropping your torso into a full squat. You tend not to use the skill of balancing your weight around your centre line when you slump into a chair.

Picture a juggler as he goes into action. He starts an object moving and then follows it with another one, timed in good rhythm. He can keep two or more objects in the air by properly timing the distance, between them and understanding the effect of gravity on each. You have bones in your body with which to carry out a similar skill. Start with the centre-line as it is the body's best guide in the launching of any well-aligned and efficient movement.

Sit down from standing

Use a wooden chair or bench as it will give greater freedom of movement while you are learning a new way of sitting down. The movement is as follows:

1. Stand in front of the chair with your back towards it.

2. In your imagination picture the central line. Relax your left sitting bone and then the right one.

3. Place the heel of one foot two or three inches nearer the chair than is the other.

4. Imagine that the sitting bones are leading you down to the chair. Give them the go signal. Your skull follows your vertebrae by following the trajectory of the centre line. Make a gentle controlled landing onto the surface of the chair.

5. Slide back in the chair by first relaxing the left sitting bone and placing it back a bit, and then by relaxing the right sitting bone as you place it back a bit. Continue to slide back in this way until you are comfortably seated. This exercise uses your deep abdominal muscles close to your centre line. It will flatten your abdomen.

To stand up from sitting:

1. Imagine the centre line to be lengthening downwards. Relax the shoulders and rest your hands in your lap, palms down.

2. Relax the left sitting bone and think 'up' to slightly lift the bone and place it forward a trifle. Relax the right sitting bone and think 'up' to very slightly lift that bone and place it forward a trifle. Continue with one side and then the other until you are near to the edge of the chair.

3. Place one heel two to three inches behind the other.

4. Keep your head in the centre line as it takes the lead in going up.

5. Think 'up' and squeeze the anal sphincter as you rise to your feet. You can feel the sphincter but several internal muscles that are less sensate come into play as well as your thighs. The sitting bones need first to relax under you before the internal pelvic muscles and legs can take over to provide the lifting thrust. After this is mastered the deep pelvic muscles can also be activated in the process of sitting down, which you can then do as slowly as you like.

exercise **Sitting Down and Getting Up 2** It is easier to sit down or get up if the centre of the thigh - knee - ankle joints follow one another in sequence from the top down. So that the movement at one joint carries the impulse to the others. The first impulse in movement should come from deep in the abdomen where the thigh transmits motion to the spine via the pelvic girdle. From the thigh socket, it falls to the knee and then to the ankle. This allows flexibility of the lower leg and greater ease of movement at the ankle. The reason the middle line of the legs is a good image to follow is because it allows action to follow in sequence through all three aligned leg joints; thigh - knee - ankle.

Many people instinctively use the folding movement in tying their shoelaces. It is a good exercise for keeping the leg joints supple because of the fact that it is a daily necessity it doesn't become boring or forgotten. **Instructions for tying shoelaces with a focus on alignment:** Stand sideways at the front corner of a chair after you have put your shoes on and are ready to fasten them. Stand close to the chair, but give yourself room to swing your leg next to the chair directly forward. Swing your leg forward visualising the action as high in the Psoas Major muscle, which is deep within the pelvis. When, through the bending of the knee, the foot is on a level with the chair seat, drop your foot onto the seat. Now with the foot resting on the chair you are in a favourable position to do the squatting action. Do this by lowering the body.

Think of the centre line and when you have an awareness of it, including the balance of your head, lower the line as straight down as you can toward the floor. Your position is now low enough to put your hands in place to begin tying your shoelaces. The inner edge of the shoe should be parallel with the edge of the chair seat. To tie the other shoe, stand in front of the chair and follow the same instructions.

This movement done every day will be very rewarding in keeping the joints supple and in maintaining good body alignment. It relaxes muscles which are often over contracted and strengthens those that are weak.

exercise **Sitting to Work** Checklist:
- Make sure the chair is close enough to the table.
- Lean forward from thigh joints rather than bending in the back.
- Feet are best placed 'in step' rather than side by side. Crossed legs causes restricted circulation.
- Relax the shoulders especially on the side of the writing arm.
- The best chair back supports the back of the pelvis and lumbar area rather than the upper back.

exercise **Just Sitting** Just sit quietly and contemplate the following instructions:
- Centre the weight of the torso on the pelvic rockers. Imagine you are sitting on a one-legged stool; without muscle tension or 'trying' keep this image in your mind.
- Level the top of the rib cage. A friend can check you on this; it commonly means moving the first rib circle up in front.
- Allowing the spine to move forward, at the level of the twelfth Thoracic vertebra, to the centre of the trunk. This ensures the back isn't unnecessarily flattened.
- Be aware of breathing and a relaxed but toned belly. A slighter tension is preserved that gives strength for the whole trunk to stay relaxedly erect.

STANDING EXERCISES

exercise **Standing Still or 'Tadasana'** BKS Iyengar, the Yoga master, accused the human race of not paying attention to how to stand well. People he said, often have their weight thrown on one leg or back on the heels, or to the side. He advises us to look at how our shoes wear to see evidence of imbalanced weight distribution. These things have effects on the elasticity of our spine. Feet should tend to be kept parallel, with hips turned in and chest forward. He claims this gives a feeling of lightness and even gives the mind more agility. Poor standing fatigues the body and soon the mind becomes dull.

It is therefore, he says, essential to master the art of standing correctly. Standing practice in Yoga is 'Tadasana'.

1. Stand with feet touching, the body held erect.
2. Tighten the thighs to pull on the kneecaps and 'contract the hips'.
3. Keep the stomach firm; pull the chest forward; gently stretch the spine whilst keeping the neck straight.
4. Distribute body weight evenly on the soles of both feet.
5. The arms can ideally be stretched out over the head, but it is acceptable to hold them down with palms facing thighs.

Paraphrased from 'Light on Yoga' by B.K.S. Iyengar

This should be really done with a set of Yoga Asanas finishing with relaxation.

Note: Japanese Hara, the culture of the belly centre seems to go a stage on from this exercise. Having stretched the knee muscles and made the legs firm as tree trunks the strength is then with drawn from the legs up to the lower belly. It is then said that one places the feet on the ground by the strength of the 'koshi' or lower belly centre alone.

exercise **Standing 1**

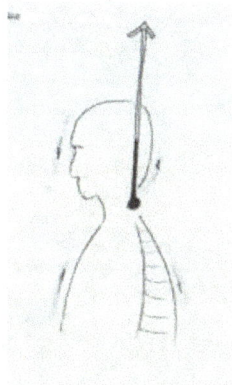

The simplest direction towards postural improvement is the visualisation of spinal lengthening without effort being made. If one 'tries' as well as visualising, wrong muscles are tensed. The aim of the 'lengthening' is to use only the muscles concerned with spinal support and not the muscles involved with larger movements of the torso. When these muscles are successfully reactivated the spine becomes an autonomously structured unit able to act as the flexible and responsive basis of an efficient erect posture.

An image often used is that of a cord from heaven attached to the base of the neck. The spine elongates up in that direction and at the same time is relieved of the weight of the head. The back of the neck feels perceptibly longer. These visualisations should not be accompanied by any muscular effort.

exercise **The Small Dance** If you have poor skeletal alignment when standing, as is common, fatigue will soon occur. This is caused mainly by the pressure of tight muscles restricting veins, especially in the lower limbs. With better posture the weight is supported dynamically through the skeletal framework and frequent small sways distribute muscle tension and aid circulation around joints. This subtle movement was called 'the small dance' by North American dancer Steve Paxton.

When standing for a long time it is better to stand in slight step position and allow these tiny movements to continue to happen and to become aware of them as you might if you were enjoying free dancing. Rather than shifting from one uncomfortable distorted position to another, which is the common pattern when standing around unawarely, the micro-movements become more fluid and become a source of pleasure. I found this a great thing to practice whilst waiting for buses.

Meditation on these small movements also gives us a more detailed awareness of our standing postures.

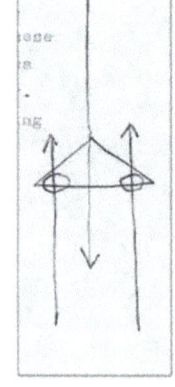

exercise Standing Posture: a summary

1. Correct pelvis tilt: The pelvis is commonly tipped too far forward. A good image to hold is to imagine the pelvis as a bowl full of water that needs to be held level.

2. Centre weight at the thigh joints: Be aware of 'the small dance' especially as it occurs around the thigh joints. Relax breathing so the belly participates in the breathing motion. Now move very slightly to one side so that your weight travels predominantly down through one thigh joint. Then with the subtlest hip movement transfer weight to the other leg. Do this until you can accurately place your weight on either leg. Then work on becoming aware of sharing weight equally between the two joints.

3. Improve the use of your Psoas Major muscles: These deep muscles control the relationship between spine and pelvis.

4. Achieve a better balance of spine and head position: Awareness of breathing will often give us the most profound reassurance of our present time safety and allow the tensions to temporarily slip away. As this dynamic relaxation occurs a shift of the spine/neck/head relationship will often be felt. The chin will tuck in and the back of the neck be felt to lengthen and the head will feel lighter and physically empty. These effects are noticed through relaxation rather than by trying to do them.

Work on posture may be started by breathing relaxation and solo visualisation of imagery, but radical progress needs to be monitored by a postural teacher, and accompanied by psychotherapy work on the original emotional causes of postural rigidities.

This guide although limited in scope can at least be a guard against the amount of incorrect knowledge that abounds in this area of therapy.

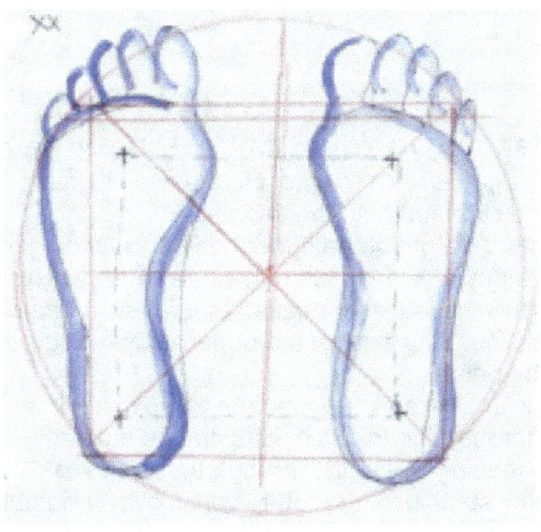

exercise **Standing 2** Stand with your feet parallel. Weight should be equally on both feet with weight slightly forward so that about three quarters of your weight is going into the ground through the front of the foot and about one quarter through the heel.

Very slowly shift your weight from one foot to the other. Returning to the centre when the body weight is felt equally on both feet. Then shift the Centre of Gravity from front to back; then reestablish the centre.

Repeat on the diagonal.

Finally take your weight in a circle and around the edge of the feet spiral slowly in to find the centre again. Pause. Spiral outwards.

Do this slowly and with as much awareness as possible.

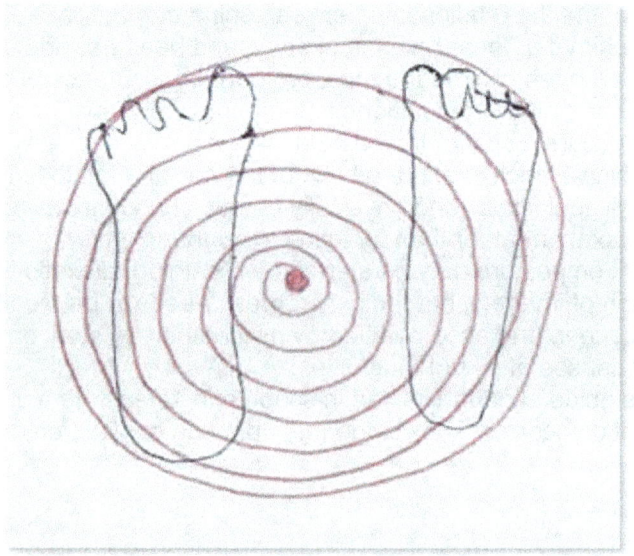

exercise **Standing in Your Centre** Establish the image of a long centre line. Now put all your attention to the two hip joints. Sense the weight equally distributed onto the thighbones.

The centred weight of the upper body is balancing on these two bones. Release any tension felt in buttocks and neck. This upper body weight goes down the legs into relaxed feet felt as pyramids of soft clay. As you exhale imagine the weight of the upper body falling down the centre line, through the pelvis.

- Once this image is established, as you exhale, imagine support rising through the thigh sockets. Image the centre line as stationary and extending down and through the floor.
- Taking tiny steps begin to rotate very slowly around this axis. At first initiate the rotation from the hip. Later it may be initiated from other

parts of the body.

- After two or three revolutions walk forward a few steps; keeping hold of the centre line image.
- Reverse direction and repeat.

It is essential to do this VERY slowly.

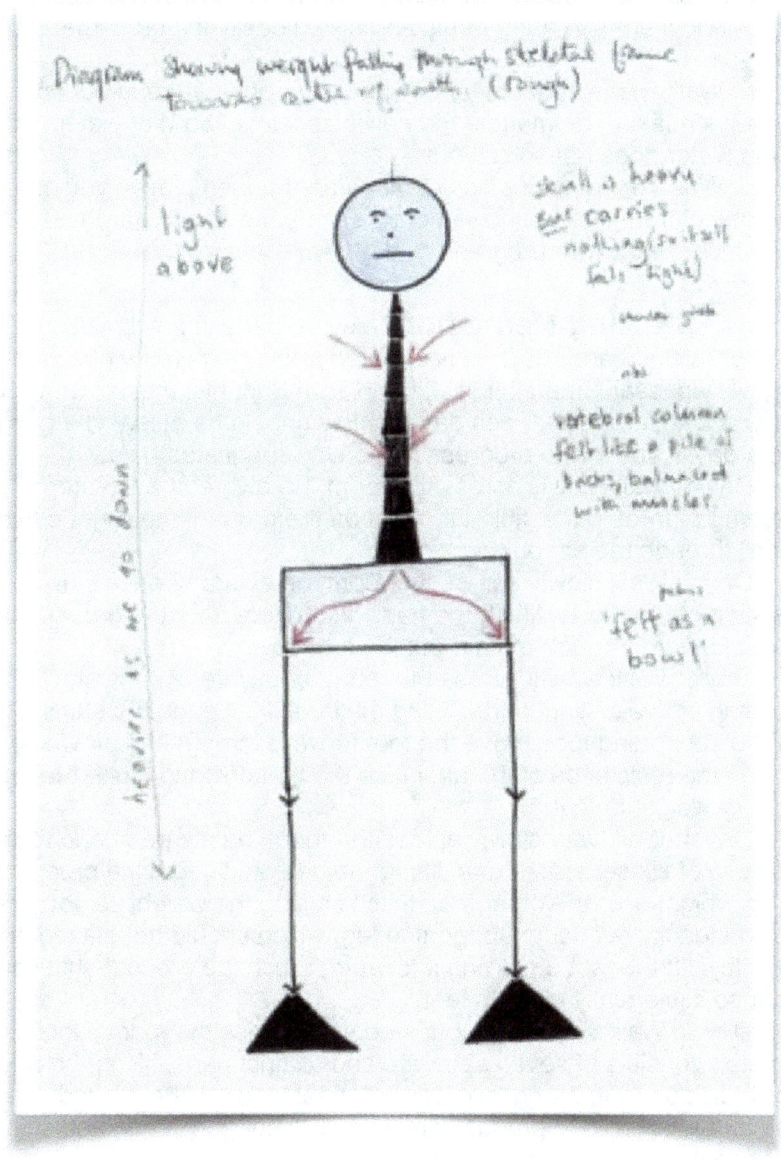

WALKING EXERCISES

exercise **Priorities for Efficient Walking**

1. Direct the toes straight ahead with relaxed feet.
2. Relax shoulders completely. Your strength should come from a minimal muscle tone in the flexible lower belly.
3. Allow arms to hang freely and swing easily to counterbalance leg motion.
4. Walk with an imaginary bowl of water on your head but check your neck stays relaxed; or imagine the pelvis as a level bowl of water. Walk so that the water does not splash out.
5. When good mechanics of movement are employed you can pick up an object from the ground without loss of pace or awkwardness. Use this as a check on your progress.

exercise **Walking Meditation** May be done in any small space and is best practiced barefoot. This is adapted from my memory of a week of intensive Vipassana meditation with the Thai Buddhist master Chao Khun Dobhana Damatsabutsi. Each day practice should be at least half an hour, twice a day, if you are to progress in the way suggested below.

Day 1: Walk slowly across the room. Be aware of each step consisting of three parts: lifting the foot off the ground; moving the foot forward through the air; putting it down.

Day 2: Walk slowly across the room, be aware of each step consisting of four parts: lifting the heel; lift the foot from the ground; swing the foot forward through the air; put the foot down.

Day 3: Walk slowly across the room, be aware of each step consisting of five distinct parts: lifting the heel; lift the foot up shifting weight onto the supporting foot; move the foot forward through the air whilst trying to notice the resistance of the air; place the foot down to touch the ground; shift your weight onto it.

Day 4: Walk very slowly across the room, be aware of each step consisting of six separate parts; lifting the heel and begin the process of shifting weight onto the other foot; finish shifting the weight so you are centred steadily over your supporting leg, which should be relaxed and not held stiffly; lift the foot up; swing it forward; touch the ground; shift your weight so it is equally on both feet.

Day 5: Walk very slowly but smoothly across the room. Notice that each step consists of seven separate and distinct parts: lifting the heel; shift weight; pick up foot; swing foot forward; heel touches the ground; the rest of the foot rolls forward gradually making firm but gentle contact; shift your weight so it is felt equally on both feet.

Day 6: Walk extremely slowly across the room. Each step has eight parts: first send energy into the foot, which means that the relevant muscles are tensing in preparation of flexing the foot to begin shifting your weight; lifting the heel; shift weight; pick up the foot; swing foot forward; heel touches the ground; the rest of foot touches the ground; the weight shifts to centre. By this time but there should be no pause between 'parts'.

Day 7: By now you are moving at less than a snails-pace across the room. Arms hang loose, breathing is easy, you body is amazingly light. You are aware of every change in your body and your walk consists of one continuously changing unity of fluid coordinated movement!

exercise **The Essentials of Walking**

1. The transference of body weight through the spinal column to each leg alternately. All the while the upper body is balancing on the very top of the thighbones.

2. The use of the internal Psoas muscles to lift the thighs (see diagram). The lower end of the Psoas may be located with the fingers. Place left fingers in centre front of thigh crease and the right-hand forefingers on the right side of the spine at waist level. Walk slowly and you can feel the action of the Psoas.

3. Be aware of an easy seesaw action in the relaxed moving foot. Whilst moving forward in the air the foot is almost completely relaxed with just enough tone to adjust the foot the right position. As the foot reaches the ground muscle action comes into play.

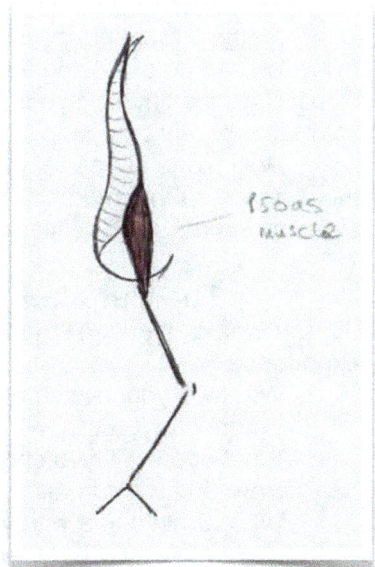

exercise **Use of the Psoas Muscles for Walking** Strengthening the use of the Psoas muscle is best done in the critical rest position. Try various images to initiate the movement of the knee towards the chest without tensing in the stomach. Some images work better for different people. Examples: Sliding the calf towards the chest or letting the knee fall into the chest. The other leg may tense to brace the frame but the outer abdominal muscles should remain relaxed.

It will help to have a well-developed sense of the centre line. Especially an image of lengthening down the back. If you have got this clearly in place from previous exercises go for a simultaneous narrowing up the front of the abdomen from pelvis to sternum and up the length of the sternum. This image relates to the use of a ligament called the Linea Alba which connects the pelvis to the sternum or breast bone.

exercise **Use of the Feet in Walking** For short periods everyday walk barefoot on your heels. Start by very slowly walking backwards being aware of how you use your heel bone. Then walk backwards and forwards with your weight on your heels. Keep the feet relaxed so that the toes droop down.

exercise **How Fast are You Walking?** If you know your average walking speed you can work out how far away a place is by seeing how long it takes for you to walk there. If the distance is known you can work out how long it would take for you to get there. In this way you can use walking as a measure of space and time.

<u>Method</u>. Measure out 528 feet along a path – this is one tenth of a mile. You can do this using the length of your stride or by counting paving slabs. Start the timer on your phone or watch and walk at an even pace. Do the maths or rely on a step counter app.

Do it alone or you may be influenced by someone else's pace. Try the distance sauntering or walking quickly. This will give you knowledge of your current range of walking speeds.

exercise **The Marathon** Walk a hundred miles. It might take you days or weeks; it doesn't matter. Think of nothing but the walk as an experience.

    What will your route be?
    Where will you stop?
    What boots will you choose to wear?
    How long will it take?
    Who would come with you?
    How will you record your experience?

If you dedicate this trip to walking you will find that afterwards walking will never be quite the same.

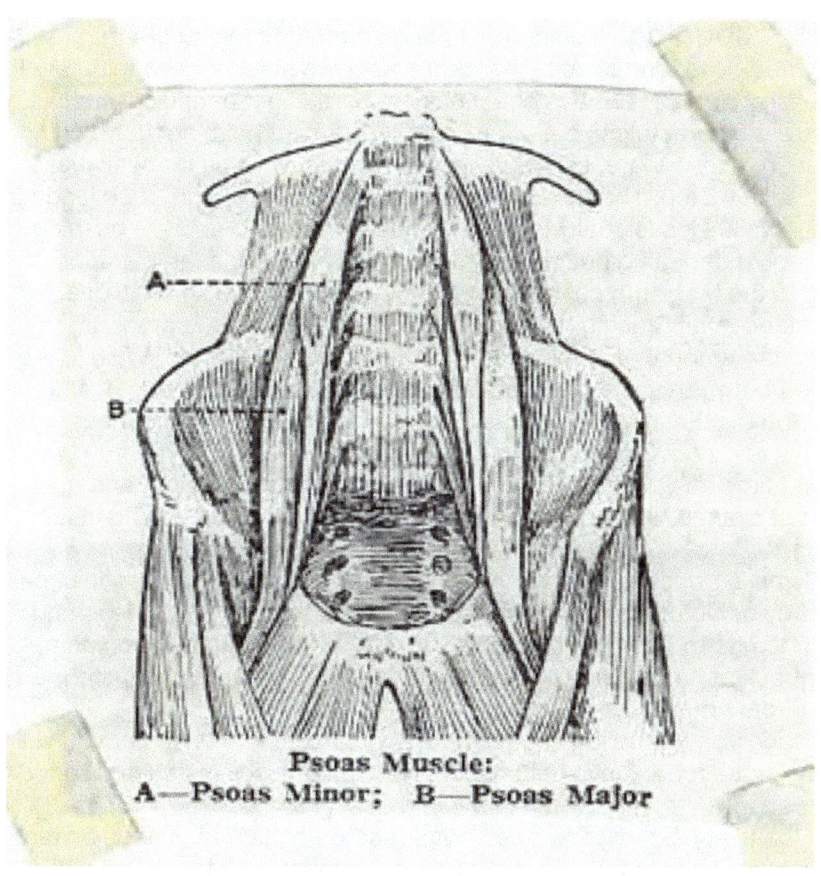

Psoas Muscle:
A—Psoas Minor; B—Psoas Major

RUNNING EXERCISES

exercise **Jogging** A guide to starting your own running programme; Unfit? Check your condition by walking and down stairs for two minutes. If you feel sick or dizzy or have chest pains after this get a medical check up. If you are a bit breathless but otherwise OK and you have not done any exercise in recent years, start daily periods of fast walking for two weeks.

Step by Step: The next step in the third week is to introduce jogging into your walk. Occasionally jog between lamp posts so you are pushing yourself but not getting out of breath. Soon you will reach the stage of jogging to the first lamp post and walking to the next and so on. Covering your distance half running half walking. The next stage is to gradually increase the amount of jogging. Jog between two lamp posts. Walk to the third. Jog between three lamp posts, walk to the fourth. Don't be over keen. Relax. You should be able to have a conversation whilst on the move.

Try to go out 3 or 4 times a week. When you arrive home from work is a good time as you can follow the run with a shower or wash and a change of clothes. Those who work at home may prefer first thing in the morning.

Time & Space: Rather than trying to make it around a chosen circuit start off by going out for a set time. Start off with ten minutes or less and build up to fifteen and then twenty. If you use the same route each time, turning back at half time, you can monitor your progress by the distance you get from home in a set time.

Once you are fit, jogging all the way and getting a bit faster you will probably settle for a convenient circuit. Round the block is usually a good notion because it means you can avoid crossing roads.

Health check: Jogging need not speed up and can be just a bit faster than walking. Then you may want to increase the amount of time gradually. At first you can expect achy legs but your chest shouldn't hurt. Only when your legs are in condition should you start to increase your pace and start breathing more deeply.

Pulse rate is a good guide to how fast you should work. Subtract your age from 200. Then subtract a handicap of 40 for unfitness, unless you are fairly fit from other physical activity. This gives you a beginner's maximum pulse rate. In other words, whilst or immediately after jogging your pulse rate should not exceed this figure. If it does you are pushing yourself too hard. Count your pulse for 15 seconds and multiply by 4.

Jogging is not recommended if you are pregnant.

exercise **More running tips** If your rhythm of breathing doesn't coincide with the rhythm of stride allow it to be independent. Breathing should be allowed to respond naturally to need. Breathe in easily through nose and when necessary mouth. Your face should feel relaxed.

It is important to find your own pace and feel good about it. A good pace to take is one at which you feel that you could almost run all day.

Don't worry whilst jogging. Keep your mind either on postural images or notice things that you are passing. If you still don't feel quite with it, try appreciating your speed as you pass stationary objects and think, "I'm here! I'm here!" Be right there in the physicality of the activity.

It is best to go out before eating or drinking anything but water. Eating or drinking alcohol even two hours beforehand can cause stitch and other discomfort.

Wear warm clothes. Veer on the side of having too much on. It is better to sweat than be too cool. Sweating encourages a general dilation of the pores and organs that is an important benefit of jogging.

exercise **Running Without Pain** Whilst running think of the following directions:

All the leg joints from hip through knee to ankle are imagined as if air could pass between the lightly articulating surfaces.

Your feet should meet the ground firmly but without tension. At first as you relax your feet you may feel you are running flat footed.

The legs do not need to push. The back leg should not be straightened. The trailing leg is relaxed and the trailing foot feels empty.

There is a void above the top of the head, the skin of the face drops down whilst the skin at the back of the head glides upwards. The back of the neck and spine e l o n g a t e.

Exhale from the belly.

No effort should be made. Running is perpetual falling with the legs gently catching you from falling down. The whole body is at ease.

The torso swings easily to counterbalance the alternating support of each leg.

Notes from a class by Miranda Tufnell and Eva Karzag in late 1970s

"Only because there is no strength in the belly does one get out of breath when running." Okada Torajiro

exercise **Running like a fish (once you are fairly fit)** Run 10 minutes on day one; run 20 minutes on day two; 30 minutes on day three.

You might notice that on the third day after 20 - 25 minutes of running you get a 'second' wind. It is often more than an extra burst of energy. Exhilaration may sweep through your body. Your legs become light and bouncy. Where there was breathlessness minutes before, now you feel like quickening your pace, even leaping. Arms and head become weightless.

It seems that this 'second wind' is a healing and creative space. The euphoria may be followed by a deep relaxation.

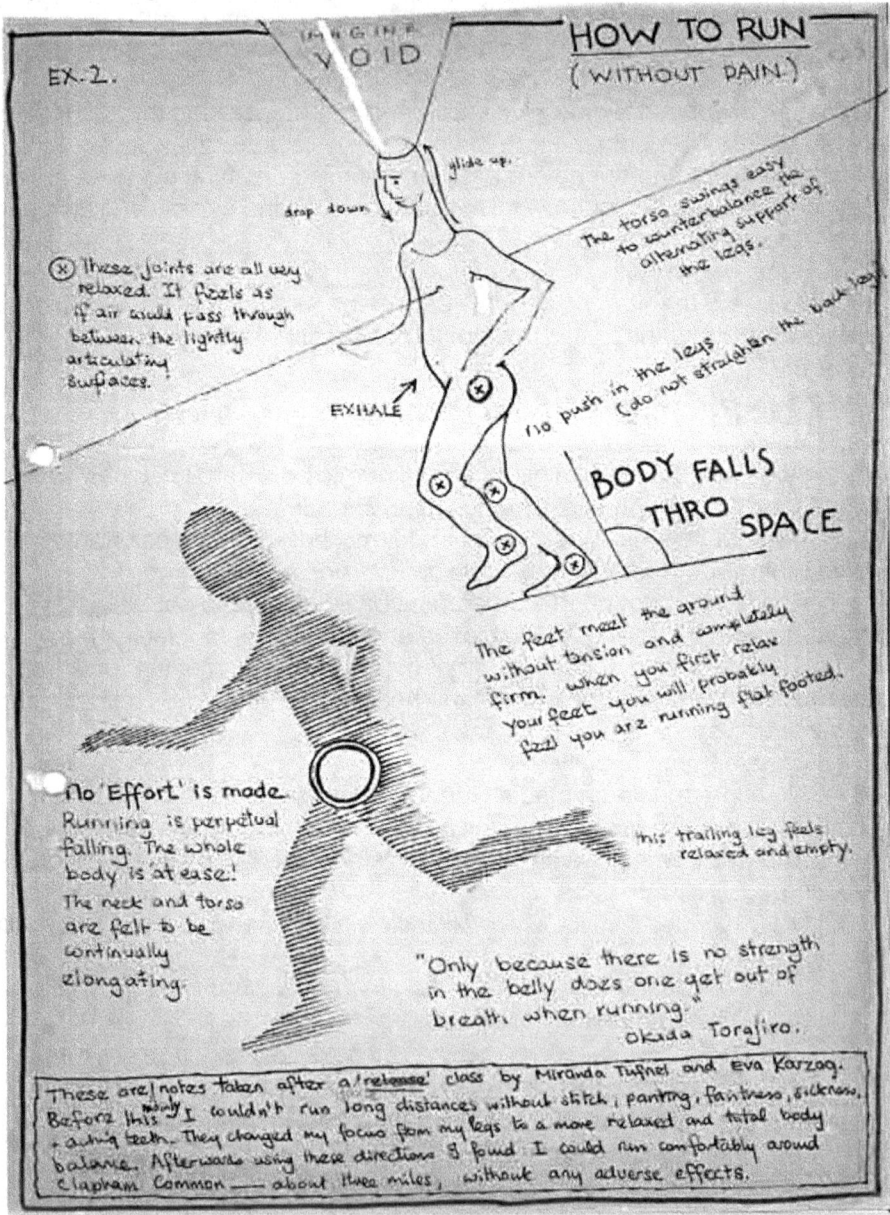

A direction or encouragement that may help you to break through this barrier is to think: '*I can run as easily as a fish swims.*'

Running is as natural to us as swimming is a fish. Trying too hard can make you a bit tense and get in the way of something our body is evolved to do very efficiently. Perhaps it is something we do better by unlearning than by learning.

The direction 'Like a fish swims' suggests being aware of the medium of air; through which we move. We also breathe the air and use its oxygen to help provide our energy.

So perhaps you may find it obstructive to have a complex set of body images as previously suggested. It might be more useful for you to simply think: 'Give up trying! Run with abandon!'

From notes of a Contact Improvisation course in Cardiff given by Mary Fulkerson in the late 1970s.

"The first five miles is a sorting out process. You think what you are going to be doing the next day. You say maybe I've got to call at the grocery stall after my workout'. The second five miles is sorting out your body. The third stage; there are creative ideas. When was a journalist I used to go out and run until I got a lead for my story. Running is great for journalists. By the time you've clocked up 20 miles you're into free floating creativity, you think about ideas and things.

As for the last few miles... You are into free floating fantasy. That is when people talk about 'a runner's high'; you're almost stoned on running. You hear a car honking, but it's like you're wearing a space helmet. You feel you could run for ever with the cares of the world away from you, you become a part of the universe."

Kathrine V. Switzer. Quoted in Guardian 1:8:80 p8.

JUMPING EXERCISES

exercise **Jumping 1** Jump to reach up as high as you can. Do a warm-up first with some jogging, knee bends or whatever. Hold a piece of chalk and score an arc at the zenith of your leap. What is the highest mark you can make?

Fold in the thigh; bend your knees; then spring into the air. Each day mark your progress along the wall. Practice for five a minutes a day until you reach a plateau.

Second version: Standing start, double foot takeoff long jump. Mark the place where your heels meet the ground.

exercise **Jumping 2** Make little jumps that gradually increase in height. Do each little jump on an exhalation, making a noise that increases in volume as the jumps increase in height.

Breathe in. Knees bend.
Breathe out. Jump and shout.
Use your feet, toes and arms as well as legs, to help your lift off.

exercise **Jumping 3** Take a long run up as if you are about to leap over a stream. At a predetermined takeoff point leap for all you're worth. Really enjoy the sensation of sailing through the air; and try to remember what it was like after you have landed.

Ideally you should arrange to land in a sandpit. If this isn't possible long grass and soft ground makes a good alternative. Of course you need to take care to land safely.

It might help to fix the sensation if you get someone to take a picture of you in midair.

exercise **Jumping 4** Preparation: The classic dance plié is an excellent training to build up strength for jumping. It is also a good warm up and preparation for the crouch and spring action which is the basis of powerful jumping. Always fold into the hip rather than bend the spine.

Try a session of imaging a centre line and use your Psoas muscles before taking this into a series of pliés and then on to some jumps.

Use the momentum gained by swinging arms to jump as high as you can.

After a good warm up do 6 to 12 leaps each day.

exercise **Step, Hop, Skip and a Jump** There are eleven simple ways of making a step, hop or jump. These form the basis of all other

pedestrian action. The eleven fundamentals are;
> A step with right foot forward.
> A step with left foot forward.
> A hop from right foot landing on left, right or both feet.
> A hop from left foot landing on left, right or both feet.
> A jump from both feet landing on left, right or both feet.

Each of these eleven fundamental moves can also be done backwards, or sideways to left or right. This gives us a total of 44 basic units of perambulation not many of which are in routine use but all of which are the raw material of dance.

Try out these fundamentals in various combinations. Note the combinations that appeal to you. The next quality we can add to the fundamentals is a change of direction or turn. Try adding various turns into the combinations you have chosen.

When you have something that feels good try it out to your favorite record or other musical accompaniment.

HANDLING EXERCISES

exercise **Hand Contact Improvisation** Manipulate one hand against the other; flexing, pressing and rolling the hands together. Find every possible combination of mutual contact and motion. Take all the routes that one hand can find rolling around the other. Vary pressure from soft to very firm.

Focus your attention on the sensations coming from each hand and allow this information to gradually build a mental map of your hands in action.

Note sensations arising from the surface of the skin and from hairs.
Note sensations from the muscle and flesh of the hand.
Note sensations from the bones.

Gently find the limits of the flexure of each joint. Allow the wrist to relax.

Spend five minutes per day on this exercise. Continue for ten days with one days rest.

exercise **Arm and Hand** Throw many different assorted objects into a bucket on the other side of the room. Choose a distance at which you are likely to achieve about 50 per cent success.

Practice for 10 mins per day. Rest every fifth or sixth day.

Continue until a screwed-up sheet of paper will stand a 90 per cent chance of finding the inside of the bin when thrown over your shoulder.

Alternatively, a darts board will fit into almost any room. Chart your progress with ten minutes a day throwing at the 20 largest segments of the board. When this is 95 percent go on other segments. Finally move on to the triple twenty or bulls eye.

exercise **Hand Reconnection Program**

Day 1. Examine your hands intently and lovingly for a full five minutes: nails, fingers, thumb, palm and back of the hand. Then for five minutes lay the hands out flat and imagine the hands lengthening. This image will allow the hands to relax to a greater degree than it is possible to will consciously.

Day 2 - 5. Use each hand to draw a map of the other hand as best you can in ten minutes. Mark the creases, scars, veins, joints and other marks carefully. Do one side per day for four days.

Day 6. Consider your right hand, relaxed and palm up. Move the fingers and thumbs slowly and resolutely, although still relaxed, towards the palm with full attention. Touch the palm and open the fingers again. Repeat six times. Repeat the above but more tensely. End up making a fist. Do this six times. With hand extended slowly splay fingers and thumb. Then return together. Do this six times. Repeat the above three exercises with the left hand.

Day 7. Rest.

Day 8 - 13. Repeat exercises as for day six.

You are connecting the hand with your conscious attention in these exercises as you first did when you were about eight to twelve weeks old. You are imbuing the hand with importance and opening channels for its powerful operation. The most important quality to apply to these exercises is concentration.

exercise **Fast Finger Parting**

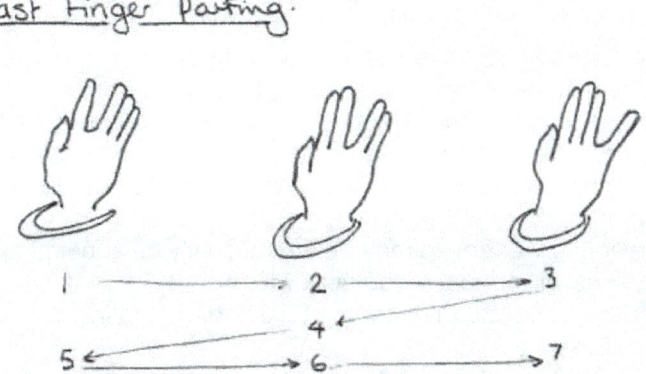

Practice this in spare moments until you can do it fast with both hands.

exercise **One-handed Task**
Prepare a simple meal with your right hand tied behind your back. Repeat with your other hand tied.

As well as giving insight into how we use our hands this is an ingenuity exercise. Barbara Clark claimed that use of the non-dominant side of the body in everyday tasks such as drinking tea, brushing teeth and combing hair will improve body alignment.

exercise **Drawing Freehand Circles**
Make the circle big enough to fill a sheet of paper or page of an exercise book. Then with a pair of compasses inscribe a circle of similar radius. This is used to check the accuracy of your hand drawn circle. Do the hand-drawn and mechanically drawn circle in different colours.

Continue the process of hand drawing circles within the

circumference of the first large circle, gradually decreasing radii to make a series of concentric circles.

    Continue this practice everyday until you become more accurate.

    Compare your first effort with one after ten days practice.

    Note: You may find it best to pause and then draw the circle quickly on an outbreath.

exercise **Hand Draw Lines** Rule some straight black lines randomly arranged on a large sheet of paper. Then with a red pen draw freehand lines parallel to the black lines. Experiment with drawing speed and distance apart.

    Repeat once each day and pin up the drawings in a row on the wall.

exercise **Hand Tracing** Take a piece of tracing paper and, with a pencil, trace a small object. Then turning to another object continue the drawing by tracing another object or shape. Keep selecting parts of convenient objects and add them to your composite tracing; working fast without thinking about the result. Adjustments may be made to the picture with an eraser.

    The first few attempts may be aesthetically disappointing, but amazing things will appear if you stick with it.

    Pleasing results can of course be tidied up and inked in.

exercise **Paired Finger Tapping**

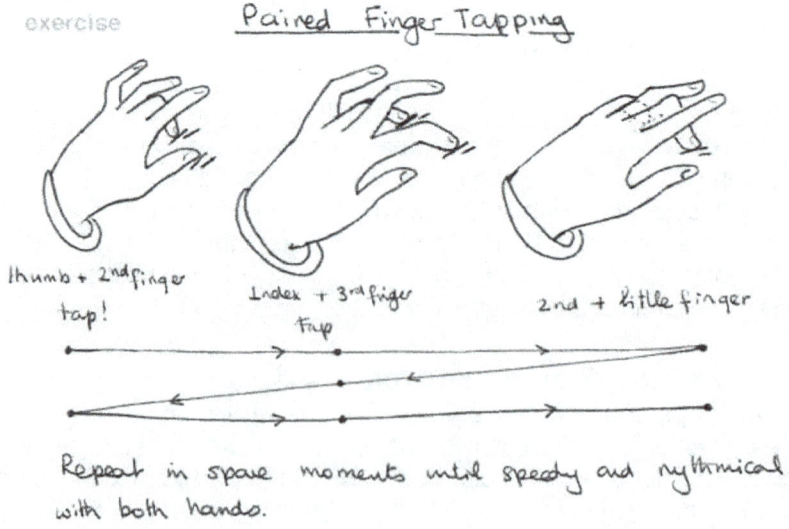

VOCALISING EXERCISES

exercise Vocalising - Lung Control Place the fingertips just below the ribs so that attention may be directed towards control of the diaphragm. Do the two exercises below daily with a break of a couple of minutes between first and second.

Part A: The idea is to gain control of an out-breath so it comes out evenly and powerfully over a measured amount of rather than all in a sudden rush then feebly.

- To gain control of the breath it is useful for it to be heard, seen, or felt.
- A whispered HAAAAHallows the exhalation to be heard.
- Breathing onto a cold windowpane allows the breath to be seen.
- Breathing into ones cupped hand, as when smelling ones own breath, allows it to be felt.

Using any of the above techniques, keep strength in the out-breath for a count of ten. Strength means gaining control so that a steady volume of air leaves the lungs. Repeat this cycle for five minutes. The front and back of the torso may be imagined as two flat boards that move together to expel the air as from a bellows.

Part B: Repeat above using a steady H I S S S S instead of HAAAAH. Check your lips, jaw, and throat; are they all relaxed? Keep this more restricted exhalation coming out steadily for a mental count of fifteen. Continue the cycle for five minutes.

exercise Vocalising - Throat Relaxation It is physiologically necessary to relax the throat in the process of yawning.

Sit in front of the mirror.

Make a yawn. A true yawn can often be induced by relaxing and making a couple of deep breaths; but if doesn't come, imitate one. Notice how the mouth and throat are wide open. Whilst still yawning, close the eyes and notice the feel of the concave tongue and arched palate that occur whilst yawning.

Relax and finish the yawn. Then, with eyes still closed, reproduce the same curved tongue and arched palate with muscle action only.

Open eyes and check in mirror.

Run though this exercise for a set period each day until the reproduction of the yawning pattern is assured.

exercise Vocalising - Tongue Articulation The tongue is a complex muscular organ with more muscles in its small space than any other part of the body.

Whistling is one of the best methods of developing tongue control. If you have a regular walk outside everyday resolve to whistle a complete tune each time you go out. If you don't have such a regular open air promenade make sure you include whistling in your weekly vocal session.

T, D, J, L, N, are letters which primarily use the tip of the tongue. Try some fast permutations of the following tongue-tip block then devise one of your own.

T - D - J - L - N

D - J - L - N - T

J - L - N - T - D

L - N - T - D - J

N - T - D - J - L

The hard C, K and Q are letters using the back of the tongue. Try some fast repetitions of the phrase '*Kitty the jocular Cock-a-Too*', and then make up a phrase of your own.

exercise **Vocalising - Roof Arch** The behavior of the roof arch is controlled by a pair of muscles in the soft palate called the 'Pillars of Fauces'; to gain control of these muscles:

Make the sound 'ING' to bring the palate and tongue together. 'AH' shoots them apart. Repeating the two sounds 'ING_AH!' to vigorously exercise the soft palate.

These may be repeated furiously for a minute or two in the manner of a mantra; or you can construct a sort of sound poem using these sounds.

TING AH... LING AH...

TING AH... LING YAH...

TING YAH...FING AH...

FING AH... FING YAH...

TING YAH... FING AH...

TING AH... LING AH...

exercise **Vocalising - Lips: Gape, pout and grin**

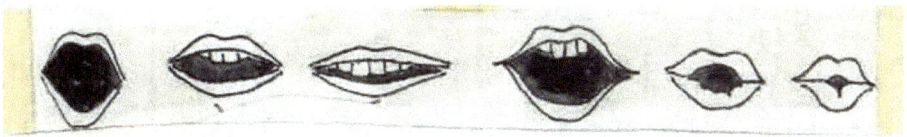

Vocalise from these lip shapes!
Ahh... Ooo... Eee... Yoo... Ahh... Yoo... See...
You are, you see.

Make a fierce muscular pout. Then draw back the lips tensely to bare the teeth. From there open the mouth wide, poke the tongue out and curve it down to touch the chin. From this full gape gather the lips slowly and stiffly inward, and only when they are firmly pursed, push them out into a pout.

When all else is said and done and practised it is the expression of the mouth that will do most to make our speech vivid and our faces look alive. A face that is alive will attract the attention we need to be brilliant.

exercise **Vocalising AHHH! AHHH...** This sound is the fundamental of speech and is an important vowel in our language. Open the mouth as if to yawn, simultaneously inhaling. Let a relaxed, resonant loud 'ARHHH' sound glide out. Repeat several times, letting each sound become longer, louder and deeper than the one before. Do this by increased relaxation.

Once you've got the hang of a really uninhibited AHHH! Try releasing the other five vowels with the same lack of restraint.

A...

E...

I...

O...

U...

Now to progressively group the vowel sounds in twos, then in threes, and finally altogether.

AH... A... E... I... O... U...

AH___A... E___I... O___U...

AH___A___E... I___O___U...

AH___A___E___I___O___U...

Then try the following permutations.

 U - O - I - E - A - AH

 I - U - O - AH - E - A

 O - I - U - A - AH - E

 E - AH - A - U - I - O

 A - E - AH - O - U - I

 AH - A - E - I - O - U

Give each vowel equal presentation.

Note: It is easy to skip this exercise because it seems too obvious but take care with these simple sounds and utter them well. They are the basis of all our English speech.

for they are the basis of all speech.

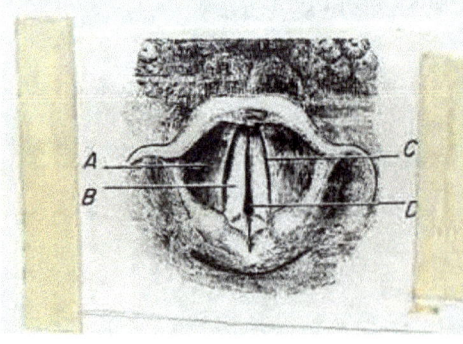

FIG. 13-49. Laryngoscopic view of vocal cords and associated parts when a high note is being sung. A, false vocal cords; B, true vocal cords; C, ventricles; D, rima glottidis (opening). (From "Morris' Human Anatomy") by Schaeffer, McGraw-Hill Book Company, Inc.)

exercise Vocalising Resonance

 A. Mouth Resonance: Repeat the vowel exercises humming between each vowel intonation. mmmAH... mmmA... mmmE... mmmI... mmmO... mmmU...

B. Nasal Resonance: Repeat the vowel exercises humming with an 'nnn' between each vowel. nnnAH... nnnA... nnnE... nnnI... nnnO... nnnU...

C. Chest Resonance: The hard 'G' suppresses the sound, forcing the resonance down into the chest cavity.

Gar Gay Gee...! Gi Go Goo...!

Gar Gay Gee...! Gi Go Goo...!

Gar Gay Gee...! Gi Go Goo...!

In the above exercises, it is important to exaggerate the resonance and really explore the possibilities of your 'instrument'. Having explored each area of resonance, practice going from one to another.

Make up a poem that takes as its main aural effect a play between these three areas of resonance.

The higher humms will resonate in the skull.

exercise **Vocalising - Neck Tension** The vocal sounds are produced in the neck region and any tension here will make the voice stilted or limited.

Relax tension around the neck area.

Let the head hang forward. Feel its weight. Shoulders are fully relaxed. Release the head completely.

Using the minimum effort necessary slowly roll it around to the side. Pause with it slumped over sideways before rolling it back continuing on around to the other side. Hold for ten. Roll carefully back to the front and repeat.

Note: We might simplify this by saying do VERY SLOW neck rolls.

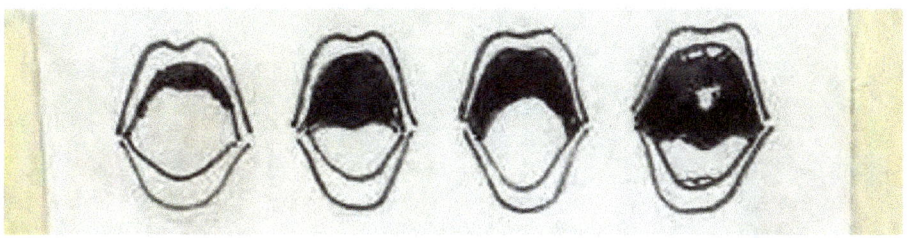

exercise **Not Vocalising or Not Speaking** Much seemingly worthless talk might have the useful function of 'getting things off your chest'. However, there is still much dull unnecessary prattle

Although the voice may be the most vivid form of communication it can also be a gate to close off more meaningful nonverbal experience. Let silence speak louder than words.

Be with another person and for a whole morning, afternoon or evening and make a pact not to speak. Don't ignore each other or constantly exchange notes but find out how to get on without words.

Later repeat the exercise but this time agreeing to allow only essential communication, things worth saying because they are beautiful in themselves. They should be poetic or melodic or bring attention to something worth sharing.

Cut out the dross leaving only worthwhile communication with silence between.

> *"The voice is at the centre of all musical activity, but it is all to easy to silence and very hard to reactivate, since those who have been silenced in this way have been wounded in a very intimate and crucial part of their being."*
> Christopher Small, *Musicking: the meaning of performing and listening*, p.212

BIBLIOGRAPHY

Human Ability - General

Callois, Roger. *Man, Play and Games*, University of Illinois Press 2000

Brown, Stuart. *Play: and how it shapes the brain, opens the imagination, and invigorates the soul*, Penguin 2009

Hills, Christopher. & Robert B. Stone. *Conduct Your Own Awareness Sessions: step-by-step instructions for 80 game-like group evenings that will change your life!* NEL 1970

Pfeifer, R., and Scheier, C. *Understanding Intelligence*, MIT 1999

Vernon, Philip E. *The Structure of Human Abilities*, Methuen 1965

SENSING General

Ackerman, Diane. *A Natural History of the Senses*, Chapmans 1990

Barlow H.B. & J.D.Mollon. *The Senses*, Cambridge U.P. 1982

Classen, Constance. *Worlds of Sense: exploring the senses in history and across cultures*, Routledge 1993

Classen, Constance. *The Color of Angels: cosmology, gender and the aesthetic imagination*, Routledge 1998

Finnegan, Mike. *Communication: the multiple modes of human interconnection*, Routledge 2002

Geary, James. *The Body Electric: an anatomy of the new bionic senses*, Weidenfield and Nicholson 2002

Geurts, Kathryn Linn. *Culture and the Senses: bodily ways of knowing in an African community*, University of California Press 2002

Hills, C. & R.I.J. Stone. *Conduct Your Own Awareness Sessions*, Signet. 1970

Howes, David. *Sensual Relations: engaging the senses in culture & social theory*, University of Michigan Press 2003

Howes, David. Ed. *Empire of the Senses*, Berg 2004

Jutte, Robert. Transl. James Lynn. *A History of the Senses: from antiquity to cyberspace*, Polity 2005

Malnar, Joy Monice. & Frank Vodvarka. *Sensory Design*, University of Minnesota Press 2004

McGough, Roger ed. *Sensational: poems inspired by the five senses*, Macmillan 2004

Ong, Walter J. '*The Shifting Sensorium*' in, *The Varieties of Sensory Experience*, ed. David Howe University of Toronto Press 1991

Smith, Mark M. *How Race is Made: slavery, segregation and the senses*, University of North Carolina Press 2006

Stafford, Barbara Maria. *Artful Science: enlightenment entertainment and the eclipse of visual education,* MIT 1994

Stewart, S. *Poetry and the Fate of the Senses,* Chicago U.P. 2002

Taussig, Michael T. *Mimesis and Alterity: a particular history of the senses,* Routlege 1993

SEEING

Benjamin, Harry. *Better Sight Without Glasses,* Health for All 1929 - 41

Elkins, James *The Object Stares Back: on the nature of seeing,* Harcourt 1996

Elkins, James *How to Use Your Eyes,* Routledge 2000

Frank, Frederick. *The Zen of Seeing,* Wildwood 1979

Gibson, James J. *The Ecological Approach to Visual Perception*, Boston, Houghton Mifflin 1979

Huxley, Aldous. *The Art of Seeing,* Triad Books 1985

Itten, Johannes. *The Elements of Colour,* Van Nostrand Reinhold 1970

Klee, Paul. *Notebooks Vol 1 The Thinking Eye,* Lund Humphries 1961

Milner, Marion. *On Not Being Able to Paint,* H.E.B. reprint 1977

Sloane, Patricia. *Colour: Basic Principles and New Directions,* Studio Vista 1967

HEARING

Leeuwen, Theo van. *Speech, Music, Sound,* Macmillan 1999

Parker Mills, Ernest. *Listening: key to communication,* Petrocelli Books NY 1974

Pinney, Rachael. *Creative Listening,* Annick Pamphlet, Toronto 1976

Ree, Jonathan. *I See a Voice: language, deafness & the senses - a philosophical history,* Harper Collins 1999

Wishart, Trevor. *Sounds Fun, Schools Council,* York University 1975

TOUCHING

Classen, Constance. *The Deepest Sense: a cultural history of touch,* University of Illinois Press 2012

Classen, Constance ed. *The Book Of Touch,* Berg 2005

Josipovich, Gabriel. *Touch,* Yale U.P. 1996

Montague, Ashley. *Touching,* Harper & Row 1971

TASTING & SMELLING

Classen, Constance et al. *Aroma: the cultural history of smell,* Routledge 1994

Dravniek, Andrew. *Atlas of Odor Character Profiles,* ASTM 1985

Moncrieff, R.W. *Chemical Senses,* L. Hill 1967

Orbach, Susie. *Fat is a Feminist Issue: the anti-diet guide to permanent weight loss,* Paddington Press 1978

Ostrom, Lizzie. *Perfume: a century of scents,* Cornestone 2015

Watson, Lyall. *Jacobson's Organ and the Remarkable Nature of Smell,* W.W.Norton 2000

WARMING AND COOLING

Chalkley & Carter. *Thermal Environment,* Architectural Press 1968

Chang, C.C. *Tibetan Yoga,* Citedal N.J. 1977 (Orig. N.Y.1963)

Heschong, Lisa. *Thermal Delight in Architecture,* MIT 1979

Pallasmaa, Juhani. *The Eyes of the Skin: architecture and the senses,* Academy Editions 1996

ACTING AGAINST GRAVITY

Clark, Barbara. *Body Proportion Needs Depth,* Clark Manuals, Tempe, Arizona 1975

Feldenkrais, Moshe. *Awareness Through Movement: health exercises for personal growth,* Pelican 1980 (Orig. 1972)

Fulkerson, Mary. *Language of the Axis,* Dartington Theatre Papers. No. 197 c1978

Lanworthy, Orthello. *The Sensory Control of Posture & Movement,* Williams & Wilkins. Baltimore 1970

Shawn, Ted. *Every Little Movement: a book about François Delsarte,* Dance Horizons 1954

Sweigaard, Lulu E. *Human Movement Potential: its ideokinetic facilitation,* Dodd, Mead & Co 1974

Todd, Mabel Ellsworth. *The Thinking Body,* Dance Horizons c1970

Wells, Katherine Fuller et al. *Kinesiology: Scientific Basis of Human Motion,* McGraw-Hill Publishing Co. 2001

PAIN (The senses give pleasure - pain is the antithesis)

Melzack, Ronald & Patrick D. Wall. *Handbook of Pain Management,* 2nd Edition (A Companion to Wall and Melzack's Textbook of Pain), Churchill Livingstone 2003

Scarry, Elaine. *The Body in Pain: the making and unmaking of the world* Oxford U.P. 1989

Wall, Patrick. *The Science of Pain and Suffering,* Weidenfeld and Nicholson 2000

THINKING General

Anon. *The Mind Gym: wake up your mind*, Time Warner Books 2004

Barclay, Glen. *Mind Over Matter: beyond the bounds of nature*, Arthur Barker, London 1973

Bono, Edward de. *The Use of Lateral Thinking*, Pelican 1978 (Orig. 1967)

Bono, Edward de. *The Five Day Course in Thinking: introducing the L game*, Pelican 1970 (Orig 1967)

Bono, Edward de. *Practical Thinking*, Pelican 1979 (Orig. 1971)

Bono, Edward de. *The Six Value Medals*, Vermillion 2005

Berger, John. *Ways of Seeing*, Penguin BBC 1972

Blackmore, Susan. *Conciousness : an introduction*, Oxford 2004

Blakemore, Colin. *The Mechanics of Mind*, Cambridge 1977

Buzan, Tony. *Use Your Head*, BBC 1974

Buzan, Tony. *How to Make the Most of Your Mind*, Colt Books 1977

Cade, C. Maxwell. & Nona Coxhead. *The Awakened Mind: biofeedback and the development of higher states of awareness*, Wildwood House 1979

Campbell, H.J. *The Pleasure Areas*, Eyre Methuen 1973

Cohen, Martin *Wittgenstein's Beetle: and other classic thought experiments*, Blackwell 2005

Droit, Roger-Pol. *101 Experiments in the Philosophy of Everyday Life*, Faber & Faber 2003

Gerhardt, Sue. *Why Love Matters: how affection shapes a baby's brain*, Brunner-Routledge 2004

Golemann, Daniel. *Social Intelligence: the new science of human relationships*, Heinmann 2006

Haddock, Frank Channing. *Power of Will: a practical companion book for enfoldment of the powers of the mind*, Pelton 1919 (orig. 1907)

Hamblin, Henry Thomas. *The Power of Thought*, The Science of Thought Press, Chichester 1924

Kamin, Leon J. *The Science and Politics of I.Q.* Penguin 1977

Masters, R.E.L. & Jean Huston. *Mind Games*, Turnstone 1973

Maund, Barry *Perception*, Acumen 2003

Rose, Steven. *The 21st Century Brain: explaining, mending and manipulating the mind*, Jonathan Cape 2005

Searle, John. *Mind, Language and Society: philosophy in the real world*, Weidenfeld & Nicolson 1999

Searle, John R. *Mind: a brief introduction*, Oxford U.P. 2004

Smith, Alistair. *The Brains Behind I.T.* Network Educational Press 2002

Stafford, Tom & Webb, Matt *Mind Hacks: Tips and Tricks for Using Your Brain*, O'Reilly Media 2004

Williamson, Judith. *Decoding Advertisements,* Marion Boyars 1978

MEMORISING

Brown, M.E. *Memory Matters,* David & Charles 1977

Hunter, I.M.L. *Memory,* Pelican 1964

Lorayne, Harry. *Remembering People,* Stein & Day 1975

Small, Gary. *The Memory Prescription: Dr Gary Small's 14-day plan to keep your brain and body young,* Hyperion Books 2004

Spence, Jonathan D. *The Memory Palace of Matteo Ricci,* Penguin 1985

Wicks, Rev.B.J. *The Art of Remembering: hints on memory training,* Arthur H. Stockwell, London c1920s

Yates, Frances A. *The Art of Memory,* Peregrine 1966

MEDITATING

Benson, H., and M. Stark. *Timeless Healing: the power and biology of belief,* Scribner 1996

Forem, Jack. *Transcendental Meditation,* Allen Unwin 1974

Kabat-Zinn, Jon. *Full Catastrophe Living: how to cope with stress, pain and illness using mindfulness meditation,* Piatkus 1990 - 2006

Naranjo, Claudio. & Robert E. Ornstein. *On the Psychology of Meditation,* Allen Unwin 1973

Rooy, J de. *Tools for Meditation,* (Christian) Grail 1976

AUTO-SUGGESTING

Baudouin, C. *Suggestion & Auto-Suggestion,* Allen Unwin 1949

Powers, M. *Self-Hyphosis,* Thorsons 1956 - 66

DREAMING

Freud, S. *The Interpretation of Dreams,* Allen Unwin 1913

Fromm, E. *The Forgotten Language,* Gollancz 1952

Garfield, Patricia. *Creative Dreaming,* Futura 1976

Jung, C. *Man and His Symbols,* Picador 1978 (Aldus 1964)

Watkins, Mary M. *Waking Dreams,* Harper Colophon 1977

IMAGINING

Arnheim, Rudolf. *Visual Thinking,* Univ. of California 1969

Catterson-Smith, R. *Drawing from Memory & Mind Picturing,* Pitmans 1921

Howard, Vernon. *Psycho-Pictography,* Parker N.Y. 1965

Llewelyn, John. *The Hypocritical Imagination: Kant and Levinas,* Routledge 1999

McKellar, Peter. *Imagination & Thinking,* Cohen & West 1957

Rugg, Harold. *Imagination,* Harper & Row 1963

Sacks, Oliver. *Musicophilia: tales of music and the brain,* Alfred A. Knopf 2008

Somner, Robert. *The Minds Eye,* Delta 1978

INTUITING

Ayres, Ian. *Pervasive Prejudice?: unconventional evidence of race and gender discrimination,* Chicago U.P. 2001

Barron, Frank. *The Psychology of Imagination,* Scientific American, CXCIX, September 1958

Damasio, Antonio. *Descartes' Error: emotion, reason, and the human brain,* Putnam 1994

Ekman, Paul. *Emotions Revealed: recognizing faces and feelings to improve communication and emotional life,* Henry Holt 2003

Gigerenzer, Gerd & Peter M. Todd and the ABC Research Group. *Simple Heuristics That Make Us Smart,* Oxford 1999

Gladwell, Malcom. *Blink!: the power of thinking without thinking,* TimeWarner 2005

Hogarth, Robin M. *Educating Intuition,* Chicago U.P. 2001

Klein, Gary. *Sources of Power: how people make decisions,* MIT 1998

Klein, Gary. *Intuition at Work: How to use your gut feelings to make better decisions at work,* DoubleDay 2003

Myers, David. *Intuition: its powers and perils,* Yalebooks.com 2002

Prevost, Edwin. *No Sound Is Innocent,* Copula (the imprint of Matchless Recordings), 1995

Wegner, Daniel. *The Illusion of Conscious Will,* MIT 2002

Wilson, Timothy D. *Strangers to Ourselves: discovering the adaptive unconscious,* Harvard U.P. 2002

RATIONALISING

Ayers, A.J. *Language Truth & Logic,* Pelican 1936 - 78

Carrol, Lewis. *Symbolic Logic,* Harvester 1977

Chomsky, Noam. *Language and Mind,* Harcourt Brace Jovanovich 1972

De Leeuw, Manya and Eric. *Read Better, Read Faster: a new approach to efficient reading,* Pelican 1967

Carey G.V. *Mind the Stop: a brief guide to punctuation with a note on proof correction,* Penguin 1971 (orig. Cambridge U.P. 1939)

Fesch, Rudolf. *How to Write, Speak and Think More Effectively,* Signet 1960 (Orig. 1946)

Gowers, E. *The Complete Plain Words,* David R. Godine 2002 (Orig. HMSO 1954)

Gullan-Whur, Margaret. *Within Reason: a life of Spinoza,* Jonathan Cape 1998

Jackins, Harvey. *Logical Thinking about a Future Society,* Rational Island, 1990

Jeffrey, Richard C. *Formal Logic: its scope & limits,* McGraw Hill 1967

Mace, C.A. *The Psychology of Study,* Penguin 1962

Maddox, H. *How to Study,* Pan 1963. (Orig. Methuen 1932)

Morrison, Malcolm. *Clear Speech: Practical Speech Correction and Voice Improvement,* A. & C. Black 1977

Onians, R.B. *The Origins of European Thought,* Cambridge 1951

Russell, B. *Problems of Philosophy,* OU 1980 (Orig. 1912)

Ryder, T.A. *Efficient Thinking, Reasoning and Conversation,* Elliot Right Way Books 1963

EXPRESSING EMOTION

Bernard, William. & Jules Leopold. *Test Yourself: a handbook of self-analysis based on modern psychological methods,* Souvenir Press, 1964

Brook, Roy. *The Stress of Combat, The Combat of Stress: caring strategies towards ex-service men and women,* The Alpha Press, Brighton / Portland 1999

Cohen, David. *Aftershock: the psychological and political consequences of disaster,* Paladin 1991

Cohen, Ted. *Jokes: philosophical thoughts on joking matters,* Univ. of Chicago Press 1999

Durant, John. & Jonathan Miller. *Laughing Matters: a serious look at humour,* Longman 1988

Evans, Dylan. *Emotion: the science of sentiment,* Oxford U.P. 2003

Golemann, Daniel. *Working with Emotional Intelligence,* Bantam Books 1998

Freud, Sigmund. *Collected Papers Vol 4* Basic Books 1959

Haidu, Peter. *The Subject of Violence: The Song of Roland and the birth of the state,* Indiana U.P. 1993

Hjort, Mette. & Sue Laver eds. *Emotion and the Arts,* Oxford U.P. 1997

Karp, Joan. *Counseling on Early Sexual Memories,* Rational Island Pamphlet, Seattle 1992

Lutz, Tom. *Crying: the natural & cultural history of tears,* Norton 1999

Mason, Micheline and Alan Sprung. *Healing the Hurts of Capitalism: from isolation to connection,* YouCaxton 2015

Masson, Jeffrey. *The Assault on Truth: Freud and Child Sexual Abuse* Fontana, 1992 (Orig. 1984)

Music, Graham. *Affect and Emotion,* Icon Books, 2001

Nickerson, Dan. *An Introduction to Co-counselling,* Rational Island Pamphlet, 1994

Van Slyke, Erik J. *Listening to Conflict: finding constructive solutions to workplace disputes,* AMACOM 1999

Zautra, Alex J. *Emotions, Stress and Health,* Oxford U.P. 2003

TIMING & RHYTHM

Barnard-Way R. & Noel D. Green. *Time and its Reckoning,* Wells Gardener Darton & Co. Redhill, Surrey UK 1951

Lefebvre, Henri. *Rhythmanalysis: space, time and everyday life,* Althone 2004

Sacks, Oliver. *Musicophilia: tales of music and the brain,* Alfred A. Knopf 2008

ACTING /muscle action general

Lawther, John D. *The Learning of Physical Skills,* Prentice Hall 1968

Man-ching, Cheng. & Robert W. Smith. *Tai-Chi: the supreme ultimate exercise for health, sport and self-defense,* Tuttle 1967

POSTURE

Clark, Barbara. *Body Proportion Needs Depth,* Clark Manuals Tempe, Arizona 1975

Critchley, Duncan with Nicholas Spahr and Kelly Ridley. *Spinal Stabilisation Training: your pathway to a stronger back,* Guy's and St Thomas' Hospital 2005

K.G. von Durkheim. *Hara: the centre of personality,* 1960

Gelb, Michael. *Body Learning: An Introduction to the Alexander Technique,* Aurum Press, 2004

Shadmehr R. *A computational theory for posture and movement in a multi-joint limb,* Technical Report 91-7, Centre for Neural Engineering, Univ of S. California 1991

BREATHING

Morris, Margaret. *Breathing Exercises: in diagrams and words,* (Men's edition) Margaret Morris 1935

SLEEPING

Ambrogetti, Antonio. *Sleeping Soundly,* Allen & Unwin 2001

Kryger, Meir H. et al. *Principles and Practice of Sleep,* Medicine W.B. Saunders Co. 3rd edition 2000

RELAXING

Benson, Herbert. *The Relaxation Response,* 1975 (Avon Books 2000)

Jacobson, Edmund. *Progressive Relaxation,* 1929

Schultz, J.H. & Luthe, W. *Autogenic Therapy: Vol. 6. Treatment,* 1969

SITTING

Clarke, Barbara. *Let's Enjoy Sitting - Standing – Walking,* Clarke Manuals, Tempe, Arizona 1963

Loori, John Daido. *The Art of Just Sitting: essential writings on the Zen practice of Shikantaza,* Wisdom 2002

STANDING

Clarke, Barbara. *How to Live in Your Axis Your Vertical Line,* Clarke Manuals, Tempe, Arizona 1968

Iyengar, B.K.S. *Light on Yoga,* Schocken 1973

WALKING

Man, John. *Walk!: it could change your life,* Paddington 1979

Pope, Simon. *London Walking: a handbook for survival,* Ellipsis 2000

Solnit, Rebecca. *Wanderlust: a history of walking,* Verso 2001

Sussman, Aaron. & Ruth Goode. *The Magic of Walking,* Simon & Shuster 1980

Zipfel B. & Berger L.R. *Shod versus Unshod: the emergence of forefoot pathology in modern humans,* The Foot, Volume 17, Issue 4, Pages 205-213 2007

RUNNING

Spino, Mike. & Jeffrey Earl Warren. *Mike Spino's Mind/Body Running Programme,* Bantam 1979

JUMPING

Platt. Geoff. *Beating Dyspraxia with a Hop, Skip and a Jump: a simple exercise program for home and school,* Jessica KIngsley 2011

HANDLING

Latash, Mark L. & Michael T. Turvey eds. *Dexterity and Its Development,* Lawrence Erlbaum Associates, 1996

Irwin, Greg. *Finger Fitness: The Art of Finger Control,* Handhealth.com 1988

Sennett, Richard. *The Craftsman,* Allen Lane 2008

VOCALISING

Hellier, Marjorie. *Release Your Voice and Find Your Personality,* Elliots 1968

EATING

Orbach, Susie. *On Eating,* Penguin 2002

Fisher, MFK. *The Art of Eating* Wiley 2006

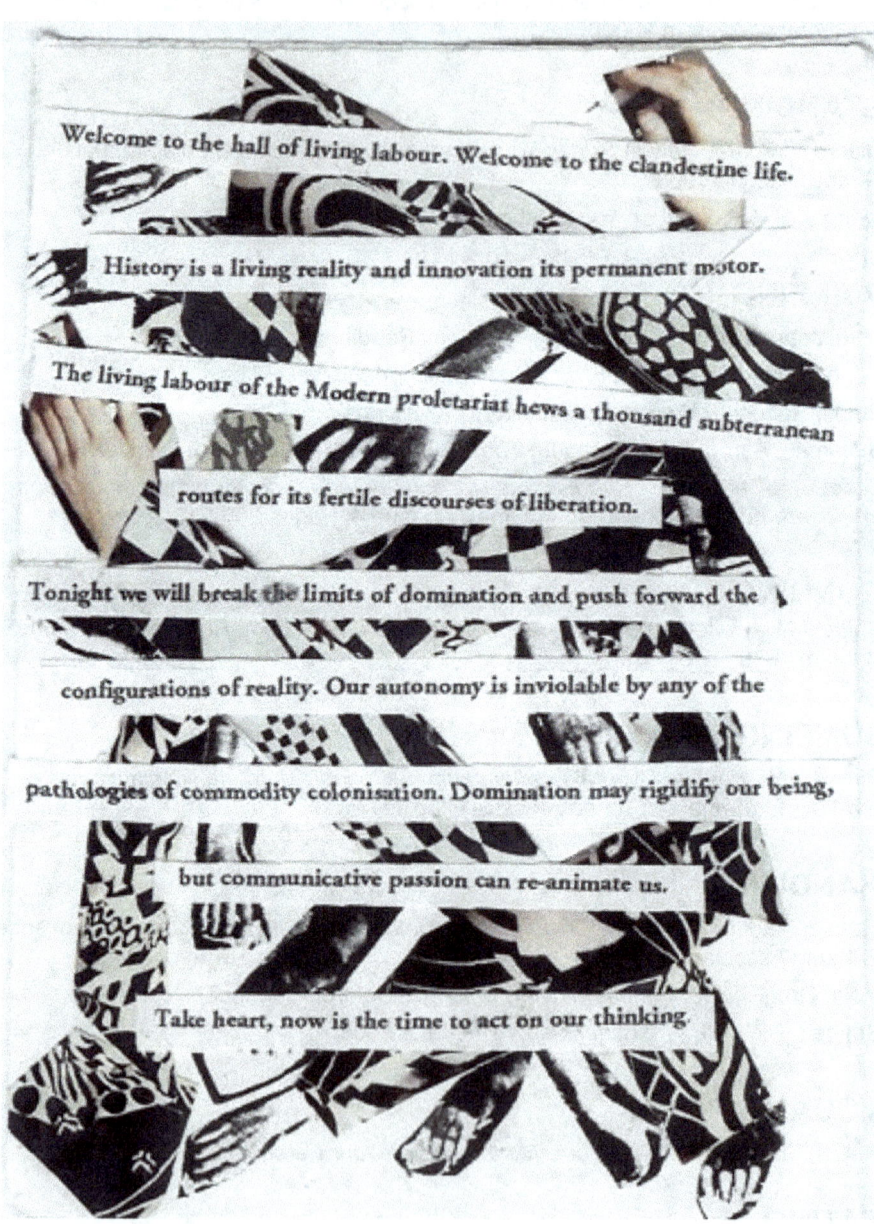

Other **Routine Art Co** imprint publications include:

'The Conspiracy of Good Taste: William Morris, Cecil Sharp and Clough Williams-Ellis and the repression of working class culture in the C20th' 2nd edition, illustrated. 177pp Pbk. ISBN 9781870736718

'Global Music?' free ebook http://payhip.com/b/K48n

'Nature Study Notes Revisited: improvisation and collective process' Illustrated. ISBN 97818870736961

Routine Art Co. publications are also available as ebooks. http://payhip.com/b/3TKf

Other publications by Stefan Szczelkun may be found via http://www.stefan-szczelkun.org.uk

www.ingramcontent.com/pod-product-compliance
Lightning Source LLC
Chambersburg PA
CBHW071343080526
44587CB00017B/2947